Conte...

Digital Video
with Windows· XP

Greg Perry

SAMS
Teach
Yourself

Sams Publishing, 800 East 96th Street, Indianapolis, Indiana 46240 USA

Digital Video with Windows XP in a Snap

International Standard Book Number: 0-672-32569-1

Library of Congress Catalog Card Number: 2003102930

Printed in the United States of America

First Printing: March 2004

07   06   05   04   4   3   2   1

Trademarks

All terms mentioned in this book that are known to be trademarks or service marks have been appropriately capitalized. Sams Publishing cannot attest to the accuracy of this information. Use of a term in this book should not be regarded as affecting the validity of any trademark or service mark.

Warning and Disclaimer

Every effort has been made to make this book as complete and as accurate as possible, but no warranty or fitness is implied. The information provided is on an "as is" basis. The author and the publisher shall have neither liability nor responsibility to any person or entity with respect to any loss or damages arising from the information contained in this book.

Bulk Sales

Sams Publishing offers excellent discounts on this book when ordered in quantity for bulk purchases or special sales. For more information, please contact

U.S. Corporate and Government Sales

1-800-382-3419

corpsales@pearsontechgroup.com

For sales outside of the U.S., please contact

International Sales

1-317-428-3341

international@pearsontechgroup.com

Acquisitions Editor
Betsy Brown

Development Editor
Jonathan Steever

Managing Editor
Charlotte Clapp

Senior Project Editor
Matthew Purcell

Copy Editor
Seth Kerney

Indexer
Larry Sweazy

Proofreader
Kathy Bidwell

Technical Editor
Dallas Releford

Publishing Coordinator
Vanessa Evans

Designer
Gary Adair

About the Author

Greg Perry is a speaker and a writer on both the programming and application sides of computing. He is known for his skills at bringing advanced computer topics to the novice's level. Perry has been a programmer and a trainer since the early 1980s. He received his first degree in computer science and a master's degree in corporate finance. Perry has sold more than 2 million computer books worldwide, including such titles as *Sams Teach Yourself Windows XP in 24 Hours*, *Absolute Beginner's Guide to Programming*, *Sams Teach Yourself Visual Basic 6 in 21 Days* as well as the phenomenal bestseller, *Sams Teach Yourself Office 2003 in 24 Hours*. He also writes about rental property management, creates and manages Web sites, loves to travel, and enjoys home life with his lovely wife Jayne and their two fluffy dogs Casper and Zucchi.

Acknowledgments

I want to send special thanks to Betsy Brown for putting up with me on this project. She was the driving force behind the work and I cannot express how glad I am that she wanted me to do this project.

Dallas Releford had to wade through all the problems I put into this book's first draft. Any problems that might be left are all mine. In addition, the other staff and editors on this project, namely Matt Purcell, Jon Steever, and Seth Kerney, made this book better than it otherwise would have been.

Finally, I want to express my thanks to the readers who keep coming back to my titles. Teaching you how to do something that I love, such as shooting and editing movies, is nothing but a pleasure for me. If you have any suggestions, ideas, or new ways of using Movie Maker, I'd love to hear from you!

—Greg Perry
Greg@SimpleRentHouses.com

We Want to Hear from You!

As the reader of this book, *you* are our most important critic and commentator. We value your opinion and want to know what we're doing right, what we could do better, what areas you'd like to see us publish in, and any other words of wisdom you're willing to pass our way.

You can email or write me directly to let me know what you did or didn't like about this book—as well as what we can do to make our books stronger.

Please note that I cannot help you with technical problems related to the topic of this book, and that due to the high volume of mail I receive, I might not be able to reply to every message.

When you write, please be sure to include this book's title and author as well as your name and phone or email address. I will carefully review your comments and share them with the author and editors who worked on the book.

Email: consumer@samspublishing.com

Mail: Mark Taber
            Associate Publisher
            Sams Publishing
            800 East 96th Street
            Indianapolis, IN 46240 USA

Reader Services

For more information about this book or others from Sams Publishing, visit our Web site at www.samspublishing.com. Type the ISBN (excluding hyphens) or the title of the book in the Search box to find the book you're looking for.

PART I

Introducing Digital Video and Movie Making

IN THIS PART:

1

✔ Start Here

These days, anybody with a video camcorder and a PC manufactured in the past few years can create high-quality video productions. As the cost of required hardware and software drops, two things happen:

1. More and more video content is available for independent movies, instructional videos, home videos, event videos (for occasions such as birthdays and weddings), and just about anything you can imagine.

2. The overall quality decreases as the quantity increases!

That last statement might be slightly cynical, but it does contain lots of truth. Entire college courses are available for photographers and *videographers*. Bookstores contain shelf after shelf of books about shooting quality video (although none are as good as *this* book!). Several magazines are devoted to video and still-image photography. The Web contains scores of related sites. These courses, books, magazines, and Web sites exist to turn a newcomer with a video camcorder into a skilled videographer.

The existence of these materials proves that owning a camera is not enough to know what to do. It's not elitist to state that anyone can shoot videos, but without knowledge of some fundamentals related to lighting, focus, motion, exposure, and so forth, the videos are never as good as they are after the camera owner learns the basics.

The quality of equipment is far less important than the quality of the videographer.

In the world of video moviemaking, a little knowledge can be valuable. By understanding the basics of shooting video—the basics you'll learn right here in the next two jam-packed chapters—you'll rise above the crowd and begin creating much improved videos.

After the Shoot

After you shoot your videos, what then? Even expert videographers cannot shoot a quality video in one take. They must shoot extra footage, reshoot some more, and even then they realize that hours or days of editing lie ahead of them. Fortunately, every person who owns a PC can edit video because Microsoft gives away Movie Maker, a surprisingly simple and feature-packed editing program that you will master through this book's tasks.

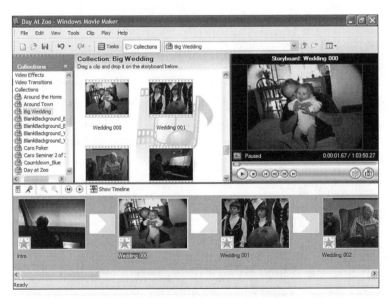

Movie Maker contains all the features you need to turn raw video footage into a final movie.

Your Equipment

This book uses the terms *camera*, *video camera*, and *camcorder* interchangeably.

What do you need to make videos, edit them, and produce a final movie? Simply put, you only need a video camera, a computer, and Movie Maker. Each of the next three sections explores these elements of movie making.

Your Video Camera

Obviously, the more features your camera has, the more you can reduce problems at the source. For example, some cameras allow you to control how much light enters the camera during filming. If you have to shoot in poor lighting conditions, this light feature can help improve your video—if you understand how to take advantage of it (**see 13 Light Your Video Properly** and **16 Take Low-Light Movies**). However, if your camera does not adequately support controlling the entry of light, you can do some editing in a video editing program to help reduce the problem.

The world of video cameras has dramatically changed in the past few years, and that change appears to be speeding up, not slowing down. With the rapid change, a list of desirable features from last year is now standard on this year's models. This year's desirable features will be standard next year.

Suffice to say, a video camera you purchase new today will certainly be adequate for starting out on your videography journey. After you master the basics, you might want to step up to a more expensive, but more feature-packed, camera.

TIP

If you bought a video camcorder a few years ago, don't worry. It will work fine for your first foray into videography.

NOTE

Given that today's bare-bones, inexpensive cameras contain plenty of the features you need to make quality videos, this section won't offer a comparison of specific cameras or features you need to look for. Instead, a broad overview of camera types is all you need to make your first purchasing decision.

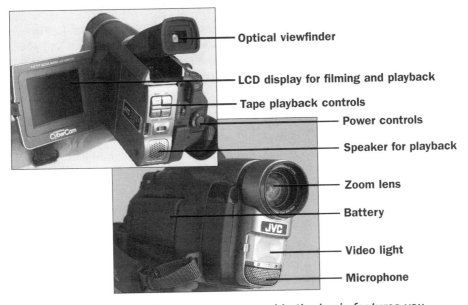

- Optical viewfinder
- LCD display for filming and playback
- Tape playback controls
- Power controls
- Speaker for playback
- Zoom lens
- Battery
- Video light
- Microphone

Even inexpensive and older camcorders provide the basic features you need to get started making movies.

Digital Video Cameras

One feature that will make life simpler for your first movie-making forays (although certainly not a requirement), is a *FireWire connection*. A FireWire connection is the primary distinguishing aspect between an *analog camera* and a *digital camera*. If your camera has a FireWire connection, you almost certainly have a digital camera, or perhaps a hybrid analog and digital camera. (The hybrids are good if you have several older analog video camera tapes you shot years ago that you want to transfer to your computer.) As long as your computer also has a FireWire connection (and if it does not, FireWire expansion cards are inexpensive), you can plug your camera directly into your computer and send it all your videos quickly and easily. A program such as Movie Maker controls the process and does the job effortlessly.

The most important advantage to digital video as opposed to the original analog camcorder video is that you can move your digital videos from camera to computer to camera to DVD to hard disk and back again, and you can make as many copies as you want, without any loss in sound or picture quality. If you've ever seen a copy of a copy of a VCR tape, you've seen the drawback to copying analog video—the quality diminishes with each copy.

Prosumer and Consumer

In the old days (less than a decade ago), the difference between professional video cameras and consumer models was simple to spot. All you had to do was look at the price tag. The pro models might command thousands of dollars more than a high-end consumer model, which might price at a little more than $1,000.

These days, ordinary and inexpensive consumer models that cost $500 and less have many features that used to be exclusive to the pro models. Yet there still exists a divide between high-end professional cameras and consumer models. Fortunately, consumer models produce excellent video, and can be the basis for fairly high-quality productions. Today, a third category called *prosumer* has arisen that can give you near-professional results at just a little more cost than everyday consumer models.

Here are some of the ways that prosumer models differ from consumer models:

- Wider range of values for depth of focus, white balance (see **14 Control Your Depth of Focus** and **15 White-Balance Your Scene**), zoom, and exposure settings.

- More dials and knobs, so you have more precise control during shooting, as opposed to the same controls on consumer models that generally require you to select from a menu on the LCD screen.

- Greater audio options.

- Better color depth, control, and pureness.

- Multiple lens attachments for different shot requirements.

- Greater camera weight.

TIP

A general rule of thumb is that a prosumer model costs about one-third that of a professional camera, and about twice as much as a typical consumer camera.

Even if you have yet to purchase a video camera, and even if you have money to burn, don't buy a prosumer model if you're just starting out in videography. There are two reasons to buy only a high-end consumer model now and get the prosumer model later:

1. You can't know which prosumer features you need most until you've shot lots of video. Different features help different movie makers. Learn what features you need most before looking at prosumer models. If you buy a prosumer model first, you might find it lacks the feature set you need most, or perhaps it implements that feature set in a more complicated way than another model.

2. After you use a consumer model for a while and learn the features that are most important to the kinds of videos you shoot, you not only will make a more knowledgeable prosumer purchase, but the price you pay for the prosumer model will probably be less a few months from now than it is today (that always seems to be the case).

TIP

The greater weight of prosumer models is actually a benefit in spite of the fact that manufacturers tout lightweight camcorders to the public as a benefit. Professional videographers agree that added weight helps them balance the camera and keep it steadier during filming.

Your Computer

Most of today's low-to-medium priced PCs can handle the needs of routine video editing. Higher-end models certainly are equipped to help even the most ardent video pros capture and edit their movies. If you own an older computer, you might be able to upgrade your PC to handle your editing needs.

Generally, the following specifications are the minimum you need to edit videos without too much trouble:

TIP

Hardly any upgrade helps speed your video editing work more than adding computer memory. "I have too much computer memory" is not a phrase ever uttered in the history of computer video editing.

- An 800MHz or faster processor, although some experts say that 1GHz (1,000MHz) is the minimum speed.

- 256MB of RAM, although with today's inexpensive prices, you should settle for no less than 512MB if you plan to edit videos over 10 to 15 minutes in duration.

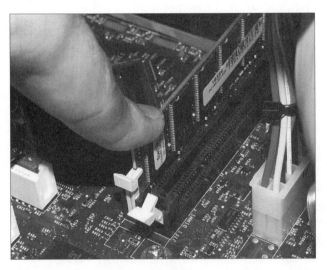

The more memory you add to your computer, the shorter your video editing session will last, because your computer can process more information faster with the added memory space to work in.

- A 17-inch monitor is a minimum if you want to be able to see both your movie and the video editing controls at the same time easily. The larger the monitor, the greater your ease of editing will be. Today's Windows-based PCs enable you to add a second graphics card and a second monitor to your computer. If you can do that, you will really go to town with video editing, because you can watch the video on one monitor while editing and controlling the production on the other.

- A video graphics card with at least 64MB of memory. (This memory is sometimes called *video memory*, *video RAM*, or *VRAM*.)

- A video capture card that captures analog video and converts it to digital. If you want to edit from any analog video source, such as a VCR or from an analog video camera, you must have a capture card. If all your video will come from a digital video camera, you do not need a capture card because you can use the FireWire connection to port the video to your computer. If you can get a capture card with an S-video connector, do so because the quality gained by using the S-video connector over the other video input jacks is significant when coming from a source such as a VCR. If you ever want to use a high-end video-editing program such as Adobe Premiere Pro, be sure to read the software's video card requirements to ensure that your card will work properly.

A video capture card enables you to pull video from your VCR or older video camera into a digital video format your computer can read and work with.

- An 80GB hard disk will get you started, but if you plan to store a lot of video on your computer, you will quickly run out of space. Consider adding 200GB to your primary editing hard disk. Today's removable hard disks, which connect to your computer's USB 2.0 or FireWire port, are large, fast, and simple to connect, so you may opt to buy them as you need them instead of spending the time and effort upgrading your computer's internal hard disk.

- A DVD or CD burner is necessary if you want to store your videos on DVD or CDs. Most computers sold in the past few years have CD burning drives, but only the recent ones are equipped with DVD burners.

🔦 TIP

If you have a digital video camera with analog input jacks (called RCA phono jacks), you can forgo a capture card! Connect your VCR, for example, to the camera's input phono jacks, and connect your digital camera's FireWire cable to your computer. The camera decodes the analog signal to a digital video signal that your computer can understand.

NOTE

It's okay if your computer has only one FireWire connection. You can plug one FireWire device (such as your video camera) into another FireWire device (such as an external disk drive), and only the first device in the chain needs to be attached to your computer's single FireWire port.

In addition to the hardware, you must ensure that you have either the Windows XP Home or the Windows XP Pro operating system. Movie Maker 2 requires Windows XP.

If you want to get a DVD burner, you should familiarize yourself with the formats. Unlike audio and data CDs, no single DVD standard exists. You can very easily store a video on a DVD that can play only on your computer's DVD player, but will not play in most non-computer DVD players. You want the world to be able to play your videos!

Table 1.1 describes the five DVD formats available. Pay close attention to the third column, because it describes each format's compatibility with the DVD players found in most homes today.

TABLE 1.1   **Not All DVD Burners Are the Same**

Format	Read or Write	Compatibility
DVD-RAM	Multiple rewrites	Generally only readable by other DVD-RAM drives. Perfect for data storage, but not great for sharing videos.
DVD-R,+R	Writable once	Compatible with most DVD players.
DVD+RW,-RW	Multiple rewrites	Generally compatible with most DVD players sold today.

Video Editing Software

As long as you have computer hardware that matches or surpasses the minimum requirements mentioned in the previous section, you can edit videos you capture to your computer. Editing involves far more than just splicing together different videos or removing pieces of them.

Video editing software enables you to do all the following and more:

- Add narration to video
- Add a soundtrack to the start and end of a movie
- Add music and sound effects throughout a movie
- Create transitions between scenes to fade in, wipe out, swirl, turn, and change from one scene to another in a fancier way than just switching from the end of one scene to the start of the next scene
- Add opening titles, subtitles, and ending movie credits

- Slow down parts of the movie and speed up other parts

- Add special video effects throughout the movie

- Capture still photo images from any frame in the movie

If you have a closet of home videos, you can finally put together a video collection that your family can watch, enjoy, and treasure. If all this sounds like an advertisement for video editing, it's only because of my excitement that the capability to edit video is finally so widely available. Computers could be used for video editing even through the late 1990s, but the process was neither inexpensive nor simple. Today, with software such as Microsoft's Movie Maker, video editing is virtually effortless.

Editing Movies with Movie Maker

Although Microsoft introduced Movie Maker in Windows 98, it wasn't until the second version, Movie Maker 2, that Movie Maker began to be noticed as an excellent video editing tool. Although nobody argues that Movie Maker lacks features found in other more expensive editing packages, Movie Maker certainly contains all the basic features that you'll need to get started.

This book is not about Movie Maker, but most of its chapters are devoted to teaching Movie Maker tasks. After you master Movie Maker—and you *will* master Movie Maker if you tackle the tasks throughout this book—you will understand the concept of almost all other video-editing programs on the market. Those programs, which are far more costly than Movie Maker (Movie Maker is free), all use a screen layout similar to Movie Maker's. The final chapter, "Taking Digital Editing to the Next Step," explores more advanced video-editing software programs you might want to move to after you master Movie Maker.

Getting Movie Maker 2

If you've owned your computer for a while and have been upgrading your computer's operating system as Windows advances, you probably have at least the first version of Movie Maker. Honestly, the original Movie Maker left a lot to be desired, and you shouldn't waste time with it.

> ⚓ **TIP**
>
> If you plan to perform fairly advanced video editing on your computer, you should master Movie Maker before moving to a more comprehensive package, such as Adobe's Premiere Pro, which costs a few hundred dollars (see **110** About Editing Professionally with Adobe Premiere Pro). Movie Maker is a great launching pad that introduces you to video-editing skills. Although Movie Maker works with virtually any video card, you might find that upgrading to a more powerful software package also requires that you upgrade your video card, too.

To see which version you have, follow these steps:

1. Select **Start**, **All Programs**, **Windows Movie Maker**. If Movie Maker does not appear on your **Windows All Programs** menu, you might have to select **Accessories** and possibly **Entertainment** before you locate the **Movie Maker** option.

2. After Movie Maker starts, select **Help**, **About Windows Movie Maker**.

Make sure you have the latest Movie Maker before editing video.

3. Read down the **About** dialog box until you see **Windows Movie Maker Version X.XX**. If the version number begins with 2, such as **2.03**, you have Movie Maker 2. If you have the first version, you need to upgrade to version 2 immediately.

All you need is an Internet connection to upgrade Movie Maker to version 2. Select **File**, **Exit** to quit Movie Maker version 1 and follow these steps to upgrade to Movie Maker version 2:

1. Point your Web browser to www.microsoft.com/windowsxp/moviemaker/default.asp, Microsoft's Movie Maker Web site.

2. Scroll to the **Downloads** section.

3. Click the link labeled **Movie Maker 2**.

Download Movie Maker 2 if you have the previous version.

4. Click the **Go** button on the right side of your screen (assuming you want the English version). If you want to download a different language, first select the language and then click **Go**.

5. Click the **Download** link on the right side of your screen. A download dialog box opens.

6. If you want, you can download the Movie Maker upgrade to your computer by clicking **Save** and selecting a location. You really don't have to save the file unless you want to have it to upgrade other computers you own, or in case you have to re-install Movie Maker 2 later. If you don't elect to save the file, click **Open** to start the installation. If you save the file first, click **Open** after the file is saved.

7. Follow the installation instructions as they walk you through the process.

Getting to Know Movie Maker

After you ensure that Movie Maker 2 is installed on your computer, you're ready to start the program and take a quick tour. If Movie Maker is not running, select **Start**, **All Programs**, **Windows Movie Maker** to start the program.

NOTE

If you've never edited video, Movie Maker's screen might seem confusing at first. After you learn the fundamentals, you'll see that the screen is easy to navigate and understand.

The rest of this book teaches you all you need to know about using Movie Maker. A quick preview will make you more comfortable with Movie Maker's screen. Depending on the start-up settings and **View** options selected, your screen might differ somewhat from the ones shown in this chapter. Also, the figures here show Movie Maker during a video-editing session—when you start Movie Maker for the first time, your video-editing session will be blank. Nevertheless, you can learn the parts of the screen now so that you'll better understand subsequent discussions throughout this book's tasks.

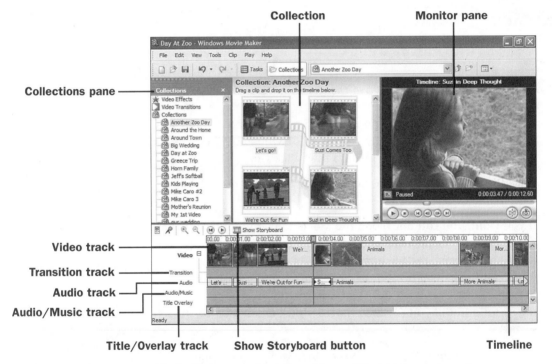

Movie Maker provides the video editing tools you need.

Take a few seconds to locate and review the following major sections of the typical Movie Maker screen:

- **Collections pane**—A Movie Maker window pane that contains various transitions, special effects, video, and audio content that you can select from for your video. When you import video into Movie Maker, the video's name appears in the **Collections** pane. You can drag any item from the **Collections** pane to the **Collection** to see individual video clips that you then can add to the video you're currently producing (**see 17 About Collections, Contents, and Projects**). Some video-editing programs have a similar pane called the *asset pane* that holds a repository of content you can pull into your current project to add to your movie.

- **Collection**—When you drag an item from the **Collections** pane to the **Collection**, usually the item breaks into multiple clips. You then can choose to insert one or more clips into your movie in any order.

- **Monitor pane**—Also called the *monitor*, the **Monitor** pane is like a small video screen where you can preview clips, pictures, special effects, transitions, and movies (**see 24 Watch Your Video in the Monitor**).

- **Timeline**—A row of clips that define the order and timing of your movie. As you add and remove clips, sound, transitions, and special effects from the movie you're currently creating, the timeline updates to reflect the order and timing of your movie (**see 36 Place a Clip on the Timeline**).

- **Video track, Transition track, Audio track, Audio/Music track**, and **Title Overlay track**—As you add items to your movie, the various items (such as transitions or background music or audio narration) appear on various timeline tracks.

TIP

If some of the window panes appear to be missing when you start Movie Maker, you can use the **View** menu to display the missing panes.

NOTE

It's unfortunate that the **Collections** pane and the **Collection** share a common name. The Collections pane contains all the items available for your video production. The **Collection** contains only those specific video, audio, and still picture clips you want to select from to make your current movie.

NOTE

The *storyboard* is the timeline's sister, and is viewable by clicking **Show Storyboard** atop the timeline. The storyboard shows your movie's clip order and contents, but does not show the timing of those clips. The storyboard is more useful than the timeline when viewing your movie's overall sequence.

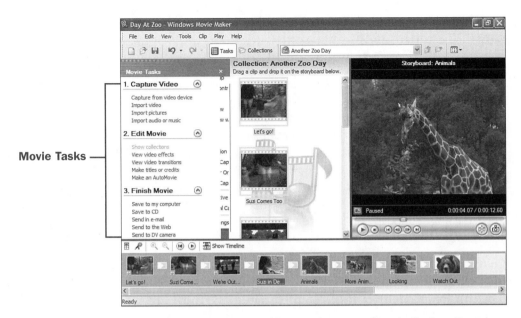

Movie Maker's tasks provide step-by-step wizards that walk you through all major movie-making features.

A Word on File Formats

Movie Maker is fairly generous in its support for files from all sources. You can capture any kind of video and audio file, as long as you can pull that file from your FireWire connection. Most digital video cameras sold today allow this connection. You can capture video and audio from any video or audio source if you use a video capture card (or if you have a digital camera that supports analog input).

Perhaps just as important as Movie Maker's capability to capture video content is its capability to import from video and audio files that you might already have stored on your computer:

- Movie Maker can import any of the following video file formats: **.asf**, **.avi**, **.mpeg**, **.mpg**, **.m1v**, **.mp2**, and **.wmv**.

- Movie Maker can import any of the following audio file formats: **.aif**, **.aifc**, **.aiff**, **.au**, **.mp3**, **.snd**, and **.wav**.

- Movie Maker can import any of the following still image formats: **.bmp**, **.gif**, **.jfif**, **.jpe**, **.jpeg**, and **.jpg**.

NOTE

Still images play important roles in moviemaking as opening credits, advertisements, and as special breaks from the action. In addition, Movie Maker supports the creation of an entire movie filled with still images that so you can create an online scrapbook of picture memories.

After you create a movie, you must save the movie in some format. Movie Maker is quite a bit more limited in its output formats than in its input formats. Movie Maker can only save your movie in the **AVI**, **WMA**, and **WMV** file formats.

Usually, you'll want to do more than just save the movie to your disk for later playback. After you finish creating a movie, you can send the movie to any of the following output locations:

- To your computer's hard disk

- To a video server on the Web so others can watch your movie

- To someone via an email file attachment

- To a digital video camera via the FireWire connection (You must save your video in the **AVI** format to send it to your digital camera)

- To a CD

- To a DVD

Surprisingly, Movie Maker does not directly support the output of a movie to DVD. Several reasons for this exist, but the primary reason is that Windows XP contains no native support for writing to a DVD (the next version of Windows should). Although you'll surely want to send some movies to DVD, you must use a third-party, non-Microsoft program to do this. The program, such as Sonic's MyDVD and CD & DVD Creator (**see 108 Produce DVDs with CD & DVD Creator**), should support Windows Media Player file formats (**WMA** and **WMV**) because those are the file formats Movie Maker outputs best.

Not only will you want to obtain a DVD-writing program, you will probably want to get other programs that enhance your Movie Maker experience. Microsoft offers two that complement Movie Maker's features, one that's free and one that retails for less than $20. You can download the *Movie Maker Creativity Fun Pack* (**see 93 About the Movie Maker Creativity Fun Pack**), which adds new titles, credits, and special sounds to your Movie Maker Collection pane. Microsoft's *Plus! Digital Media Edition* is a program that adds new transitions, special effects, and a DVD and CD label generator that can accentuate your movie making (**see 100 Install Microsoft Plus! Digital Media Edition (DME)**).

NOTE

Keep your video under one megabyte in size if you want to send it to a Web server or through email to respect others' download speeds. On a dial-up connection, downloading a complete movie can be very slow.

Use programs like Sonic's MyDVD to store your movie productions on DVDs others can play.

PART II

Shooting Videos Like a Pro

IN THIS PART:

2

Making the Best Video Possible

IN THIS CHAPTER:

After you master the tasks provided here, you will be well-grounded in the beginning fundamentals of shooting digital video. Many people with a digital video camera have little or no training—and their videos make it obvious! The good news is that you only need a short primer in shooting digital video to rise above the crowd and create audience-grabbing videos.

This book fills in any gaps you might have. If you're a complete novice or if you used to be fairly good with a video camera years ago, this book brings you up to date and up to speed quickly. You'll learn only what you have to learn to make, edit, and produce digital videos.

This chapter and the next provide a quick background in taking the best digital video you can take. You'll master the roadmap that takes you from using your digital video camcorder to capturing video into your computer, editing that video, and publishing it. You'll learn about lighting and audio considerations. You will see that with only a little preparation, your video's lighting and audio are greatly improved.

1 Walk Through a Digital Video Production

See Also

→ **2** Plan Your Video

→ **6** About Shooting Tirelessly and Editing Relentlessly

→ **15** White-Balance Your Scene

Video editing is not as complicated as it might seem at first. If you've never studied digital video production, some terms might be new to you. You'll also need a short primer on lighting and sound and getting the right shot.

This task provides more of a sneak peek at what lies ahead. By laying out the steps you should expect when making digital videos here, you will be more comfortable with the rest of the book when you see the details of this task's overview.

KEY TERM

Storyboard—A storyboard shows a movie's planned sequence of events. The storyboard might be sketches of proposed scenes, or snapshots of pictures with actors posing for the scenes.

1 Create a Plan

Most producers use a plan called a *storyboard*. The storyboard can be a sketch of scenes you draw to help you focus into the movie's sequential events (**see** **2** **Plan Your Video**).

② Install Ample Memory

Make sure your computer has the horsepower to handle the movie's editing job. Memory is a lot like good looks—you rarely can have too much. The more memory your computer has, the faster your editing process will go and the smoother your videos will play onscreen. Although Movie Maker requires only 128 megabytes of memory to run, your digital editing sessions won't begin to go smoothly until you get at least 512 megabytes of memory. Add even more and you will be able to do other tasks on your computer while you capture or save your movies without a noticeable slowdown.

③ Check Hard Drive Space

Check your My Computer window's status bar to make sure you have at least two gigabytes of free disk drive space. Click on the disk drive where Movie Maker is installed (normally this is your C: drive) and read the free space remaining at the bottom of your screen on your My Computer window.

④ Install Video Capture Card

You must be able to move your movie from your digital video camcorder to your computer. If you plan to capture video from a VCR or from an older digital video camera that has no FireWire connection, install a video capture card in your computer.

⑤ Shoot Video

Load the proper film cartridge in your video camcorder, perform a white balance to ensure you've got good color balance in your video, and start shooting! (**See** 15 **White-Balance Your Scene.**)

⑥ Capture Video

You now must grab the video from your video camcorder and capture it, or download it, to your computer. Once on your computer, you can edit the video (**see** 18 **Start a Movie Maker Project**).

 TIP

Use a bulletin board for your storyboard layout so you can easily rearrange your movie as you plan it.

 NOTE

Movie Maker provides a digital storyboard that lets you rearrange clips after you shoot your movie (see 28 **About Movie Maker's Storyboard**).

 NOTE

An hour of video can consume as much as five gigabytes or more. A hard disk upgrade is a must for serious video editing. Consider one of the large capacity multi-gigabyte external USB 2.0 or FireWire hard drives if you plan to keep all your movies on disk as your video library.

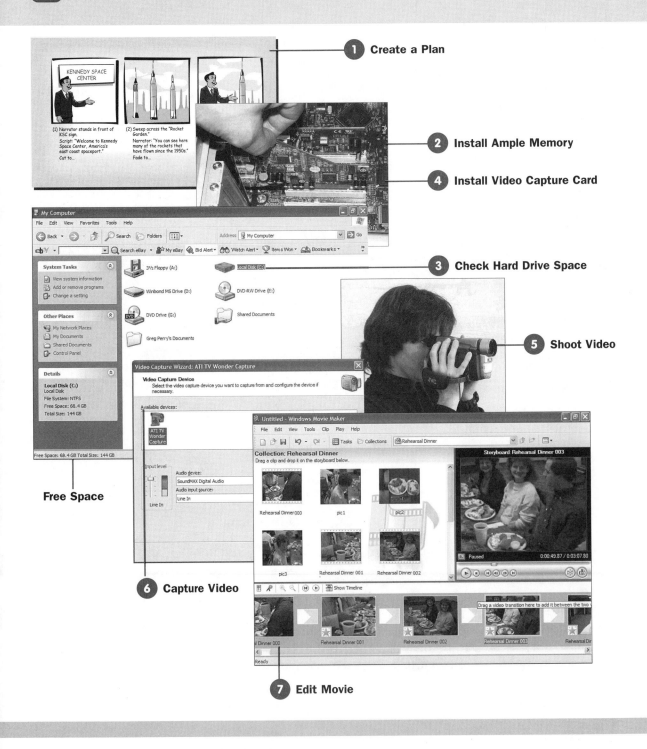

1 Create a Plan

2 Install Ample Memory

4 Install Video Capture Card

3 Check Hard Drive Space

5 Shoot Video

Free Space

6 Capture Video

7 Edit Movie

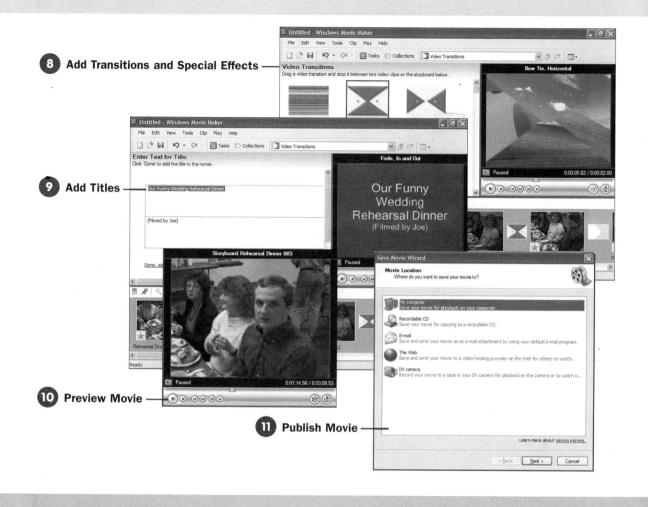

8 Add Transitions and Special Effects

9 Add Titles

10 Preview Movie

11 Publish Movie

---

7 **Edit Movie**

Organize the video clips you've just captured to your hard drive by referring to Movie Maker's storyboard (**see 20 Capture Video into Movie Maker**). You can drag clips to the storyboard and rearrange them to order your video into the sequence you prefer.

8 **Add Transitions and Special Effects**

Transitions can offer elegant ways to move from scene to scene. Choose from your editing software's vast array of wipes, fades, and dozens of other effects (**see 69 Transition from Clip to Clip**).

Just be sure you use transitions in moderation so they do not distract from the message of your movie. To add pizzazz, a few special effects will capture your audience's attention (**see** **65** **Add a Special Effect to a Clip**).

9 Add Titles

You can add opening credits, titles on still video clips, subtitles, and captions to help identify your video to your audience. At the end of your movie, you can add closing credits, too (**see** **72** **About Titles and Credits**).

10 Preview Movie

At any point in the production, you can preview your video creation on your computer from within Movie Maker to get a rough idea of what the movie will eventually look like (**see** **81** **Preview Your Final Movie**). After you've completed your movie and are ready to publish the final product, preview the entire movie in Movie Maker to ensure your movie contains exactly the footage you intend it to contain.

11 Publish Movie

After you've reviewed the entire movie and decided your creation is complete, generate the finished movie by saving it to your computer, sending it via email, storing it on the Web, or sending it to a CD or DVD (**see** **92** **About Putting Movies on DVD**).

---

2 Plan Your Video

Before You Begin

✔ **1** Walk Through a Digital Video Production

See Also

→ **6** About Shooting Tirelessly and Editing Relentlessly

Most video projects, including Hollywood blockbusters, benefit from a bit of planning and preparation. One of the first things you should do when you set out to make a video is to storyboard it.

The storyboard describes the events of your movie in a *thumbnail* form. By looking through, changing, replacing, and rearranging the thumbnail images and descriptions on the storyboard, your movie plan shapes up, and you'll waste less time and film later when you're ready to shoot your movie.

If you do a good job creating a storyboard, you'll have an easier time filming your video. Remember, however, that you might need to revise your storyboard when you get into the editing stage. Be thinking about special effects, music, and titles which you won't add during the storyboarding stage but you will need to add in the editing stage.

① Sketch the Key Scenes

Think of your storyboard as a cartoon that describes, scene by scene (or even frame by frame), what happens in your movie. Draw all the events depicting the video from key camera angles you intend to shoot. You can use a storyboard as a road map to filming the video.

② Add Narrative

Under each frame, describe what is happening, who is in the scene, and what everyone is saying. You can also describe the mood or any other key elements.

③ Write the Script

At this stage, it's also important to write a script that identifies what everyone is going to say. The script will help identify any weaknesses in the storyboard and flesh out the video you are about to film.

④ Build the Props List

Describe in detail any costumes, props, and other essential items under each frame of the storyboard where appropriate. Keep adding storyboard items to flesh out your video. Between scenes, add transitional effects you'd like to see and make notes of special effects you'd like to add to the video on certain scenes. Also, make notes of soundtrack music you might want to add in certain places if you think of something special. When done, your storyboard panels will appear, when you place them side-by-side, like a cartoon that shows your movie's sequence and requirements.

KEY TERM

Thumbnail—A small picture that represents a scene or a larger picture.

NOTE

Movie makers often use the term *storyboard* as a verb, as in "to storyboard a movie." They think they sound cool when they do that.

NOTE

Obviously, if you're planning to shoot an event such as a birthday party, storyboard planning is overkill. For any instructional or entertainment video, however, you will save a great amount of time and frustration by storyboarding.

NOTE

Your storyboard is not only a sequential layout of your movie, but it's also a great place to put notes you'll refer to during the movie's filming and post-filming production.

1 Sketch the Key Scenes

Close up of Susan.

Zoom out as Peter enters scene and they look at each other.

Script: Susan: "Where's the money?"

Peter: "I couldn't get it away from Tony."

3 Write the Script

Close up of Susan.

Zoom out as Peter enters scene and they look at each other.

2 Add Narrative

Close up of Susan.

Zoom out as Peter enters scene and they look at each other.

Script: Susan: "Where's the money?"

Peter: "I couldn't get it away from Tony."

Props: Peter has gun

4 Build the Props List

3 About the Camera's Perspective

Before You Begin

✔ **1** Walk Through a Digital Video Production

✔ **2** Plan Your Video

See Also

➜ **4** About Your Video's Audience

Your camera sees the world differently from the way you see the world. The camera's *peripheral vision* is more limited. Begin looking at your subject matter from the camera's viewpoint. By doing this, your videos will more accurately reflect what you want them to portray. By limiting the peripheral vision, your video might need more *panning* to capture a scene's contextual meaning. For example, a flag waving amid tombstones in a cemetery portrays a much different effect from a flag waving atop a baseball stadium. Unless you pan or zoom out from the flag, your camera will catch only the flag, and its context will be lost.

The camera's eye sees less peripherally than you do.

KEY TERM

Peripheral vision—The area of vision outside the center of focus. You can look straight ahead and see some things off to either side. Those things are in your peripheral vision.

Panning—Moving the camera left and right to film subject matter that is not currently in the camera's eye.

You'll quickly learn, especially when you're trying to tell a story, as you'd do in a movie or when creating an instructional or sales video, that small improvements in the way you film will greatly enhance the look of your production. Although you can read about shooting effectively, it will be the school of hard knocks that really drills proper video techniques into your head.

For example, *jump cuts* often occur in amateur films. The producer might not even notice that a jump cut occurred. Even the audience might not notice it—consciously. Unconsciously, a sloppy jump cut can break the flow of the movie. You'll want to stay alert to ensure that a person's position in one shot matches the same position in the next shot if you want to eliminate jump cuts in your movies. If you're shooting live action taking place in front of you, you won't be able to eliminate jump cuts, but if you're in control of the subject matter, teach your subjects to keep their hands and bodies in the same position from shot to shot if you must take multiple shots in the same scene.

Jump cuts in audio can occur as well as in video, so make sure the sound levels and surrounding noise don't differ too much from shot to shot within the same scene's time period.

KEY TERM

Jump cuts—A quick cut from one shot back to the same shot again when the actor's position has changed, breaking the scene's continuity.

 TIP

If you cut from and back to a moving subject, jump cuts pose far less of a problem because the audience realizes the subject's position has changed between cuts.

Before Cut   **After Cut**

The subjects' positions changed too much between shots because of the jump cut.

TIP

If you want to record a scene with two people speaking and you only have one camera with which to shoot the scene, align your subjects diagonally so the camera can easily see both speakers. You'll reduce panning.

Panning is used conservatively in most movies and television shows. The pros don't move their camera often, and neither should you (see **5** **About Reducing Motion and Relying on Your Subjects**). In addition, one of the common mistakes video camera owners make is zooming too much (see **11** **Zoom Effectively**). In some home movie videos, the camera is constantly zooming in and out. The end result is the audience must focus on where the zoom is taking them next versus the scene itself. The ride on which lots of excessive zooming takes an audience is not a good one.

4 About Your Video's Audience

Before You Begin

✔ **2** Plan Your Video
✔ **3** About the Camera's Perspective

See Also

➔ **6** About Shooting Tirelessly and Editing Relentlessly

Even before you plan your video, you need to have your audience firmly in mind. Who are you shooting for? What is your target audience? What will be their expectations for your video? Even if you shoot home movies to show friends and family, put yourself in their shoes to decide what they might want to see.

Shoot your movies using as many kinds of shots as possible. Shoot from various angles if possible. Don't just interview wedding guests—show them walking in the church, talking with greeters, and moving to their seats. You can't do this with every guest, but the variety of following at least one group to their seats adds interest to your video. When the outside lighting is good, capture a few shots of the church from different angles. You can cut these shots between some of the inside shots at times to keep the audience's focus on the overall event.

Your audience will appreciate your videos much more if you follow this chapter's simple tasks to improve your shoots. Use titles when necessary (but don't overuse them). Travel videos are more interesting when your audience can read the name of the current site or where the tour is taking them. Movie Maker simplifies title creation so much that adding enhancing titles for your audience is virtually effortless (see **76** **Put a Title on a Clip**).

TIP

Tell a story! No matter what your video's subject matter is, even if it's a wedding reception video, try to shoot your video like a story with a beginning, middle, and end. You'll help your audience stay in tune with the tone you want to portray. Get there early to show guests arriving. Stay late to watch them leave. You'll thus add a wrapping to either end of your video that makes it more enjoyable.

Spelling out a location in a title helps plant the scene in your audience's mind.

5 About Reducing Motion and Relying on Your Subjects

If you know nothing else before you begin your foray into video filmmaking, know that moving your camera too much is bad. Except in rare cases where you want to add variety, let your camera record the action from a distance far enough away to allow your audience to see what takes place—without the camera moving with the action. In other words, let your subjects move and keep your camera still.

Most of today's modern digital video cameras include a stabilization control that acts like a shock absorber. When you walk while filming, for example, the stabilizer attempts to keep your camera's picture steady. Although a stabilizer can be effective, a stabilizing feature does not substitute for a steady hand. Keep your camera as still as possible while filming. Move your body and not your hands during a shoot.

Before You Begin

✔ **3** About the Camera's Perspective

✔ **4** About Your Video's Audience

TIP

One way to tell whether a movie you're watching was made in the 1970s is the overuse of camera motion and zoom (and bell-bottom pants).

TIP

Using a tripod mount for your camera not only keeps your shots steady, but it also reduces your urge to move the camera too much during a scene.

Keep your scenes stable. Try to remain balanced and focused. Some novice videographers try to help their audience by moving the camera's eye with the scene, but doing so only confuses the audience's eyes. You want your audience to concentrate on your movie's content, and not on the movie's production. You don't even want your audience to know they are watching a movie; instead, you want them immersed. Even for simple family videos, keeping this idea in mind while you shoot greatly enhances the videos you make.

Not only does camera movement cause your audience viewing problems, your camera's focus can suffer as well. A blurred video or lighting that starts bright white before settling down often occurs when the camera moves too quickly from one subject to another, especially when those subjects are different distances from the camera.

Blurring and lighting problems can result from an unsteady camera.

When you must pan your camera left to right, move from your waist and not with your hands. The pan will be much smoother and less jerky. In spite of all this discussion on the importance of limiting camera movement, some shots require movement, panning, and zooming. Let the scene determine what's needed, and don't impose movement when none is warranted.

KEY TERM

Tight shots—Another name for a close-up shot that shows a subject up close and in detail without showing much of the periphery.

One way to change your camera's perspective without zooming or moving the camera is to shoot from different shot distances. Combine wide sweeping shots with medium shots and close-up shots (called *tight shots*) to give your video more depth.

6 About Shooting Tirelessly and Editing Relentlessly

When filming, shoot anything and everything. At events such as parties, weddings, and plays, you cannot reshoot a scene later if you miss it the first time. As a videographer, you will learn to enjoy such events through your camera's eye. If you don't learn to shoot continuously as much as possible, you risk missing key scenes that would make your video more enjoyable.

Shoot from as many different vantage points as possible to add spice to your production. If you've ever had to sit through a friend's travel video, shot entirely from a bus window, you know how stale watching scenes from the same viewpoint can be.

Scenes comprised of shots from different perspectives make your movies more interesting.

Shoot peripheral elements at your event. If you film your daughter's graduation, also shoot the parking lot as people arrive and leave. Take shots of the front entrance and of the sign. You can cut some of these extra shots throughout the graduation itself. Your video does not have to be entirely linear. A judicious use of jumping to and fro can spruce up an event as long as the event itself remains the primary focus, and as long as you don't make too many cuts to peripheral scenes.

After you have as much as possible on film, and after the event is over, you can edit to your heart's content. With Movie Maker, for example,

Before You Begin
✔ **2** Plan Your Video
✔ **4** About Your Video's Audience

See Also
→ **32** Rearrange the Storyboard
→ **44** Set Trim Points

TIP

Carry fully charged spare batteries. Don't miss an event's highlight because you ran out of juice. Also, carry a screw-on clear lens (called a *UV lens*) and camera cover for shooting outdoors when it starts raining.

KEY TERM

UV lens—A screw-on clear lens that protects your camera's built-in lens from scratches and weather. The lens filters none of the camera's vision, so your videos are unaffected by its presence.

TIP

If you can afford a second video camera, even if it doesn't have the bells and whistles of your primary camera, give it to another person at the event to get shots from locations other than where you'll be. You can later edit in some of these shots to add another perspective to your scenes.

you'll easily be able to rearrange shots, transition from scene to scene, shorten clips, add special effects, and cut spare footage from the video. It's the cutting of spare footage that is perhaps the most important task you'll perform during the editing of your movie.

"Less is more," is a phrase good writers have understood for years as they write their novel in draft form and then cut, cut, and cut some more to trim excess wordage. Use the same technique for your movies. If you've ever sat through a movie you thought was too long, it's because you felt the same movie could have been made using much less film. Don't make your audience think your videos are too long. Trim shots and keep only the most attention-grabbing elements for most of your scenes.

Sure, if you're shooting your sister's wedding, she will want the entire ceremony without one second dropped. Nevertheless, you are free to be creative in the before-and-after scenes of the groom's pre-wedding jitters and the bride's payback for those jitters as she crams an entire piece of cake into his mouth at the reception.

When filming, remember to give yourself room to work during the editing process. Start each scene or shot with four or five seconds of lead time. Keep the camera on a few seconds longer than you need to when shooting a scene. Doing so can give you background audio that you can keep playing during a fade-out effect or during a transition to another scene. Also, the extra footage gives you more edit points that ensure you don't have to cut a scene too short, thus cutting the tone of the scene off too soon.

TIP

Shots under 25 to 30 seconds often hold your audience's attention far better than longer shots. Even when shooting the same subject, break up the shot when possible. Try to change the video shot in some way (without relying solely on special effects, panning, or zooming) every few seconds of footage.

KEY TERM

Cutaway shots—Shots that correlate to a scene but are not imperative to the scene. Cutaway shots help to keep a scene moving without being too distracting.

Shoot many *cutaway shots*. You can embed the cutaway shots between other shot changes. For example, you could shoot your daughter walking onto the stage and performing her recital and then walking off. Sometime before the production ends, shoot the audience reacting to something similar as a cutaway shot. You'll later be able to cut to the audience's "reaction" and back to your daughter performing (while keeping your daughter's audio continuing through the cutaway).

Before Cutaway   **Cutaway Shot**   **Continue with Original Shot**

Use cutaway shots judiciously to help your audience focus on the scene as well as the scene's surroundings.

7 About Making Audio a Priority

Rarely is a new video maker concerned with sound. Rarely is a professional video maker *unconcerned* with sound. Good sound often goes unnoticed by the audience, and that's exactly what the professional wants in many cases. The sound is there, especially a background music soundtrack and **ambient sound**, but the sound is to keep the audience focused on the video. You never want to audience to focus on a sound, but on the action (unless, of course, you're filming a piano recital).

Your camera's built-in microphone is fine for capturing the sound of many events for home movies and family travelogues. Actually, the microphones of most digital video cameras do a better-than-expected job at capturing the proper sound. Having said that, even when filming informal events, you must stay focused not only on your video but also on the sound.

If you shoot in a crowded environment, such as from the bleachers of a sports arena, the audience around you will certainly detract from any sound being made on the field. People talking next to you can drown out action in the game. Often there is little you can do to mask these sounds. It's a shame that you cannot zoom a microphone into the sound you want most, as you can zoom a camera lens into a scene to specifically shoot what you want.

If you're shooting more important video, such as an independent film-maker would consider himself doing (indies *always* think they're making

Before You Begin

✔ **2** Plan Your Video

✔ **4** About Your Video's Audience

See Also

→ **46** About Movie Maker Audio

→ **48** Add a Soundtrack to Your Video

→ **52** Add Narration to Your Movie

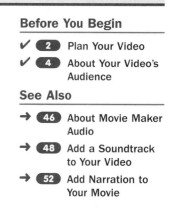

KEY TERM

Ambient sound—Background sound such as a car motor, birds singing, and water rippling. A scene completely devoid of ambient sound often seems lacking.

TIP

You might find that an external directional microphone helps eliminate surrounding noise while focusing on your subject's sound.

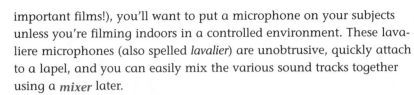

Mixer—An audio device with multiple microphone input jacks that enables you to combine several sound sources into one balanced soundtrack.

important films!), you'll want to put a microphone on your subjects unless you're filming indoors in a controlled environment. These lavaliere microphones (also spelled *lavalier*) are unobtrusive, quickly attach to a lapel, and you can easily mix the various sound tracks together using a *mixer* later.

If shooting a movie or instructional video, you should make preliminary videos at each location in your production before starting the actual filming. Review each of your test videos to see how ambient sound interferes or enhances the picture. You might be surprised at how much of a role, for good and bad, ambient sound will play. For example, when you shoot a beach scene, it would be wonderful to capture the sound of waves hitting the beach while your two subjects speak to each other. The problem you'll find with that, however, is that waves share a similar sound spectrum with human voices. Instead of accenting the moment, the waves will overwhelm (I would say drown, but that would be far too easy of a pun) your speakers' voices.

When you find that ambient sound detracts, you might have to shoot your film and request that your actors dub their lines over the video later.

Narration is wonderful when shooting travel videos. You'll tell your audience what they are seeing and you can offer background history. You can also tell anecdotal stories about what happened to you when traveling or about local customs and food.

NOTE

Movie Maker makes adding narration simple. You can watch your video playback while adding the narration so you time your scenes properly and synchronize the sound with the video (see **52** **Add Narration to Your Movie**).

For travel video buffs who love to record their trips for others to watch, the built-in video camera's microphone is great for speaking about the shoot during the shoot. In other words, if you're shooting a bartender making cappuccino in Venice's great plaza, you can talk about the people, the weather, and the excitement of the city as it passes you by while you await your scrumptious drink. Your knowledge of the place from where you're shooting is rarely better than at that moment, so record your thoughts then. Having said that, rarely will that audio be very good. You'll stumble over some words, and even find yourself saying some silly things. After all, you are trying to stay focused on your subject while describing the environment. Use what you record during the shoot as a basis, or draft script, for your final narration. Transcribe what you say and tighten the wording and fix your grammar mistakes, then record your voice once again over the video. You'll retain the same material, but the narration will be more focused and enjoyable.

3

Shooting Videos Like a Professional

IN THIS CHAPTER:

So many things can make the difference between a quality video and an amateur one. If you're new to digital video filmmaking, you need to learn about and avoid some of the possible pitfalls of shooting digital video. For example, many times newcomers struggle with either overusing a feature or avoiding it altogether. Excessive zooming is one of the most common mistakes beginners make; however, zooming is not something to stay away from entirely—just don't overdo it. When used effectively, a good zoom can focus the audience on exactly what it should focus on.

The lack of adequate lighting is another common mistake beginners make. Yet, if you've ever been to a photography studio, you know that professionals use lots of heavy-duty lighting. Why would they waste all that money on electrical bills if they did not greatly enhance the pictures?

This chapter contains several tasks that help you improve poor or mediocre videography skills, and the effort you must put into your skill-building is fairly light. A little knowledge gained from this chapter's tasks will dramatically improve the movies you shoot.

8 Reduce Camera Shake

Before You Begin

✔ **5** About Reducing Motion and Relying on Your Subjects

See Also

➜ **12** Blur Your Video's Motion

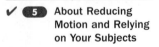

Digital image stabilization—Built-in camera movement sensors that act as shock absorbers. If you move the camera in a jerky motion, the digital image stabilization corrects for the movement and attempts to keep the picture steady.

Many digital cameras come with a feature known as *digital image stabilization*. Image stabilization can be used to reduce the apparent jitters or shakiness in a scene, especially when you're using the zoom. (When you zoom in to an image, any camera movement is magnified on film.)

This task offers ways to stabilize your camera's image that work to improve upon the camera's built-in stabilization that might be there. Digital image stabilization cannot correct for every move you make. This task shows you how to reduce any shakiness while filming.

Sometimes you will not want to use digital image stabilization. Most digital video cameras enable you to turn off the feature. Unfortunately, some digital artifacts can be obvious when using this feature. Avoid stabilization when shooting in low light, when using digital zoom, or when shooting scenes with lots of obvious stripes (such as Venetian blinds). All these situations increase the potential for digital noise on film if your camera is set to use its electronic stabilization feature.

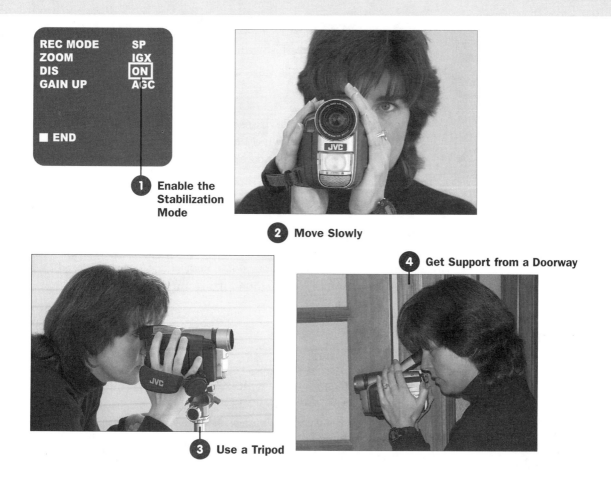

REC MODE   SP
ZOOM   IGX
DIS   ON
GAIN UP   AGC

■ END

1 Enable the Stabilization Mode

2 Move Slowly

4 Get Support from a Doorway

3 Use a Tripod

1 Enable the Stabilization Mode

When you're in a situation where you want to minimize the jitters that come from camera shake, enable your camera's digital image stabilization mode. You can find it on your camera's menu; refer to the manual for details if you cannot locate your camera's stabilization section.

2 Move Slowly

Regardless of whether you're using electronic stabilization, try to move the camera slowly and steadily. Don't jerk the camera

NOTE

Adequate lighting cannot be stressed enough. You learn here that low lighting deteriorates the otherwise positive effects of a stabilizer. Many cameras cannot handle low lighting situations well so try to shoot with a well-lit subject when you have a choice (see **13** Light Your Video Properly).

NOTE

Your camera's digital image stabilization (DIS) screen will probably differ from the one in the picture.

TIP

Tighten all screws securely on your tripod except for the head elements to ensure a solid base. Make sure you mount your tripod on solid ground.

around. Note that fast zooming can induce motion sickness in your audience. Zoom slowly and keep any zooming you do to a minimum.

3 Use a Tripod

The best way to stabilize a scene is by mounting your camcorder on a tripod. Leave the swivel head loose so that you can move the camera from side to side and up and down while you shoot your video.

4 Get Support from a Doorway

If you can't use a tripod, try leaning your body against something solid (such as a doorway, a fence, or a post) for support. You'll be surprised at how much more stable your videos are as opposed to the ones you shoot while standing on your own.

---

9 Mask with a Blue Screen

Before You Begin

✔ **3** About Your Camera's Perspective

See Also

➔ **15** White-Balance Your Scene

KEY TERM

Blue screen filter—Also known as a *chroma key transparency filter*, a blue screen filter enables you to create a useful special effect by embedding one video inside another. Weather newscasters often use the blue screen effect to stand in front of a map of moving weather elements, when in reality, a second camera is shooting the map elsewhere and they are actually standing in front of a blank, colored screen.

A warning is in order for this task. This book's focus is on taking quality digital videos and editing them with Movie Maker. The concepts you learn here are not limited to Movie Maker. For example, Movie Maker does not support the use of the *blue screen filter* described in this task although more advanced video editing programs do support blue screen editing. Programs such as Adobe Premiere Pro do (**see 110 About Editing Professionally with Adobe Premiere Pro**). Blue screens can be used so effectively in some video situations that you need some exposure to the concept and this task gives you that exposure.

By filming your video's action in front of a specially colored backdrop, you can put another video layer in the background. Some practice and planning is necessary to produce a good blue screen effect. The blue screen does not have to be a backdrop. This task intentionally makes the subject hold a blue screen matte so that you can see the effect of adding a layer of video at some random location in the scene.

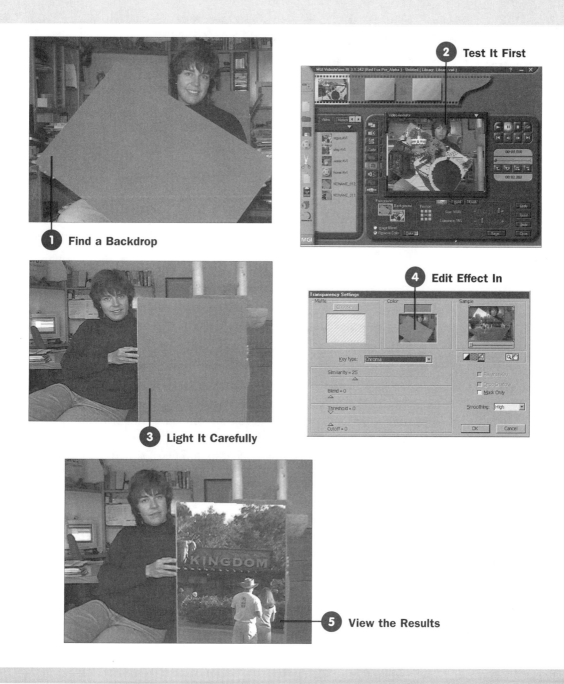

1 Find a Backdrop

2 Test It First

3 Light It Carefully

4 Edit Effect In

5 View the Results

NOTE

The blue screen doesn't have to be blue! To prove that point, this task's pictures use a red backdrop as the "blue screen."

Special video effects such as blue screens are the most fun and rewarding parts of experimenting with a camcorder. Extremely good blue screen matte effects are hard to generate, though. To get your feet wet, try filming one person in front of a solid wall. You might also try putting a piece of brightly colored poster paper on the wall to get an evening news "weather map" effect. If you have success with that, step up to shooting moving action against a colored backdrop.

1 Find a Backdrop

Your backdrop doesn't have to be blue but it should be a very different color than anything else in the scene. You needn't fill the whole background with the backdrop; a small square can serve as a weather map or window.

2 Test It First

Before you count on your backdrop working, test it first. Film the backdrop with your camcorder and then import the clip into a video editing program that supports blue screening.

3 Light It Carefully

Your backdrop should be lit evenly, with no obvious shadows or highlights. It might take more than one backlight or lighting reflector panel to illuminate the backdrop properly. Make sure that any people in front of the backdrop don't cast shadows on the material.

NOTE

When you first watch a blue screen-based scene you've shot, the scene might seem strange to you, even though you expect the results! There's something eerie about watching a scene with missing content, when you saw that content clearly throughout the filming and editing process.

4 Edit Effect In

After you have your video on tape, you'll need to use the chroma key transparency filter in your video editing program to let another layer of video see through the backdrop. Read your video editing program's instructions for blue screen or chroma key to see how to do this in that specific program.

5 View the Results

Watch the resulting video to ensure that your blue screen produced the desired results.

Transitions can be as simple as a fade-out after a scene ends or as complex as seeing one clip fly off the screen as another clip enters the picture. In reality, every scene transitions to the next, but unless you specify a different transition effect, your movie will simply switch from the final frame of one scene to the opening frame of the next scene and continue playing.

Depending on your video camera's capabilities, you usually have the ability to generate these two kinds of transitions:

- **Camcorder-Based Transitions**—You might be able to enable simple transitions in your camcorder. When you end one scene and start shooting the next, your camcorder will insert the transition. When your camera automatically generates the transitions that you want, you have less work later during the editing process.

- **Software-Based Transitions**—Programs such as Movie Maker can insert many kinds of transitions into your video and place them right where you want them to appear. You have more freedom and a far greater selection than video cameras can offer.

This task explains how to turn transitions on using your camera's transition effects. Generally, if you won't be able to edit your video for some reason, perhaps such as when you're shooting an event and the event's sponsors want the video as soon as the event ends, you should set up transitions in your camera so the scenes smoothly transition between each other. If you are able to edit the video, don't set up special camera transitions because such transitions make it more difficult to separate scenes into clips during your editing process.

① **Enable Fades or Wipes**

Refer to your camcorder's manual and find the menu setting that enables the automatic transitions, usually called a *fade*, or *wipe*. You should see a short menu of possible options to choose from.

Before You Begin

✔ **3** About Your Camera's Perspective

See Also

➔ **69** Transition from Clip to Clip

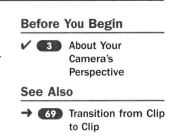

KEY TERM

Transitions—Graphical segues that signal the end of one scene and the start of the next. Transitions are often called *wipes*.

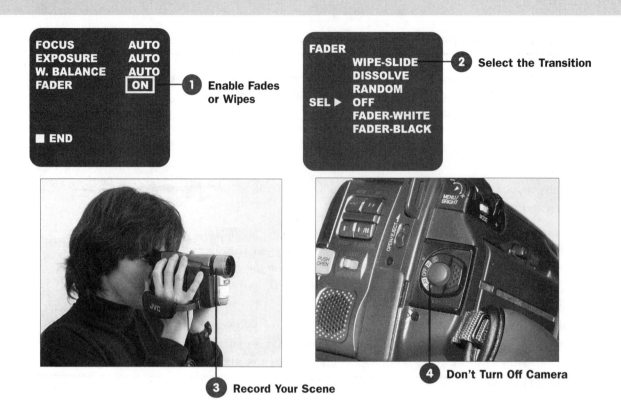

FOCUS AUTO
EXPOSURE AUTO
W. BALANCE AUTO
FADER ON ——— **1** Enable Fades or Wipes

■ END

FADER
  WIPE-SLIDE ——— **2** Select the Transition
  DISSOLVE
  RANDOM
SEL ▶ OFF
  FADER-WHITE
  FADER-BLACK

4 Don't Turn Off Camera

3 Record Your Scene

2 Select the Transition

🖲 **TIP**

For more complex transitions, you'll have to rely on Movie Maker.

Pick the transition you'd like to use. A fade "fades" from black or white; a *wipe* or *slide* physically moves the new video into the frame while displacing the old video. A *dissolve* fades from one video to the next.

3 Record Your Scene

The transition effect happens automatically when you press your camera's **Record** button to start and stop recording. When you are done with the effect, remember to turn the transition feature off in the camera's menu.

4 Don't Turn Off Camera

If you turn off your camcorder after filming a scene, the ending position will be lost and the camera can't use a transition to ease into the next scene you film.

NOTE

If you fade out of a scene, feel free to power off your camera. The start of the next scene will not need to match the end frame of the scene from which you faded out.

11 Zoom Effectively

In spite of proper warnings against the overuse of zoom, and in spite of the horrid videos beginners make when they use zoom too much, your camera's zoom feature is a valuable tool you can use to compose your shots and to capture proper elements of the subject. For example, specific *focal lengths*, shot from a consistent distance, will give your movie a different look from one shot more conventionally. By shooting at a far-off focal length, for example, your movie will take on a more voyeuristic tone where your audience feels less like a part of the action.

In general, the more you zoom out, the less in-focus your subject will appear. Close-up zooms also amplify inadvertent camera movement (see **8 Reduce Camera Shake**). People often purchase a particular camcorder because it offers massive zoom—something along the lines of 200× or 300×. In reality, that number refers to a digital zoom and not an optical zoom. An optical zoom uses your camera's optics to enlarge the image, but a digital zoom uses electronic trickery to magnify the image, and the results too often are grainy and ugly. Avoid using digital zoom too often; try to stick within the limits of your camera's optical zoom.

Because a camera's resolution suffers at higher zoom levels, when possible keep a wide angle and walk toward a subject if you want to get the camera closer than your current focal point allows.

1 Use the Zoom Button

Your camera should have a level or dial for controlling the zoom. Press it one way to zoom toward wide angle, and in the other direction for telephoto. Note that many cameras use one dial or level to do several things, such as change volume and zoom the lens (as the **VOL** dial does in this picture).

Before You Begin

✔ **5** About Reducing Motion and Relying on Your Subjects

See Also

➜ **12** Blur Your Video's Motion

KEY TERM

Focal length—The distance from the camcorder lens to the subject.

TIP

If a subject is coming toward you, you can utilize zooming to keep the subject approximately the same size inside your framed camera eye.

MODE MENU

REC MODE
ZOOM 16x 64x 400x ———(2) **Enable Digital Zooming**
DIS ON
GAIN AGC

■ END

(4) **Focus Manually**

(1) **Use the Zoom Button**

(3) **Zoom Slowly**

TIP

Remember to use optical zoom if possible to get the best zoomed resolution. If your optical zoom is not powerful enough, switch to digital zoom to get the close-up you need.

(2) Enable Digital Zooming

Your camera probably has a digital zoom mode that extends your ability to zoom well past the optical zoom of the camera. You'll probably have to refer to your manual and enter the camera's menu system to turn on this zoom feature, which can enable you to magnify the view up to as much as 300×. (Optical zooms generally max out at about 12×.)

(3) Zoom Slowly

Zooming takes patience and restraint to do well. Generally, you should zoom slowly (abrupt changes in zoom look bad on film) and zoom only once or twice in a scene. Watch television to see how professionals zoom—they do not overuse this technique. In fact, try to zoom between shots so that the viewer doesn't see the zoom happen.

4 Focus Manually

If you use the digital zoom mode and perform some extreme magnifications (such as 64× or more), the camcorder might have a hard time focusing automatically. If that's the case, you can disable your camera's auto-focus mode to focus manually, usually by turning a dial or ring. Refer to your camera manual for how to do this.

12 Blur Your Video's Motion

It's difficult to get the impression of speed in video—even when you're filming something that's going 100 miles per hour it can look relatively stationary on a small television screen. That's why you should master *motion blur* to give your audience a sense of something quickly moving when you need the effect. For example, you could use motion blur to record a horse race to show your audience the equestrians' speed.

When blurring, you will find yourself panning your camera quickly. Except when blurring, you usually want to maintain slow pans. In addition, you'll find that slowing your camera's *shutter speed* will help blur the background but you also should use a steady hand (and preferably a tripod) to keep your subject in the same position inside your camera's lens.

1 Set a Slow Shutter Speed

You can get decent motion blur even with your camera set on full automatic shutter speed, but the slower your shutter speed is set, the better your results will be. Try setting your camcorder's shutter to manual mode and try 1/30 or 1/60 of a second.

2 Set for Manual Focus

In certain situations, you might not be able to keep the moving subject in the middle of the frame, where the auto-focus sensors are located. If so, set your camera's focus to manual and dial in the focus to where the moving subject will be when you start shooting.

Before You Begin

✔ **5** About Reducing Motion and Relying on Your Subjects

✔ **8** Reduce Camera Shake

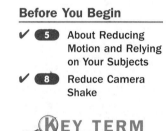

KEY TERM

Motion blur—The effect of tracking a speeding object and thus blurring the background due to the motion.

KEY TERMS

Shutter speed—The time between the opening and closing of your camera's shutter, determining how many frames per second your camera records.

Shutter—Blades that open and close, exposing your subject to your camera's film, creating one frame of video each time the shutter opens.

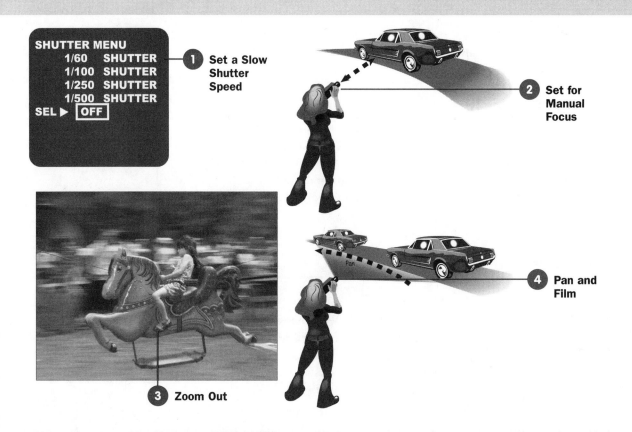

SHUTTER MENU
1/60 SHUTTER
1/100 SHUTTER
1/250 SHUTTER
1/500 SHUTTER
SEL ▶ OFF

① Set a Slow Shutter Speed

② Set for Manual Focus

④ Pan and Film

Pan

③ Zoom Out

NOTE

Your shot's background provides a stable image behind your motion blur. If your motion blur is weak, one of the first things to try is zooming out for a wider background shot.

③ Zoom Out

Before the shot begins, make sure that you're not zoomed in too far. If you can't see enough of the background, the effect of the motion blur will be lost.

④ Pan and Film

When it's time to get the shot, start recording and pan with the moving object. Ideally, the object will move from left to right (or right to left) across your field of view. Just turn with the moving object to keep it in the frame throughout the shot.

13 Light Your Video Properly

Properly exposing video film to a subject differs a bit from setting the exposure on a still camera, but the principles are the same. You can keep your camera in auto mode all the time, or you can take control and get better results with manual overrides. Every camcorder is different; to learn how to access your camera's manual exposure mode, refer to the documentation that came with your camera.

A camera exposes a scene by balancing between the shutter speed (**see** **12** **Blur Your Video's Motion**) with the *aperture setting*. The larger the aperture's *f-stop*—expressed as f/2, f/5.6, or f/22 for instance, the smaller the aperture opening.

Many lighting options are available to the filmmaker. You can purchase a large, collapsible reflector from any camera store to put additional light on your subject. Reflectors fold up small enough to fit in a camera bag, but unfurl quickly to put indirect light on your subject. If you can, consider multiple light sources. The room or setting's primary lighting source works best when you combine that light with filler light that you add, reflecting the filler light off another surface to soften the added light. A backlight reflected off your scene's background adds a sense of distance between the subject and the background.

❶ Stay in Shade

When you shoot outdoors, direct sunlight can overwhelm your camcorder and create unflattering lighting or harsh shadows on your subject. Shoot in a shaded area when possible and keep the sun to your left or right and never allow the sun to shine directly in front or behind you.

❷ Go Manual When Moving

When you move from indoors to outdoors within a scene, the sudden change in lighting conditions can radically underexpose or overexpose the subject for a few seconds while the camera adjusts. To avoid that problem, set the exposure manually and leave it there through the scene transition. Your scene's background is far less important than the subject!

Before You Begin

✔ **3** About the Camera's Perspective

See Also

→ **15** White-Balance Your Scene

→ **16** Take Low-Light Movies

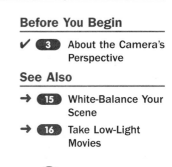

KEY TERMS

Aperture setting—The size of the opening that lets light through the lens.

F-stop—Numbers that indicate the size of a camera's aperture opening. The formula for an f-stop is a fraction which makes the larger the f-stop number, the smaller the aperture opening and the less light can enter the camera.

🔅 TIP

Several Web sites specialize in lighting accessories for your shoots. Wolf Camera (**http://www.wolf-camera.com**) provides a huge assortment of amateur and professional lighting accessories. If you know exactly what you're looking for, don't forget eBay (**http://ww.ebay.com**), where you can sometimes pay just pennies on the dollar for new or like-new accessories.

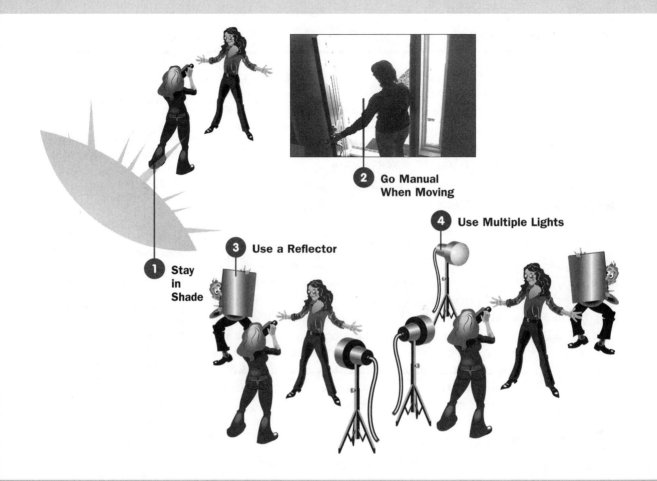

2 Go Manual When Moving

4 Use Multiple Lights

3 Use a Reflector

1 Stay in Shade

NOTE

If you have a choice, don't shoot an indoor subject standing in front of a window (in the daytime). The window's natural light will wash out your shoot. Lighting a subject in front of a window with bright sun coming through is virtually impossible.

3 **Use a Reflector**

A reflector is especially useful outdoors where you can position someone who is holding it off to the side of your subject. This kind of light is more flattering to people than harsh, direct sunlight.

4 **Use Multiple Lights**

When filming indoors, you have a lot more control over the lighting. If you're in a really controlled situation, such as shooting a talking head for an interview, use two or three lights to illuminate your subject.

14 Control Your Depth of Focus

Beginning videographers rarely think about the subtleties of filmmaking, but it's the little things that can really make your projects look professional and have that extra punch. One such aspect is *depth of field*. Creative use of depth of field can have a powerful, dramatic role in your films.

Your video's depth of field depends on both the amount of zoom you've set and the current aperture setting (**see 13 Light Your Video Properly**). Use depth of field to isolate your subject from the foreground and background or to keep the entire scene in focus. Unlike the process with a regular 35mm film-based camera, you don't have to do anything to check the depth of field you are filming; what you see through the viewfinder is what you get on film.

1 Zoom In for Less Depth

An easy way to reduce depth of field to isolate your subject is to work at the telephoto end of the optical zoom on your camera. However, note that zooming in to the digital zoom ratios on your camera has no effect on depth of field.

2 Zoom Out for More Depth

You achieve the most depth of field by zooming out to the camera's most wide-angle setting. At this setting, virtually all of the scene should be in sharp focus.

3 Open Aperture for Less Depth

If you can switch to the camcorder's manual mode, opening the aperture to admit more light also has the effect of reducing depth of field. In this picture, note that although the camera lens is zoomed out to capture both children, the wide-open aperture setting narrows depth of field so that the focus is only on the child in front.

Before You Begin

✔ **3** About the Camera's Perspective

✔ **5** About Reducing Motion and Relying on Your Subjects

✔ **11** Zoom Effectively

 KEY TERM

Depth of field—The amount of a scene that is completely in sharp focus at any one time.

TIP

The more you zoom in to a subject, the steadier your camera must be to keep camera shakes from the audience's eyes. A tripod works wonders to reduce zoom-in camera shake.

1 Zoom In for Less Depth

2 Zoom Out for More Depth

3 Open Aperture for Less Depth

4 Close Aperture for More Depth

4 **Close Aperture for More Depth**

In manual exposure mode, if you shut down the aperture to smaller values, you reduce the light entering and simultaneously increase depth of field, putting more of the scene in focus. In this picture, notice that the lens is zoomed out about the same as it was for the children in the preceding step, but the smaller aperture setting forces a deeper field of focus.

15 White-Balance Your Scene

Video camcorders have to be tuned to the particular color of light in which you are filming. Otherwise, colors (such as some flesh tones) look wrong. When your camcorder knows what color white is, all the other colors come out accurately as well. This adjustment is usually done automatically, but you can get better results by manually white-balancing your camcorder—especially indoors, in low-light situations, when using a camera light, or with unusually tinted overhead lights.

Different light sources (such as light provided by sunrise, midday sun, candlelight, and fluorescent bulbs) have different color temperatures, and this affects the way your camera displays color. An improperly balanced scene will appear reddish or bluish, depending on the color temperature.

Remember to reset your white balance whenever conditions change. If you use manual white-balance settings from indoors when you film outdoors, you'll get unusual results.

1 Enter Camera's Menu

The exact procedure for balancing whites manually depends on the kind of camera you have but most white-balancing procedures are similar. Start by entering the White Balance menu and selecting manual mode.

2 Focus on White Paper

Have someone hold a piece of bright, white paper in front of the camera. Position yourself so that the paper fills the frame and is in focus. Also, be sure that the paper is bathed in the light that you plan to shoot your subjects in so that you balance the camera properly.

3 Set Balance

Refer to your camera's documentation to learn how to set the white balance. (The JVC camera in this picture uses the Menu dial to lock in the white balance.) Then select the appropriate control on your camera to memorize the paper's color value. This sets the white balance for the current lighting conditions.

Before You Begin

✔ **13** Light Your Video Properly

See Also

→ **16** Take Low-Light Movies

 TIP

For the most accurate video, balance your whites often and do not trust your camera's automatic controls any more than you have to.

1 Enter Camera's Menu

FOCUS	AUTO
EXPOSURE	AUTO
W. BALANCE	AUTO
FADER	OFF

■ END

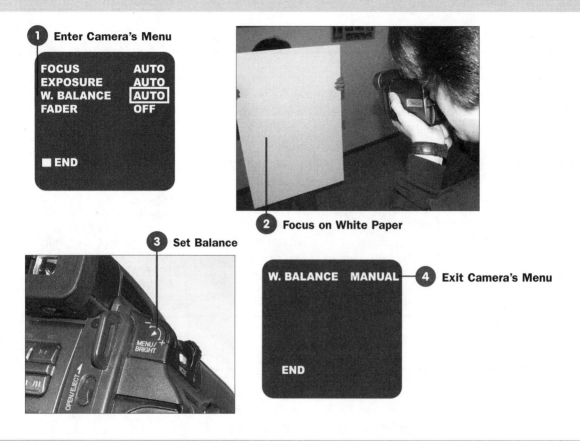

2 Focus on White Paper

3 Set Balance

W. BALANCE   MANUAL **4** Exit Camera's Menu

END

4 Exit Camera's Menu

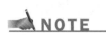NOTE

Now you might better understand why Hollywood movie production crews are so large! People are there to set white balance, set up lighting, set proper aperture, and so much more. The actual filming of a scene is simple once the rest is set up.

Finish the process by exiting the white balance menu by selecting the End or Exit option on your camera's menu. The camera is now set for filming. Remember that when you're done filming this scene, you should either set the camera back to automatic white balance or recalibrate the manual white balance for the next set of lighting conditions.

16 Take Low-Light Movies

Video camcorders are often rated by their *lux value*. Although lux values are subjective (and seem to be often exaggerated by manufacturers), a 2-lux camera can work in very low light, even in candlelight. Such shooting is not always optimum quality, however, so you'll learn from this task how to gain better quality in low-lighting conditions.

Although you can film in low-light situations with most camcorders, keep these items in mind for best results:

- Auto-focus systems fail in low light. You might need to resort to manual focusing if you're filming by candlelight.

- The quality of light varies dramatically in a dark room. When you set the white balance, put the white card exactly where you plan to film (**see** **15** **White-Balance Your Scene**).

- The quality of video recorded in low light will be dramatically lower than the quality of video recorded in daylight.

1 Set White Balance

Low-light situations are almost certainly outside the camera's pre-set white balance values. Whenever filming in these situations, the first thing you should do is set the camera's white balance. If the lighting changes during the shoot, reset the white balance as often as necessary.

2 Use Lights

Camera lights are often harsh and unforgiving, but they are essential if you're trying to film in very low-light conditions. Your camera might have a built-in light and if so, you should use it.

3 Avoid Digital Zoom

In low-light situations, the image will probably be grainy—this is digital noise that occurs when there isn't enough light to make a good shot. Digital zooming introduces noise of its own, so avoid digitally zooming when you film in low light.

Before You Begin

✔ **13** Light Your Video Properly

✔ **15** White-Balance Your Scene

 KEY TERM

Lux value—A measurement that states how low a light level can be before registering on your camera. Lux values determine how much candlelight, or unit of light, falls on a surface.

 NOTE

When you shoot action sequences, low lighting levels will more dramatically and adversely affect your filming than adequate lighting. Pay extra attention to light levels when you film movement.

 TIP

Camera stores sell clip-on lights you can add to your camcorder if your camcorder has no built-in light or if the camcorder's light is too weak to be helpful.

1 Set White Balance

W. BALANCE   MANUAL

END

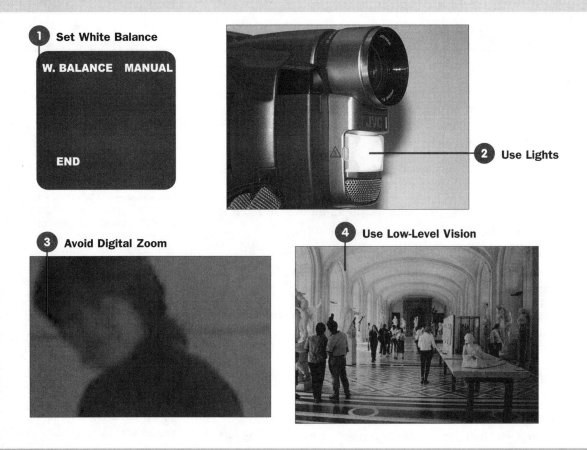

2 Use Lights

3 Avoid Digital Zoom

4 Use Low-Level Vision

4 Use Low-Level Vision

In near or absolute darkness, you might be able to use another feature: infrared recording. Some video cameras include infrared recording to help nighttime shooting. Others specifically adapt better than most to low-lighting situations. Your budget and subject matter will determine how much extra you want to pay for a camera with better nighttime capabilities.

PART III

Preparing Your Videos

IN THIS PART:

4

Getting Content into Movie Maker

IN THIS CHAPTER:

Understanding how Movie Maker's windows relate is the first step in producing videos quickly and easily with Movie Maker. Before you can produce a movie in Movie Maker, you must transfer your video and audio content to Movie Maker. Once there, you arrange the clips, add transitions, special effects, added audio (such as you might do for narration), and trim portions of the video to fit within your required playing time length.

Movie Maker supports several ways to import content into your video project. Your project does not even have to be a video; you can turn your imported audio and still photos into a slide show. To make your slide show more interesting, you can add narration and even specify how you want one slide to transition to another.

Movie Maker is simple to use, but part of its simplicity requires that you understand the workflow from raw video footage or pictures (or both) to your final movie.

TIP

You can insert still pictures between two video clips. The pictures will display as long as you have set their duration to appear (see **39** **Set a Picture Clip's Duration**). Your movie's soundtrack can continue playing during the picture's display.

---

17 **About Collections, Contents, and Projects**

Before You Begin

✔ **1** Walk Through a Digital Video Production

See Also

➜ **19** About Your Project's Content

TIP

The **Collections** pane holds the name of everything in your collection. To display the **Collections** pane, select **View**, **Collections**. To hide it, click the **Close** button in the upper-right hand corner of the **Collections** pane.

The video and audio content available for your movies resides in Movie Maker's **Collections** pane. All the video, audio, still images, transitions, and special effects that you might want to add to your final movie reside in the collection. Everything in your collection won't appear in your final video—think of your collection as a repository of all the possible things you might add to your movie.

The **Collections** pane only lists the content by name. When you click any item in the **Collections** pane, the **Contents** pane shows the contents of that collection's item, such as a thumbnail image of clips in the video, or a series of available transitions you can select. You can switch the **Contents** pane between thumbnails and details by selecting **View**, **Thumbnails** or **View**, **Details**.

Collections Pane

Click to Hide Pane

Contents Pane

Selected Item

Contents of Selected Item

The Collections pane shows every element you can add to your video.

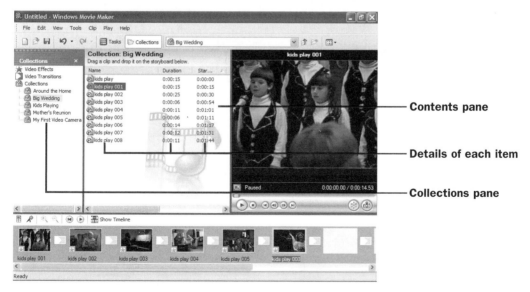

Contents pane

Details of each item

Collections pane

By displaying the Collections pane's details, you see more information about the collection's items.

NOTE

Your project holds your selected clips and special effects, as well as the order of the storyboard/timeline you've arranged. The project is not your movie. Your movie is the final output, a playable video, whereas the project is the ordered items that comprise your movie.

From the collection, you can select everything you want in your final video, edit your video's elements by trimming, merging, and ordering clips, and add special effects and transitions. Before creating your final movie, you will need to save your project. You can always load any project file back into Movie Maker to continue editing your production. Think of the project as your workspace, with all the editing you've done so far on a movie. Even if you create a final movie, you should save that movie's project in case you ever want to work on the movie again.

All collections include entries for **Video Effects** and **Video Transitions**. You might not need to add special effects or use transitions in your video, but Movie Maker always makes them available by inserting them in every collection. When you click on **Video Effects** or **Video Transitions** in your **Collections** pane, Movie Maker will display all possible elements from that collection item in your **Contents** pane.

Transitions Appear Here

Click to Select Video Transitions

Click to See Effect in Monitor

Click to Play Effect

Click to See More

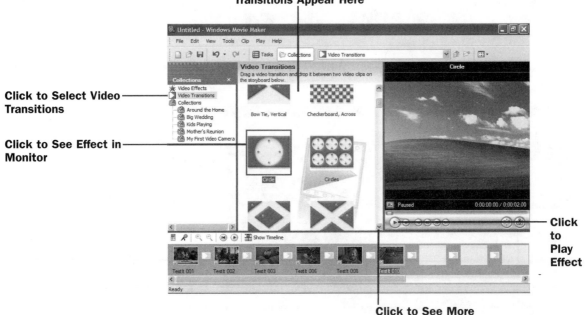

You can scroll through all possible transitions by clicking the Video Transitions entry in your Collections pane.

18 Start a Movie Maker Project

Your project holds the production script to your production. The project contains the clips your movie contains, the transitions between clips, the soundtrack, and any narration you might provide. In a way, you can think of your project as containing a description of what your story-board/timeline looks like.

Your project file does not actually contain any video or audio footage. The project does contain a description of that footage. Whereas a video you create from a project might consume four megabytes or even much more, the project file from which you made that movie might only be one-tenth the size.

 Select File, New Project

From the **File** menu, select **New Project**. You can also press **Ctrl+N** to request that Movie Maker create a new project.

2 Save Previous Project If Needed

If you have not saved a project you were already working on, Movie Maker gives you the chance to do so.

3 Select File, Save Project

Display the **File** menu once again and select **Save Project**.

4 Type a Name

You can now give your project a name. Movie Maker saves projects with the **.MSWMM** filename extension, an extension indicating that the file is a Microsoft Windows Movie Maker project file.

5 Click OK

When you click **OK**, Movie Maker saves the project.

Before You Begin

✔ **17** About Collections, Contents, and Projects

See Also

→ **26** About Cataloging Your Videos

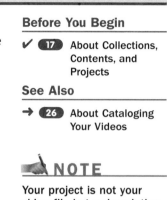 **NOTE**

Your project is not your video file but a description of your video. You can create multiple videos from the same project. You can create one video, change the project a bit, then create a second video. From one project, you thereby produce two similar but different videos.

 NOTE

You won't always create a new project for every video you create; you might want to modify an existing project file instead of creating a new one. If so, open an existing project file with **File**, **Open Project** instead of creating a new project.

 TIP

It's best to give your project a name at the time you begin the project. If you work on multiple projects, you are less likely to confuse two similar projects if you give them names when you create them instead of selecting a name right before shutting down your editing session.

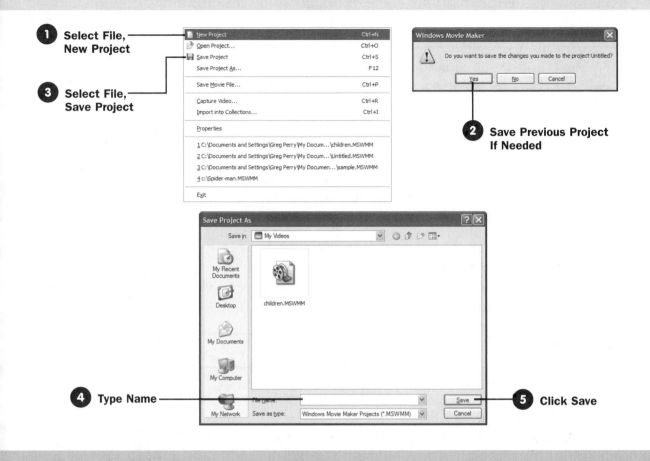

1 Select File, New Project

3 Select File, Save Project

2 Save Previous Project If Needed

4 Type Name

5 Click Save

---

19 About Your Project's Content

Before You Begin

✔ **17** About Collections, Contents, and Projects

✔ **18** Start a Movie Maker Project

See Also

→ **34** Display a Clip's Properties

When someone new to Movie Maker creates a new project for the *second time*, they are often surprised that Movie Maker does not erase the **Collections** pane. Any elements that appear in your collection, as well as the thumbnails or details shown in the **Contents** pane, are still there when you create a new project.

Keep in mind that the project is a description of your video's storyboard/timeline details. The project is not your collection. When you create a new project, Movie Maker will remove everything from your storyboard/timeline because you are instructing Movie Maker to give you a fresh video.

A project's properties often contain useful information. As you create more and more productions over time, each project's properties enable you to locate projects quickly, or search for projects that meet criteria you're looking for.

You must enter the project's property information. Select **File**, **Properties** to display the **Project Properties** dialog box after you create a new project. Movie Maker saves those properties along with the project in the future.

The Project Properties dialog box contains details that describe your project.

Here are the properties associated with a Movie Maker project:

- **Title**—The **Title** field is the name you assign to your project, which Movie Maker then attaches to the video you ultimately create. The title usually appears on the screen when someone plays your video on a computer. Movie Maker gives you room for 128 characters for the **Title** field.

- **Author**—Usually, the **Author** field holds the name of the producer, who will be you in most cases. Some playback software displays the author's name when the video is played back on a computer. Movie Maker gives you room for 128 characters for the **Author** field.

NOTE

If Movie Maker cleared the **Collections** pane, you would have to reload the **Collections** pane with content, including importing the same video again into your collection, if you wanted to create a new video based on the first one.

TIP

You might be surprised how often you create a second video based on one you made before. Highlight videos and previews (such as *trailers*) are simple to create from an existing project's content. You will thus save the movie's project and the preview's project in two files, both of which use the identical **Contents** pane for their subject matter.

KEY TERM

Trailer—A short movie preview that attempts to generate interest and a potential audience.

TIP

Select **Tools**, **Options** to fill in the **Default author** field. That name appears in the Author properties for subsequent projects you create. You can change the default name for individual projects by editing the **Project Properties** dialog box's **Author** field.

- **Duration**—The project's duration is the time that Movie Maker fills in automatically. The duration matches your timeline using the *hours:minutes:seconds:hundredths of seconds* format. The duration changes as you modify your project.

- **Copyright**—Any copyright-related information you want to enter goes in the **Copyright** field. Some players display the copyright information during playback. Movie Maker gives you room for only 14 characters for the **Copyright** field.

- **Rating**—You can rate your movie (A+ is always a good rating!) in the **Rating** field. Playback software often displays the rating when your movie is played back. Movie Maker gives you room for 20 characters for the **Rating** field.

- **Description**—The **Description** field displays the description you enter for your project. Playback software often displays the description when your movie is played back. Movie Maker gives you room for 512 characters for the **Description** field.

TIP

You can display and change any of your project's property values at any time, except for the **Duration** field, which Movie Maker maintains.

---

20 **Capture Video into Movie Maker**

Before You Begin

✔ **17** About Collections, Contents, and Projects

✔ **18** Start a Movie Maker Project

See Also

→ **22** Import Still Pictures into Movie Maker

→ **24** Watch Your Video in the Monitor

NOTE

When you capture video that already has audio, Movie Maker imports the audio as well and stores it on the timeline's Audio track.

As long as you have the proper hardware, you can capture video directly into Movie Maker. The capture device might be a capture card inside your computer that you plug a VCR or television cable into, or perhaps it's a FireWire port into which you've plugged your video camera's cable. You can even capture directly from a live signal if your video capture card has a TV tuner.

You can start a video capture by selecting **File**, **Capture Video** from Movie Maker's menu, but the **Video Capture Wizard** is probably the best place from which to capture. The **Video Capture Wizard** walks you through the steps needed for capturing properly, presenting options at the appropriate times.

1 **Select View, Task Pane**

If your **Task** pane is not already showing, select **Task Pane** from the **View** menu.

2 **Click Capture from Video Device**

Click the **Capture from video device** option. This initiates the capture procedure.

Adjust Options

If multiple capture devices are attached to your computer, select the one you want from the **Available Devices** option. The remaining setting defaults in the dialog box are probably fine as is.

 Click Next

From the options dialog box, click **Next** to enter information about the capture file you will be creating.

5 **Type a Filename**

Enter a filename. This file will appear in the **Collections** pane as one of the repositories you can go to when you want to add captured video clips to the storyboard or timeline.

6 **Select Location**

Your Movie Maker project needs to know where to look for the collection. Enter the location where you want to store the captured video.

When you save your project before exiting Movie Maker, Movie Maker saves the location of your captured file along with the project. If you ever move the captured file to a different location, you will need to import the captured file into your project so that Movie Maker will know where it is.

7 **Click Next**

Click **Next** to move to the **Video Setting** dialog box where you can specify the quality of the captured file.

8 **Select Playback Quality**

If you will primarily play back the video on your computer or one similar to yours, make sure you click to select the option labeled **Best quality for playback on my computer**. If you plan to play the video on another device such as a Pocket PC (which requires low resolution) or a high-resolution device such as a DVD player, click the option labeled **Other settings** and select a quality from the list that matches the device you're outputting to.

TIP

If you cannot see any video after completing each of these capture steps, return to this **Video Capture Device** dialog box, click **Configure**, then click **TV Tuner**. Change the channel from 3 to 4 or from 4 to 3, and close the dialog box and continue through the rest of this task. Often the default channel is set differently from your capture device's channel when you first begin capturing video from another source.

NOTE

As you select various output quality settings, Movie Maker displays more detail about the settings at the bottom of the dialog box. Movie Maker describes the selected setting's file type (such as a Windows Media Player file with the **.wmv** filename extension), the bit rate, the display size in *pixels*, and the number of frames played per second of video (the higher the number, up to 30, the better).

Pixel—Short for *picture element* and used to represent the smallest dot of resolution in your video. The more pixels Movie Maker gives to your movie's quality, the smoother your video will look and the more disk space it will consume.

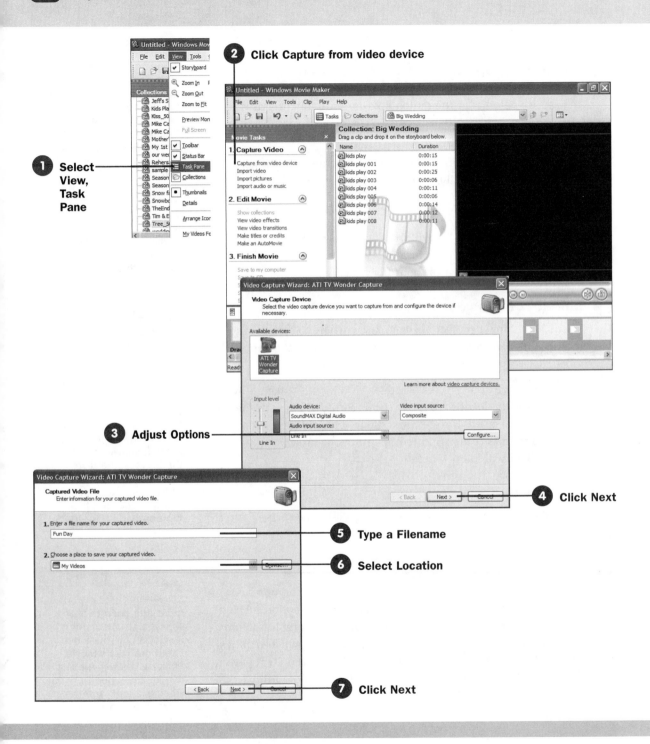

2 Click Capture from video device

1 Select View, Task Pane

3 Adjust Options

4 Click Next

5 Type a Filename

6 Select Location

7 Click Next

PART III: Preparing Your Videos

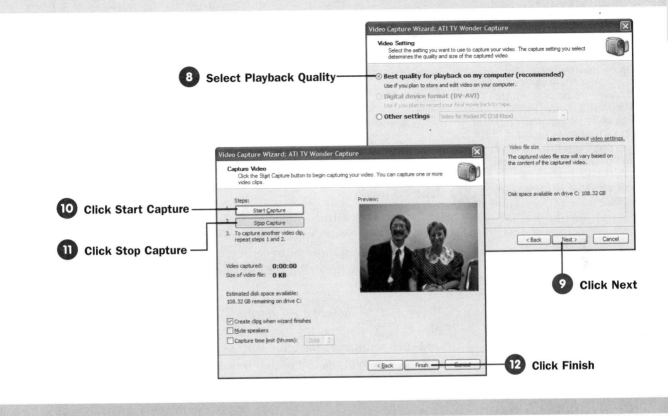

8 Select Playback Quality

 Click Start Capture

 Click Stop Capture

9 Click Next

12 Click Finish

9 Click Next

Click **Next** to display the **Capture Video** dialog box. You will stay on this box for a long time, often as long as your source video plays. It is here you see exactly what Movie Maker will capture. You must start the playback of the capture device now, and when you do, the output appears in the dialog box's monitor area. Movie Maker is not yet capturing the video; however, you must tell Movie Maker when to start and stop capturing.

10 Click Start Capture

When a scene that you want to capture appears, click **Start Capture**. Movie Maker begins capturing the video and audio at that point, and continues until you stop it.

NOTE

You don't have to divide your captured movie into clips yourself. At the end of the capture process, Movie Maker will divide the video into clips for you. Click the **Mute Speakers** option if you don't want to hear the audio while you capture the video. (Movie Maker will still continue to capture the audio.)

⑪ Click Stop Capture

Clicking **Stop Capture** stops the capture of the playback, but the video keeps playing. When another scene that you want to capture appears, you will need to tell Movie Maker to start capturing again. Continue clicking **Start Capture** and **Stop Capture** for as long as needed to capture all the footage you want into the collection file. If you miss capturing something, click **Stop Capture**, rewind the source, and begin the capture from that rewound point.

⑫ Click Finish

When you click **Finish**, Movie Maker saves the captured file and adds the file to your **Collections** pane. You will know how much disk space the captured video consumes from the **Estimated disk space available** option on the **Capture Video** dialog box where you click **Finish**.

If you want to capture a video without waiting at your computer to stop the capture at the end, click the **Capture time limit** option and set a recording time limit, such as one hour. Movie Maker will stop capturing at the end of that time limit.

---

21 Import Video into Movie Maker

Before You Begin

✔ **17** About Collections, Contents, and Projects

✔ **18** Start a Movie Maker Project

✔ **20** Capture Video into Movie Maker

See Also

→ **22** Import Still Pictures into Movie Maker

→ **47** About Importing Existing Digital Files

Importing video into Movie Maker is one of the most common tasks you'll perform when beginning a movie. After you've created a project, you must import content into your **Collections**. You can capture video from an external device, or import video into Movie Maker as described here. Note that you cannot import any video protected with *digital rights management*.

When you import video from a file, the video can be on your hard disk, on removable storage, or a networked location. Movie Maker will not make a copy of the video. When you import a video, Movie Maker imports information about the video and some scenes from the video to use for clip thumbnails.

As you work within your project, you must make sure that the imported video, called the *source file*, remains in place, and that video must be there every time you work on the project. If you move or delete the original source file, Movie Maker will no longer be able to refer to it, and the video will no longer be a part of your collection.

Through *clip detection*, Movie Maker generates many small clips as you import video into the program. Some clips might only be a couple of seconds in length, whereas others might span a minute or more.

Select File, Import into Collections

From the **File** menu, select **Import into Collections** to begin importing your source file. If you've displayed the **Task** pane (**View**, **Task Pane**), you need only click the **Task** pane's **Import video** option under the **Capture Video** heading to start the import process.

Locate File to Import

Browse to the location of your source files. You can import either video or audio content. You can also import still photos into Movie Maker (see **Import Still Pictures into Movie Maker**).

Click File to Import

Select the file you want to import. If you select multiple files, Movie Maker imports all of them.

Import multiple video files by holding **Ctrl** before clicking on file names to select more than one at the same time. If the filenames are listed consecutively in the **Import File** dialog box, click to select the first one, hold **Shift**, and click to select the last one you want, and Movie Maker selects the first, last, and all files between. Movie Maker then imports all the videos you've selected.

Click for Automatic Clips

You control Movie Maker's clip detection feature by checking **Create clips for video files** to turn the option on or off. As Movie Maker imports the file, Movie Maker will create clips from the source file to display in the **Contents** pane. If you do not request clip detection, Movie Maker imports the video as one long clip.

5 Click Import to Begin Importing

When you click **Import**, Movie Maker begins importing the source file into your project's collection. The clips will appear in the **Contents** pane.

Digital rights management—Encoding of a video or audio file that protects it from unauthorized copying or distribution by programs that recognize the digital rights management system. Also called *DRM*.

Source file—A video or audio file that you import into Movie Maker.

If you delete or move a source file after importing it, you need only import the video from its new location for Movie Maker to use it.

Clip detection—The process Movie Maker uses to split imported video into multiple clips. Movie Maker separates video into clips when it senses scene changes or major camera differences.

NOTE

Movie Maker does not use clip detection when importing audio clips.

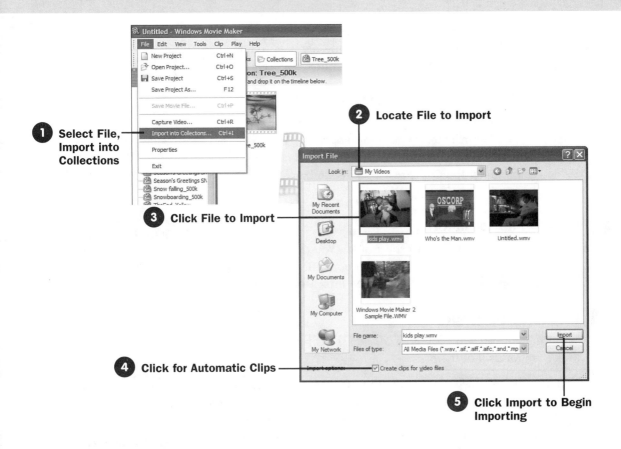

1 Select File, Import into Collections

2 Locate File to Import

3 Click File to Import

4 Click for Automatic Clips

5 Click Import to Begin Importing

---

22 Import Still Pictures into Movie Maker

Before You Begin

✔ **17** About Collections, Contents, and Projects

✔ **20** Capture Video into Movie Maker

See Also

→ **41** Take a Picture from a Clip

Importing still pictures into a Movie Maker project is rather simple because you do not need to worry with clip detection. Each still picture is considered to be a clip in your collection. You cannot divide a photo into multiple clips. Movie Maker creates a thumbnail image of the picture to use for the picture's clip.

The order in which you import pictures and video is not too important. Your import order has no bearing on the order in which your clips will ultimately appear. It's the storyboard/timeline that determines exactly which clips appear in your final video, how long they play, and in what order.

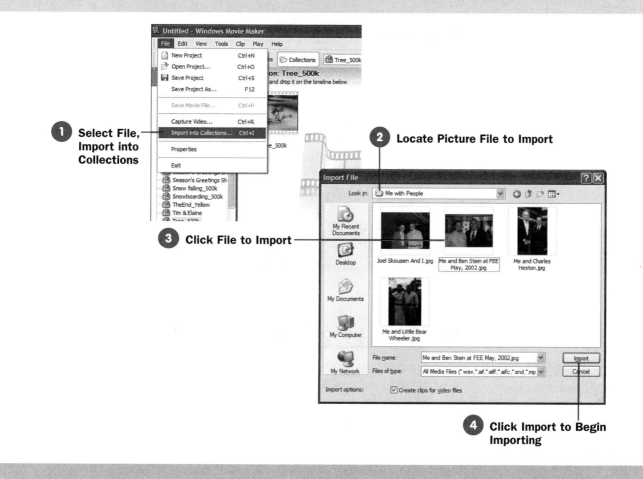

1 Select File, Import into Collections

2 Locate Picture File to Import

3 Click File to Import

4 Click Import to Begin Importing

---

1 **Select File, Import into Collections**

From the **File** menu, select **Import into Collections** to begin the importing of your source file pictures. If you've displayed the **Task** pane (**View, Task Pane**), you need only click the **Task** pane's **Import pictures** option under the **Capture Video** heading to start the import process.

2 **Locate Picture File to Import**

Browse to the location of your pictures' source files.

3 **Click File to Import**

Select the file you want to import. If you select multiple files, Movie Maker imports all of them.

Import multiple picture files by holding **Ctrl** before clicking on file-names to select more than one at the same time. If the filenames are listed consecutively in the **Import File** dialog box, click to select the first one, hold **Shift**, and click to select the last one you want, and Movie Maker selects the first, last, and all files between. Movie Maker then imports all the pictures you've selected.

 NOTE

Movie Maker does not use clip detection when import-ing picture clips.

4 **Click Import to Begin Importing**

When you click **Import**, Movie Maker begins importing the source file into your project's collection. The clips will appear in the **Contents** pane.

23 About Finding Video Content on the Web

Before You Begin

✔ **1** Walk Through a Digital Video Production

See Also

→ **94** Download the Movie Maker Creativity Fun Pack

 KEY TERM

Royalty-free—A label that indicates you can own a license to use a file any way you want, or that you are free to use the file in a specific, predefined way.

Stock footage—Video depicting a common scene or event, such as a moun-tain range or children play-ing, that you might want to use as filler video in a movie.

The Internet is full of videos from all over the world that you can watch, download, edit, and redistribute—although you cannot do all those things with all the videos that are online. In spite of the wealth of video files, many are copyrighted for specific use. Rarely do you ever actually own a video or audio file you've downloaded. Instead of owning the file, usually you only own a license to use it in some way. Be sure to read the fine print on the site where you download to discern what you are allowed to do with the file.

Several sites exist that offer *royalty-free* video content. You can use such royalty-free video as *stock footage* in your own videos when you need it. A search on the Internet for "royalty-free video" will turn up sites that offer downloadable content, as well as content available on CD-ROM and DVD that you can order.

Sites such as Fotosearch.com offer stock video footage you can purchase for use in your own movies.

WEB RESOURCE

http://www.microsoft.com/windowsxp/moviemaker/
videos/samples

While we're on the subject of video on the Web that you can use in Movie Maker, consider visiting Microsoft's Movie Maker Web site for sample movies produced with Movie Maker. You might be surprised at Movie Maker's flexibility and power.

Microsoft offers videos that demonstrate the power of Movie Maker.

More and more major studio-made movies will begin appearing on the Web with digital rights management features included. Depending on who offers the movie and the rights they allow you based on how you acquired it (bought or copied), the DRM features will determine what you can do with them. If Movie Maker refuses to import a video file you downloaded from the internet, even though that file plays perfectly in Windows Media Player, the file probably has DRM controls that disallow you from editing or using the video inside another video, so Movie Maker refuses to import the file.

KEY TERM

Newsgroups—Electronic bulletin boards, categorized by name and function, where users upload and download messages and files.

If you have *newsgroup* access, you can often find video files uploaded for others to see and use categorized by subject. Search through newsgroups that have *multimedia* in their name for possible videos you can download and use. Use Outlook Express, bundled with Windows, to access newsgroups after you learn from your Internet service provider (ISP) how to set up newsgroup access.

---

24 Watch Your Video in the Monitor

Before You Begin

✔ **20** Capture Video into Movie Maker

✔ **21** Import Video into Movie Maker

See Also

→ **31** Play Your Video on the Storyboard

→ **33** Watch a Clip

TIP

The monitor's **Play** button turns to **Pause** after you start playing a video element. **Pause** turns to **Play** when you pause the playback.

The monitor is your miniature theatre, where you'll preview your movies, clips, special effects, and video transitions as you work with them. After you select a playable Movie Maker element, such as a clip or the start of a timeline location, that element's thumbnail image appears in the **Monitor** pane.

After the thumbnail appears, click **Play** to play the whole element from the beginning. Typical playback controls such as **Fast Forward**, **Pause**, and **Stop** all appear at the bottom of the **Monitor** pane.

❶ Click to Select an Item

From the **Contents** pane, select any item. You can do this for video clips, audio clips, video transitions, or special effects that appear in the **Contents** pane.

❷ Click Play in Monitor

When you click **Play**, the selected item begins to play in the **Monitor** pane. The **Play** button turns to **Pause** so you can pause the playback if you want.

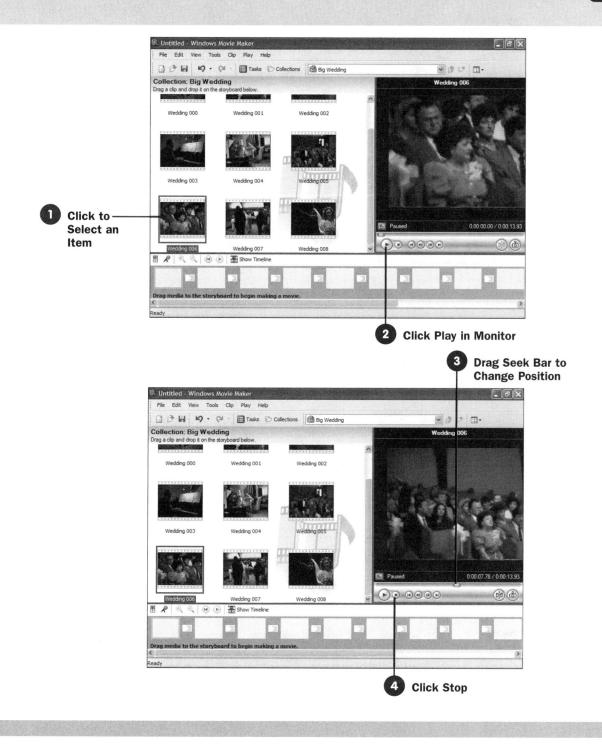

1 Click to Select an Item

2 Click Play in Monitor

3 Drag Seek Bar to Change Position

4 Click Stop

NOTE

Movie Maker uses its own background to demonstrate video transitions and effects that you play back.

Drag Seek Bar to Change Position

As you play back content, the seek bar moves to show the relative position within the playback process. You can drag the seek bar with your mouse to change the position of the playback. By dragging the seek bar slowly forward and backward, you can more accurately see minute changes take place in your video or transition.

④ Click Stop

To stop the playback, click **Stop**.

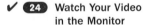 Step Through Your Video One Frame at a Time

Before You Begin

✔ **24** Watch Your Video in the Monitor

See Also

➡ **31** Play Your Video on the Storyboard

➡ **33** Watch a Clip

Whenever you play back content in your **Monitor** pane, you can watch the playback one frame at a time if you want. Doing so gives you the most detailed method for viewing every aspect of your video, transition, or special effect.

You cannot play back an audio item (such an audio file or audio clip) frame by frame and hear the playback. If you attempt to do so, Movie Maker moves the seek bar ahead one frame length, but does not play that portion of the item while doing so.

❶ Click to Select Item

From the **Contents** pane, select any item. You can do this for video clips, audio clips, video transitions, or special effects that appear in the **Contents** pane.

❷ Click Next Frame

When you click **Next Frame**, the seek bar moves right one frame length and the **Monitor** pane changes to display the next frame.

❸ Click Previous Frame

You can click **Previous Frame** to move backward in the playback by a single frame.

 TIP

At any point in the frame-by-frame playback, you can click **Play** to watch the regular playback to the end.

Click to Select Item

2 Click Next Frame

3 Click Previous Frame

5

Organizing Movie Maker Contents

IN THIS CHAPTER:

After you've planned, directed, and shot attention-getting raw video footage, you don your director's hat and begin to put your final movie together. Putting your movie together requires you to locate and organize your video files, arrange the clips into the final order in which they are to appear in your movie, and review your work along the way to ensure that your movie plays the way you want it to.

Some of your video production work won't even take place within the Movie Maker program. You'll manage much of your video collection in Windows. As you build a video library over time, your hard disk will begin to fill with video files. By using the tools available to you inside Movie Maker, such as filling out the **Project Properties** specifics when you import videos, you can begin to manage your video files outside of Movie Maker using Windows tools to locate and organize videos so your video library is easy to work within.

One place where you'll spend a lot of time working in Movie Maker is the storyboard. The storyboard is where your movie's layout begins to take shape.

26 About Cataloging Your Videos

Before You Begin

✔ **17** About Collections, Contents, and Projects

✔ **19** About Your Project's Content

See Also

→ **27** Find Your Videos Fast

You don't have to start Movie Maker to view a project file's properties. When in Windows Explorer, you can right-click on a project file and select **Properties**, and then click the **Summary** tab to view the project's properties.

Once in Windows Explorer, browse to your Movie Maker project files and select **View**, **Details** to display a project's properties. After selecting **View**, **Choose Details**, click to select **Author**, **Title**, and any other information you want to see in Windows Explorer for your Movie Maker project files. When you click **OK**, your Explorer screen displays all the details so you can more easily locate a specific project, or sort them by author, date, or title by clicking at the top of any column.

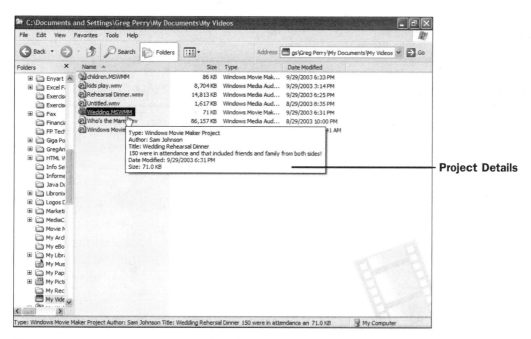

The Summary page of your project file's Properties dialog box lists
some of your project's details.

If you rest your mouse over a project file while in Windows Explorer,
Explorer displays a detail window that describes the project.

Click to Sort by Author   **Click to Sort by Title**

Windows Explorer can display the properties from all of your Movie Maker projects.

---

27 Find Your Videos Fast

Before You Begin

✔ **19** About Your Project's Contents

✔ **26** About Cataloging Your Videos

See Also

➔ **31** Play Your Video on the Storyboard

Windows contains a powerful search feature you can use to locate video files quickly. As hard disks get larger, your computer's storage system can hold many videos.

After you locate a video file you want to view or import into Movie Maker, double-click it to watch it on your screen and verify that it's the file you truly want to use. Windows Media Player opens and plays the file as soon as you double-click the filename in the **Search Results** window. If you've assigned another media playing program to play video files, that program will open instead of Windows Media Player.

 Click Start

From the Windows desktop, click the **Start** button. The **Start** menu appears.

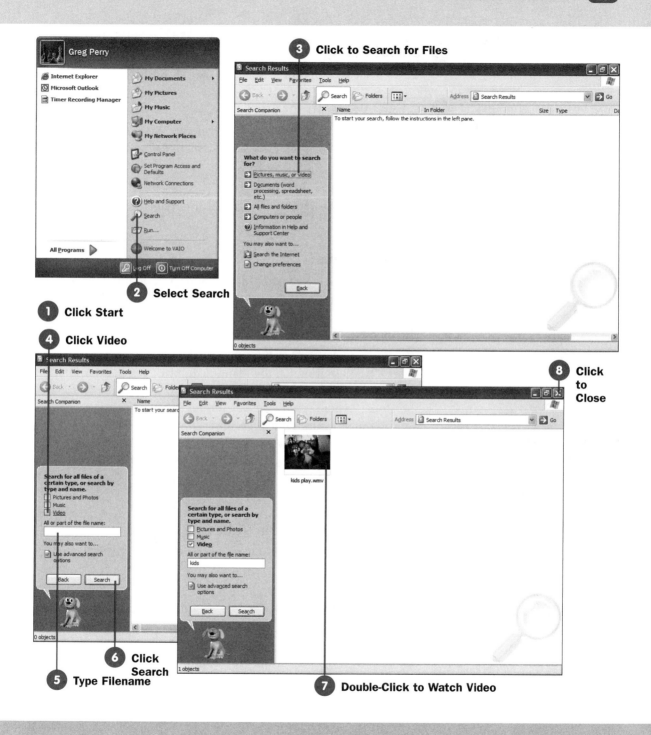

3 Click to Search for Files

2 Select Search

1 Click Start

4 Click Video

8 Click to Close

5 Type Filename

6 Click Search

7 Double-Click to Watch Video

2 Select Search

Click the **Search** option to open the **Search Results** window.

3 Click to Search for Files

Click **Pictures, music, or video** so Windows doesn't bother looking for unwanted files, such as Word document files.

NOTE

You can use the **Search Results** window to look for Movie Maker project files: Instead of clicking the **Pictures, music, or video** option, click **All files and folders**. Type *.MSWMM to limit your search to Movie Maker project files.

4 Click Video

Click to select the **Video** option to further refine the search to video files only.

5 Type Filename

Enter the filename you want to search for. You do not have to enter a filename extension.

6 Click Search

When you click the **Search** button, Windows begins its search. The items located that match the filename appear. The **Search** function will search for your search term in all or part of the filename; therefore, if your search term is **summer**, Windows locates **summer.wmv**, **summer.avi**, **summerFun.wmv**, and **summertime.wmv** if all four files are located on your disk drive. Depending on the Explorer options you currently have set in Windows, you might see thumbnails of your videos or a detailed description of the file.

7 Double-Click to Watch Video

After locating the video you want to see, double-click its filename to play the video.

NOTE

If you search for a Movie Maker project file, Movie Maker opens and automatically loads that project into its workspace.

8 Click to Close

You can close the **Search Results** window by clicking its **Close** button.

28 About Movie Maker's Storyboard

Even the biggest producers in Hollywood use *storyboarding* techniques to plan their movies. Why shouldn't you?

The Movie Maker storyboard works like a bulletin board system, with unlimited size and unlimited pins for you to place scenes from your movies, stored as clips. You'll drag clips from your **Contents** pane to the storyboard, and as you do so, you are actually arranging the scenes in your movie.

Before You Begin

✔ **17** About Collections, Contents, and Projects

✔ **24** Watch Your Video in the Monitor

See Also

→ **29** Add Clips to the Storyboard

→ **30** Delete Clips from the Storyboard

→ **32** Rearrange the Storyboard

→ **35** About the Timeline and Storyboard

The storyboard shows the order of your clips' playback, as well as any transitions and special effects you add.

🔍KEY TERM

Storyboarding—Laying out sketches or paintings of proposed movie scenes to plan and develop the sequence of events.

📝NOTE

If you see a timeline instead of the storyboard (the timeline has a sequence of time intervals across the top), click the **Show Storyboard** button to display the storyboard.

The storyboard shows your movie's ordering of clips, and you can easily rearrange the order of clips on your storyboard (**see** **32** **Rearrange the Storyboard**). The storyboard does not indicate how long each clip will play—only the sequence of clips. With the storyboard, you can review and arrange the order of events that take place in your movie. When you add clips to your storyboard, you're adding them to your final movie, although you can always remove them if you later decide you don't want them. When you do create your final movie file (**see** **85** **Start the Save Movie Wizard**), only the clips on the storyboard will end up in your production.

29 Add Clips to the Storyboard

Before You Begin

✔ **28** About Movie Maker's Storyboard

See Also

→ **30** Delete Clips from the Storyboard

→ **32** Rearrange the Storyboard

→ **36** Place a Clip on the Timeline

→ **69** Transition from Clip to Clip

💡 TIP

If you send only picture clips to the storyboard/ timeline, your project will become a slideshow, with each picture displaying for a fixed period of time that you set (see **39** Set a Picture Clip's Duration). You can insert picture clips between two video clips, as you might do if you want to evoke a style similar to the silent movie era, when caption screens indicated dialogue.

Putting clips on the storyboard requires nothing more than dragging the clips you want in your movie from the **Contents** pane to the storyboard. Movie Maker overlays the storyboard over the timeline, so if you send clips to the storyboard, the clips will also appear on the timeline. (Alternatively, if you send clips to the timeline, the clips also appear on your storyboard. Press **Ctrl+T** to switch between the timeline and storyboard views.)

The storyboard holds video clips, still picture clips, video transitions, and special effects and displays thumbnail images of everything you place there. You can drag a single clip to the storyboard or select multiple clips and drag them to the storyboard as a group. Rarely will you know exactly which clips you'll want on your storyboard until you drag some clips there and preview the results. Movie Maker makes it easy to rearrange your storyboard clips. In addition, you can easily remove unwanted clips from the storyboard.

You do not have to add all the clips you want to use in the project at once. Feel free to send some clips to the timeline and work with them, and then send one or more additional clips to the timeline when you are ready to work with them. If a clip is a picture, the picture will display for the length of its duration setting.

When the storyboard holds one or more clips, you can drag additional clips there and place the new clips at any position within the clips already on the storyboard. Movie Maker shifts the existing clips to the right on the storyboard to make room for new clips you place there.

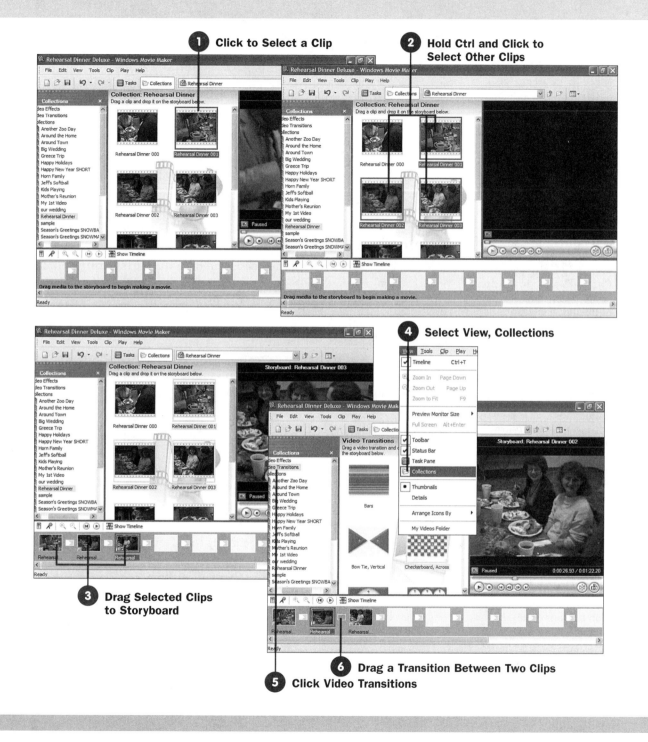

1 Click to Select a Clip

2 Hold Ctrl and Click to Select Other Clips

3 Drag Selected Clips to Storyboard

4 Select View, Collections

5 Click Video Transitions

6 Drag a Transition Between Two Clips

NOTE

Only one transition can appear between two clips. If you try to add a second transition between two clips, Movie Maker replaces the first one with the one you added.

TIP

If you want to drag all the **Contents** pane's clips to the storyboard, click to select one clip and then press **Ctrl+A** to select the rest of the clips. You can then drag every clip in your **Contents** pane to the story-board—even the clips currently out of the **Contents** pane's borders' view.

TIP

You can increase the number of clips shown at one time on your storyboard by dragging the dividing line between the **Contents** pane and the storyboard downward. The storyboard's thumbnail images will shrink, and more will be visible on the storyboard.

1 **Click to Select a Clip**

Select the first clip you want to add to the storyboard. The selected clip's border displays a darker outline than the surrounding clips to indicate that you've selected it.

2 **Hold Ctrl and Click to Select Other Clips**

To select additional clips, press and hold the **Ctrl** key and click the other clips you want to select. You can select as many clips as you want to send to the storyboard. Click the **Content** pane's scrollbars to see clips not currently displayed on the screen.

3 **Drag Selected Clips to Storyboard**

Click on any of the selected clips and drag them to the storyboard. After you drop the clips on the storyboard, a thumbnail image appears and acts as a placeholder for each clip.

4 **Select View, Collections**

Display the **Collections** pane by selecting **Collections** from the **View** menu. You can now select from another video collection or pull video transitions or special effects into your project.

5 **Click Video Transitions**

Click the **Contents** pane's **Video Transitions** option to display thumbnails of each transition available to you. These transitions will appear in the **Contents** pane.

6 **Drag a Transition Between Two Clips**

Select a transition you want to apply to a place on your storyboard and drag that transition between two clips on the storyboard. The first clip (the one to the left) will now transition into the second when the movie plays the clips. Without the transition, the second clip immediately plays after the first one, with no transitional effect.

30 Delete Clips from the Storyboard

Removing unneeded storyboard clips is one of the easiest tasks in Movie Maker. When you delete one or more storyboard clips, the clips leave the storyboard, and thus leave the final movie you can create to that point. Of course, you can always put clips right back on the storyboard if you change your mind.

When you delete a clip from the storyboard, the clip still remains in your **Collections** pane. By deleting the storyboard clip, you only shorten the video you're currently making. Whether the clip is a video clip, picture clip, transition, or special effect, you delete the clip from the storyboard the same way.

1 Click to Select

Click to select any clip on the storyboard that you want to delete.

2 Select Edit, Delete

When you select **Edit**, **Delete** (or press the **Del** key), the clip disappears from the storyboard.

3 Click Undo

Changing your mind is simple. Just click the toolbar's **Undo** button and Movie Maker puts the clip right back where it was before you deleted it. The **Undo** button will put back multiple clips you might have deleted, too. Keep clicking **Undo** as often as you want to undo an edit to your project.

4 Hold Ctrl, Then Click Multiple Clips

If you want to delete multiple clips at once, hold **Ctrl** while you click on several clips to select all the clips you want to remove. If you select a clip accidentally that you do not want to remove, hold **Ctrl** and click that clip again to deselect it.

5 Select Edit, Delete

Your selected clip or clips disappear from the storyboard when you select **Delete** once again from the **Edit** menu.

Before You Begin

✔ **28** About Movie Maker's Storyboard

✔ **29** Add Clips to the Storyboard

See Also

➔ **32** Rearrange the Storyboard

 TIP

If you want to start with a fresh storyboard, you can select all clips for deletion by clicking on one clip, and then pressing **Ctrl+A** to select all the other clips. Even the storyboard clips that don't currently appear on your screen are selected.

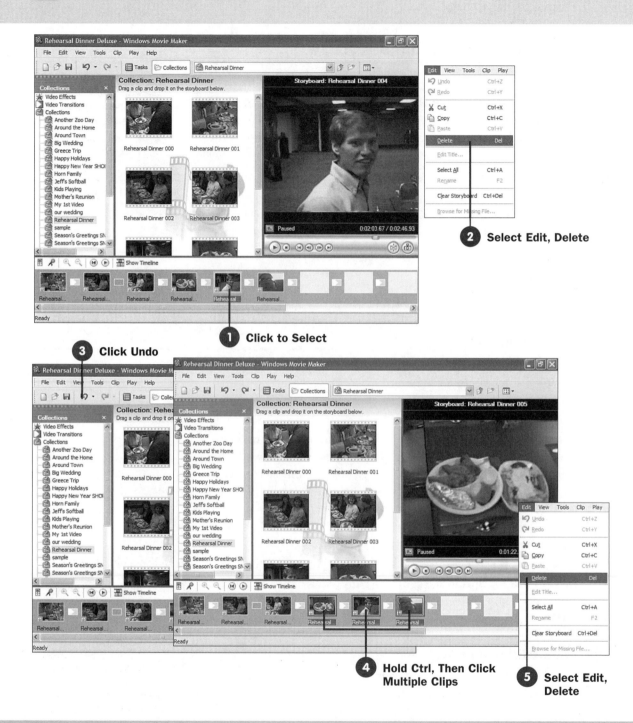

② **Select Edit, Delete**

① **Click to Select**

③ **Click Undo**

④ **Hold Ctrl, Then Click Multiple Clips**

⑤ **Select Edit, Delete**

31 **Play Your Video on the Storyboard**

As you lay out your video on the storyboard, you will want to play the storyboard to see whether the end video achieves the goal you are aiming for. Movie Maker allows you to play back clips and complete videos from several locations within the program. You might find that your work with the storyboard requires somewhat more playback and review of the video than when working with the timeline because the storyboard is for sequencing clips, but the storyboard gives no indication of time lengths; a clip that is half as long as the one next to it consumes exactly the same amount of storyboard space.

To get a better idea of the timeframe that your storyboard represents, you'll want to play the storyboard's contents. All playback appears in the **Monitor** pane, and you can control that playback using the VCR-like buttons at the bottom of the **Monitor** pane.

 1 **Click to Select**

Click to select the first clip on the storyboard. The clip's thumbnail image appears in the **Monitor** pane. The clip you select before playing the storyboard is where the playback will begin. After you start it, the playback continues until the final clip on the storyboard plays, or until you stop the playback.

 2 **Click Play**

Click the **Play** button at the top of the storyboard or on the **Monitor** pane. The storyboard begins playing. All sound, transitions, special effects, and still photos on your storyboard play in order.

 3 **Click Stop**

Stop the playback by clicking the **Monitor** pane's **Stop** button.

 4 **Click to Select**

Click a clip toward the middle or end of your storyboard. Its thumbnail image will appear in the **Monitor** pane.

Before You Begin

✔ **28** About Movie Maker's Storyboard

✔ **29** Add Clips to the Storyboard

See Also

➔ **33** Watch a Clip

 NOTE

If you were to create your final movie file now (see **85** Start the Save Movie Wizard), Movie Maker would create a final movie file that matches what you see playing on the storyboard.

 NOTE

Click the scrollbar across the bottom of the storyboard if you want to begin playing at a storyboard clip that is not currently in view.

2 Click Play

3 Click Stop

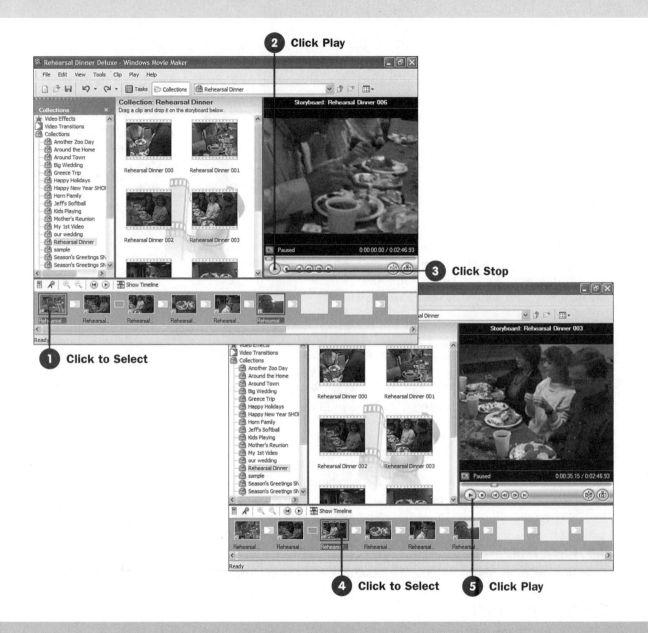

1 Click to Select

4 Click to Select   **5** Click Play

5 Click Play

Once again, when you click **Play** the storyboard's video appears in the **Monitor** pane, only the playback begins at your selected clip instead of at the first clip on the storyboard.

32 Rearrange the Storyboard

Rearranging clips is as simple as dragging cards around in Windows Solitaire. If you want to move a clip, just click and drag it to another storyboard location. When you release your mouse button, Movie Maker drops the clip into its new location.

You can select multiple clips to move at the same time. The storyboard's thumbnail images show the result of the clips' rearrangement. As soon as you rearrange the storyboard, the movie's playback is rearranged accordingly. All storyboard clips, including video, still pictures, transitions, and special effects, are available for movement on the storyboard.

 Click to Select

Click to select a clip that you want to move to a different storyboard location.

 Drag to a New Location

While holding down your mouse button, drag the clip from its original location to where you now want it to go. When you release the mouse button, the clip drops into place.

 Select Two Clips

Select two clips by holding the **Ctrl** key and clicking on each of them. You can move both of them to a different storyboard location. You can move as many clips as you select in one move.

 Drag to a New Location

Drag the two clips to the new location. When you release your mouse button, Movie Maker drops them into place on the storyboard.

 Click to See Results

Click **Play** if you want to review your storyboard's new sequence.

Before You Begin

✔ **28** About Movie Maker's Storyboard

✔ **29** Add Clips to the Storyboard

See Also

→ **36** Place a Clip on the Timeline

 **NOTE**

If you move one clip with a transition in front of it to another storyboard location, Movie Maker removes the transition. If you move two or more consecutive clips to a different location, any transitions between the moved clips will move with the clips to their new location.

 NOTE

You can only move multiple clips that are consecutive to each other. If you want to move nonconsecutive clips, you must move them one at a time to their new location.

1 Click to Select

2 Drag to a New Location

3 Select Two Clips

4 Drag to a New Location

5 Click to See Results

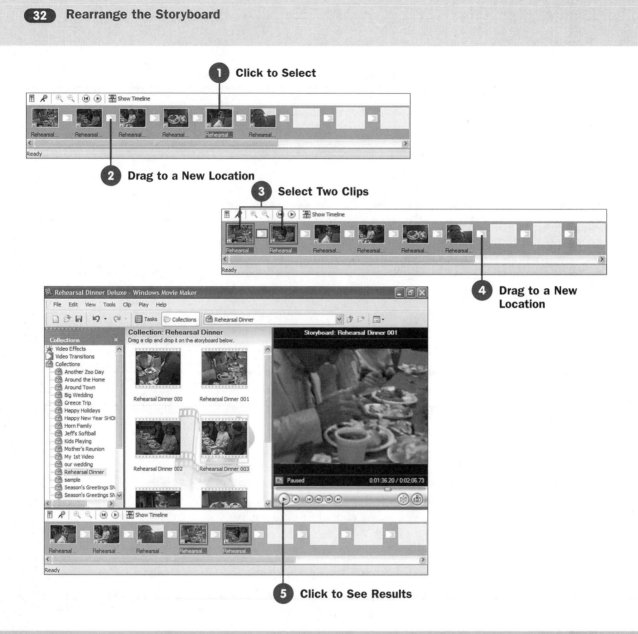

PART IV

Arranging Your Movies

IN THIS PART:

6

Working with Movie Maker Clips

IN THIS CHAPTER:

As you learned in the previous chapter, clips are small sections of video you use to produce your final video production. You can trim, merge, and arrange clips so that they appear in the order and within the timeframe you require. The better your clip-editing skills become, the more professional your resulting videos will look.

Having several clips to work with gives you flexibility when producing the final video. If you start with just one long clip, you will spend lots of time editing it to eliminate unnecessary video. If you begin with several smaller clips, you have more flexibility—you can more easily arrange the smaller clips, edit them more quickly than longer clips, and insert and delete sections of your video with less effort.

Suppose you have an hour of raw footage video from your parents' anniversary bash and you want to turn that into a 20-minute commemorative video of the evening's highlights. When you import the video into Movie Maker, instead of saving the video as one hour-long stream, Movie Maker cuts the video into multiple clips—provided that the **Create clips for video files** option in the **Import File** dialog box is selected (**see** **21** **Import Video into Movie Maker**). Movie Maker does not create clips from picture files you import. Some clips might only last a couple of seconds, and others might span a minute or more. Movie Maker separates video into clips when it senses scene changes or major camera differences.

Now that you have an assortment of numerous, small clips, you can more easily put together a video montage your parents will cherish.

---

33 Watch a Clip

Before You Begin

✔ **29** Add Clips to the Storyboard

✔ **31** Play Your Video on the Storyboard

See Also

→ **42** Split a Clip into Multiple Clips

→ **44** Set Trim Points

Often you'll watch individual video clips to see where they start and stop. Watch the clip in the **Monitor** window and use the **Play**, **Stop**, and other buttons to control the clip's playback.

Reviewing a clip is one of the simplest and most common tasks you'll do with Movie Maker. For example, you might want to watch a clip to see whether it's too long and needs trimming to a shorter length. You play back the individual clips from the **Contents** pane, but you can only play back one selected clip at a time.

1 Click a Clip

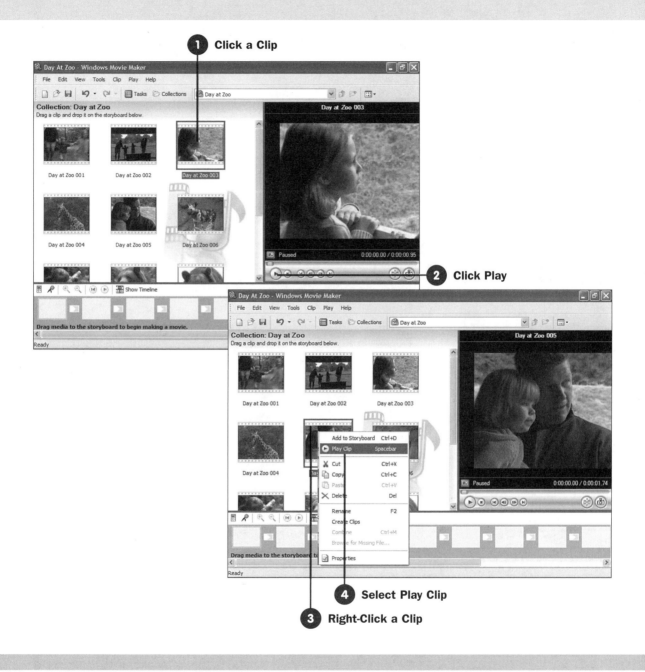

2 Click Play

4 Select Play Clip

3 Right-Click a Clip

NOTE

If you select a clip from the storyboard/timeline to watch, Movie Maker plays the entire video from the clip to the movie's conclusion and not just the selected clip only. Click the monitor's **Stop** button to keep the storyboard/timeline playback from continuing after you've seen what you want to see.

TIP

If you click to select a picture clip in the **Contents** pane, the still picture appears in the monitor.

TIP

The **Spacebar** is the shortcut key for the **Play Clip** command.

1 Click a Clip

Click a clip in the **Contents** pane. The first frame appears in the monitor.

2 Click Play

Click the monitor's **Play** button. Watch the clip in the **Monitor** window.

3 Right-Click a Clip

You can also watch a clip by right-clicking it to display a context menu with a **Play Clip** option.

4 Select Play Clip

When you select **Play Clip**, the clip begins playing in the **Monitor** window.

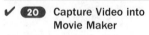

34 Display a Clip's Properties

Before You Begin

✔ **20** Capture Video into Movie Maker

✔ **21** Import Video into Movie Maker

See Also

→ **36** Place a Clip on the Timeline

KEY TERMS

Bit rate—The number of data bits, or signals, used in one second of video.

Channels—The number of separate audio soundtracks, such as two for stereo. Movie Maker supports one or two channels.

As you produce more advanced videos using Movie Maker, you will begin to pay more attention to the details of your clips. Perhaps you need to trim a few seconds from one or more clips to fit your project's length into a preset time limit.

A clip's properties describe the clip in detail. The properties include such items as the type of clip, the clip's filename and location on the disk, the file size, the *bit rate*, and details about the audio, such as the number of *channels*. By viewing these details, you will better understand how that clip affects your video's overall length and quality.

1 Right-Click a Clip

Right-click the clip for which you want to view property information. A menu appears from which you can choose options that relate to this specific clip.

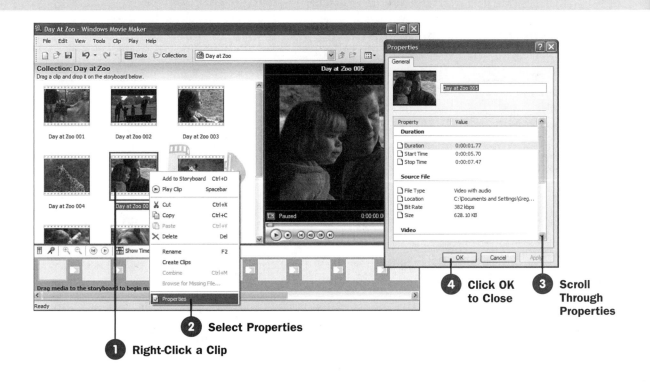

Click OK to Close **4**

Scroll Through Properties **3**

Select Properties **2**

Right-Click a Clip **1**

2 Select Properties

From the context menu, select **Properties**. The **Properties** dialog box opens to display the clip's details.

3 Scroll Through Properties

Depending on your screen resolution, you might have to click the scrollbar to scroll the information in the dialog box so that you can view all the clip's properties.

4 Click OK to Close

When you're done viewing the clip's properties, click **OK** or **Cancel**. The **Properties** dialog box closes, and you're returned to the clip in the **Contents** pane. The clip whose properties you just viewed is still selected.

TIP

Feel free to change the name of the clip from within the **Properties** dialog box.

TIP

You can close windows such as the **Properties** dialog box by pressing the **Esc** key or by clicking **OK**.

35 About the Timeline and Storyboard

Before You Begin

✔ **18** Start a Movie
Maker Project

✔ **28** About Movie
Maker's Storyboard

✔ **31** Play Your Video on
the Storyboard

See Also

→ **36** Place a Clip on the
Timeline

→ **48** Add a Soundtrack
to Your Video

Movie Maker's timeline and storyboard are similar in use and format. Yet, despite these similarities, you should know the difference between them, because each offers distinct advantages over the other.

Although the previous chapter covers the storyboard in depth (**see** **28** **About Movie Maker's Storyboard**), it's critical that you fully understand how the storyboard and timeline both work in conjunction with each other to display two different kinds of information for you. When you place clips on the storyboard, those clips also appear on the timeline. If you place clips on the timeline, the storyboard also receives the clips.

The following are the primary differences between a storyboard and a timeline:

- The **storyboard** shows a thumbnail image of the clip's first frame. Therefore, when you look at the storyboard, you can easily tell which clip is which from the picture shown on the storyboard. The sequence of your video production is also clear from those images. Only video clips and any transitions that might appear between them appear on the storyboard; no audio clips can reside on the storyboard.

Storyboard Control Buttons

Transitions Between Clips

Click to See the Timeline

KEY TERMS

Transition track—The transition effect, if any exists, between clips.

Audio track—The audio imported or captured with your video.

Audio/Music track—Audio you add to your project after you import or capture video and the audio that goes with it.

Title Overlay track—Titles and credits you add to your project's timeline.

Only the storyboard appears here; it shows video clips and transitions but no audio.

- The **timeline** is concerned more with time and less with sequence. Use the timeline to measure the length of your project's clips as you place them into your final project. The timeline displays your project's video clips on the **Video** track (depending on the clip's length, you will see some or all of the thumbnail for that clip). The timeline also shows transitions between clips on the *Transition track*, your project's *Audio track*, the *Audio/Music track*, and the *Title Overlay track*.

Timeline Control Buttons

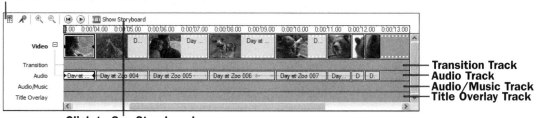

Transition Track
Audio Track
Audio/Music Track
Title Overlay Track

Click to See Storyboard

The timeline shows video clips, transitions between clips (Transition track), the video's audio (the Audio track), audio clips you've added (the Audio/Music track), and titles or credits you've added (the Title Overlay track).

You will frequently use both the Movie Maker storyboard and timeline, and you'll quickly switch between both views as you work on a project by pressing **Ctrl+T** or by clicking the **Show Storyboard** and **Show Timeline** buttons. The immediate difference between these two display areas is that the storyboard has less clutter and eases your job of arranging the clip order. You'll use the timeline to adjust the visual width of a clip's thumbnail to match its length. If a clip is short, you might not be able to see much of the first clip's thumbnail image on the timeline, but you will always see the image on the storyboard.

The storyboard enables you to manage the sequence of clips. The timeline enables you to manage the clips' timing.

The timeline shows far more details than the storyboard by displaying the **Video**, **Audio**, **Audio/Music**, **Transition**, and **Title Overlay** tracks for your movie. The timeline also enables you to see how each clip fits within the time frame of the movie.

Many references in Movie Maker's help files and related literature describe both the storyboard and the timeline as a single unit, as in *storyboard/timeline*. When presented as storyboard/timeline, a related command applies to either area, regardless of which one is showing at the time.

After you've dragged one or more clips to your Movie Maker storyboard/timeline, you have begun a Movie Maker project.

TIP

Click the plus sign on the **Video** track to display your project's **Transition** and **Audio** tracks. The plus changes to a minus sign that you can click to hide the **Transition** and **Audio** tracks.

A project has begun because there are clips on the storyboard.

36 Place a Clip on the Timeline

Before You Begin

✔ **30** Delete Clips from the Storyboard

✔ **32** Rearrange the Storyboard

✔ **35** About the Timeline and Storyboard

See Also

→ **38** Clear the Timeline

→ **39** Set a Picture Clip's Duration

→ **45** Nudge a Clip to Adjust Its Start Time

Putting clips on the timeline is about as simple as putting them on the storyboard. Actually, Movie Maker overlays the storyboard over the timeline, so if you send clips to the storyboard, the clips will also appear on the timeline. (Alternatively, if you send clips to the timeline, the clips also appear on your storyboard.) Press **Ctrl+T** to switch between the timeline and storyboard views.

You can drag a single clip to the timeline or select multiple clips and drag them to the timeline as a group. Rarely will you know exactly which clips you'll want on the timeline in your final video. Movie Maker makes it easy to rearrange your timeline clips just as you can rearrange clips on the storyboard (**see 32 Rearrange the Storyboard**). You can also remove unwanted clips from the timeline just as you can remove them from the storyboard (**see 30 Delete Clips from the Storyboard**).

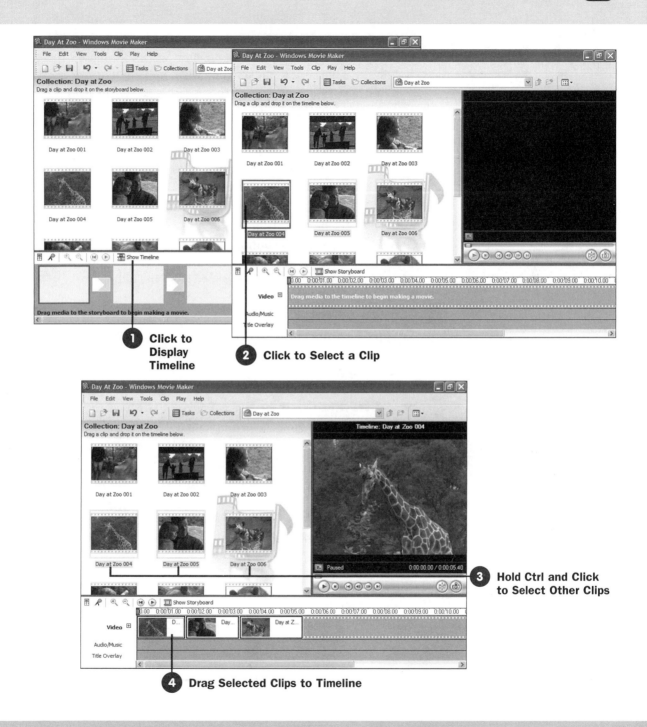

1 Click to Display Timeline

2 Click to Select a Clip

3 Hold Ctrl and Click to Select Other Clips

4 Drag Selected Clips to Timeline

TIP

If you send only picture clips to the storyboard/timeline, your project will become a slideshow, with each picture displaying a fixed amount of time that you can set.

You do not have to add all the clips you want to use in the project at once. Feel free to send some clips to the timeline, work with those clips, then send one or more clips to the timeline when you are ready to work with them. If a clip is a picture, the picture will display for the length of its duration setting (see **39** **Set a Picture Clip's Duration**).

When the timeline holds one or more clips, you can drag additional clips to the timeline and place the new clips at any position within the clips already on the timeline. Movie Maker shifts the existing clips to the right on the timeline to make room for new clips you place there.

1 **Click to Display Timeline**

Click the **Show Timeline** button atop the timeline to display the timeline. If the timeline, and not the storyboard, is already showing, you do not have to click the **Show Timeline** button.

2 **Click to Select a Clip**

Select the first clip you want to add to the timeline. The selected clip's border displays a darker outline than the surrounding clips to indicate that you've selected it.

3 **Hold Ctrl and Click to Select Other Clips**

To select additional clips, press and hold the **Ctrl** key and click the other clips you want to select. You can select as many clips as you want to send to the timeline. Click the **Contents** pane's scrollbars to see clips not currently displayed on the screen.

TIP

If you want to drag all the **Contents** pane's clips to the timeline, click to select one clip and then press **Ctrl+A** to select the rest of the clips. You can then drag every clip in your **Contents** pane to the timeline, even the clips currently out of the **Contents** pane's borders' view.

4 **Drag Selected Clips to Timeline**

Click on any of the selected clips and drag them to the timeline. Make sure that you drag the clips to the **Video** track and not another timeline track. After you drop the clips on the timeline, the clips' widths on the timeline indicate their relative length. You can also read the timeline's time track to see how much time a clip will take in the video.

37 Zoom a Timeline Clip

Your project's timeline shows how your clips fit together in your video. Whereas the storyboard shows equally-sized clip thumbnails so you can concentrate on the order of clips in your video, the timeline displays clip thumbnails in various sizes relative to how long each clip is compared to another. A clip that is half as long as the one next to it will consume only half as much space on the timeline. In addition, you might not be able to see the whole thumbnail on a short clip. (You can always press **Ctrl+T** to return to the storyboard to see the full thumbnail.)

You can adjust the time markings displayed on the top of the timeline to see more or less detail. If the times are spaced 40 seconds apart, you see more detail than if the times are spaced 3 minutes apart. You can zoom in or zoom out of the timeline to see more or less timeline detail. When you zoom in, the timeline's time intervals are smaller, and you see the timeline clips in more detail, but you see fewer of them on the screen at one time. You'll use the scrollbar across the bottom of the timeline to scroll left and right to the clips that are not showing. When you zoom out, the timeline's time intervals are larger, and you see less clip detail, but you see more clips at once. You can zoom out to see how an entire scene's clips compare with one another in time consumed.

Movie Maker provides a **Zoom to Fit** feature with which you can display your entire timeline at once, with all the clips squeezed into a single timeline view. You don't have to scroll to see timeline clips that aren't in view. The **Zoom to Fit** feature increases the timeline's time intervals dramatically so that you can see your whole timeline at once.

1 Select View, Zoom to Fit

From the main menu, choose **View, Zoom to Fit**. Movie Maker compresses your entire timeline into a single view so that you do not have to scroll to see all the timeline clips. Press **F9** to select the **Zoom to Fit** feature instead of using the **View** menu.

Before You Begin

✔ **35** About the Timeline and Storyboard

See Also

→ **44** Set Trim Points

→ **45** Nudge a Clip to Adjust Its Start Time

 **TIP**

When shooting your video, plan to create one clip for each camera angle shot. If a clip consumes a far greater amount of the timeline than most other clips, you'll quickly know to review that clip for possible trimming. Don't bore your audience with a camera focus that spends too long in one place.

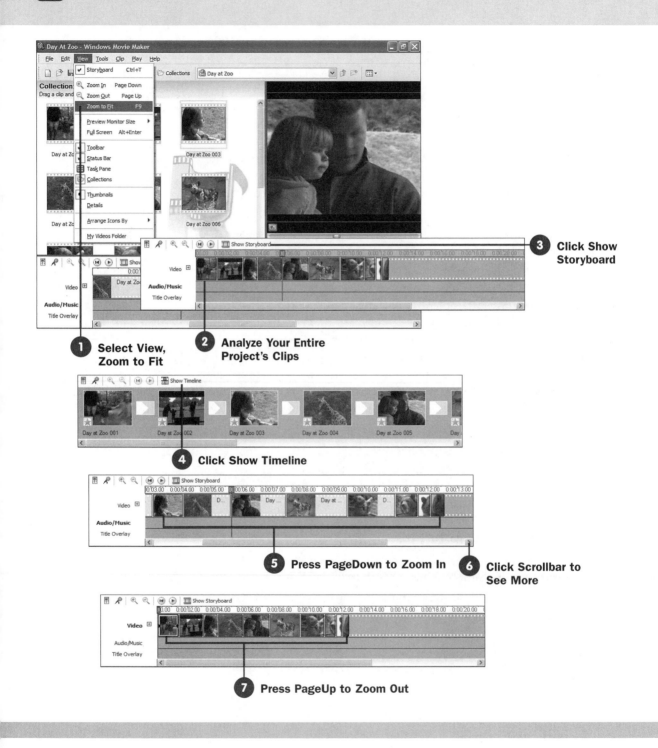

3 Click Show Storyboard

1 Select View, Zoom to Fit

2 Analyze Your Entire Project's Clips

4 Click Show Timeline

5 Press PageDown to Zoom In

6 Click Scrollbar to See More

7 Press PageUp to Zoom Out

2 Analyze Your Entire Project's Clips

By looking at your entire timeline at once, you gain better perspective on scenes that might be too long or too short. Analyze your entire project's set of clips and you'll learn how your clips relate. For example, here you can see that the third video clip is much longer than many of the other clips. Although this might not be a problem, it is a situation you could investigate to ensure that the lengthy clip doesn't contain extraneous details that you should trim.

3 Click Show Storyboard

The storyboard appears when you click the **Show Storyboard** button. You must display the storyboard and then return to the timeline after you perform a Zoom to Fit if you want to zoom back into more timeline detail.

4 Click Show Timeline

Click the **Show Timeline** button atop the timeline. The timeline once again appears, and you'll be able to zoom in and out of the timeline to see more or less detail.

 TIP

Click any time value on the timeline to see that frame in the monitor.

5 Press PageDown to Zoom In

Press the **PageDown** key to zoom in to the timeline. The time intervals between clips decrease, and you'll see more thumbnail images on the timeline's **Video** track.

6 Click Scrollbar to See More

As you zoom in, you probably won't be able to see all the project's clips on the timeline without scrolling left or right. Use the scrollbar to move along the timeline to see all the clips.

7 Press PageUp to Zoom Out

Press the **PageUp** key to zoom out. The timeline's time intervals increase, and the thumbnails get smaller and closer together so that you can see more of the timeline at once.

38 **Clear the Timeline**

Before You Begin

✔ **35** About the Timeline and Storyboard

✔ **36** Place a Clip on the Timeline

See Also

➜ **42** Split a Clip into Multiple Clips

➜ **43** Combine Multiple Clips into One

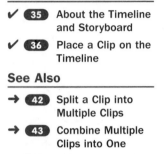 **NOTE**

You can delete both video and picture clips.

Deleting one or more clips from your project's timeline (or storyboard) requires only that you select one or more clips and choose **Delete** from the **Edit** menu. As with most Movie Maker commands, you can undo the deletion.

When you first work on a project, your video will most assuredly contain far too many clips. Removing clips is integral to producing a tight, attention-grabbing video. Remember that your clip still resides in the **Contents** pane above the timeline; if you delete a clip from the timeline and then exit Movie Maker, you will not be able to undo that deletion the next time you start Movie Maker. Yet, because the clip still resides in your **Contents** pane, you can drag the clip right back to the timeline at any time.

If you've added transitions, new audio, or titles to the timeline before you delete clips, the **Video** track, **Audio** track, and **Transition** track clips will be deleted together when you delete one or more clips from the **Video** track. The **Title Overlay** track and the **Audio/Music** track remain on the timeline. You can delete clips from the **Audio/Music** and **Title Overlay** tracks if you select clips from those tracks before selecting **Edit**, **Delete**.

① **Click to Select a Clip**

Select the clip you want to delete from the timeline. Movie Maker highlights your selected clip by darkening the clip's border.

② **Hold Ctrl and Click to Select Other Clips**

If you want to delete several clips at once, select them before you perform the delete. Press and hold the **Ctrl** key as you click to select multiple clips in the timeline.

③ **Select Edit, Delete**

From the main menu, choose **Edit**, **Delete** or press the **Delete** key to delete your selected clips. Alternatively, right-click the selected clip and choose **Delete** from the context menu that appears.

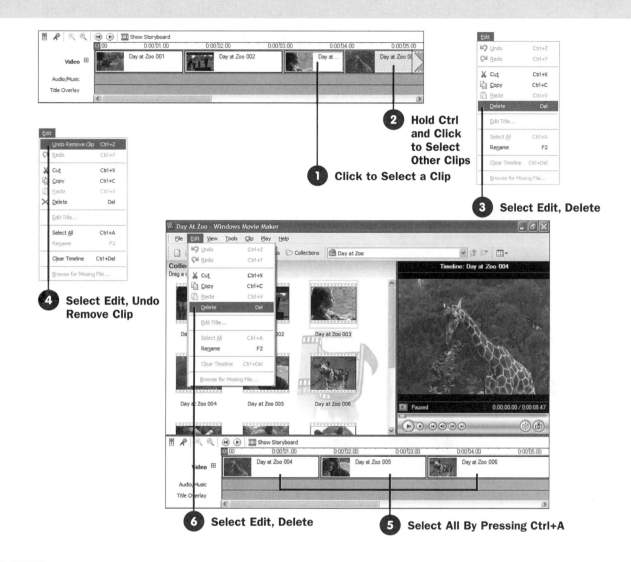

Hold Ctrl and Click to Select Other Clips

2

1 Click to Select a Clip

3 Select Edit, Delete

4 Select Edit, Undo Remove Clip

6 Select Edit, Delete

5 Select All By Pressing Ctrl+A

4 **Select Edit, Undo Remove Clip**

If you change your mind and want to undo the deletion, choose **Edit**, **Undo Remove Clip**. The clip reappears in the timeline, exactly as it was before you deleted it. You can also use the standard Windows **Ctrl+Z** keystroke to perform the **Undo Remove Clip** command without having to select from the **Edit** menu.

NOTE

If you select a clip on the **Transition**, **Audio/Music**, or **Title Overlay** track, Movie Maker removes the selected clips from that track while the other tracks remain unaffected.

5 **Select All By Pressing Ctrl+A**

If you want to clear the entire timeline, press **Ctrl+A** to select all the timeline clips—including the ones that are off the screen that you have not zoomed into.

6 **Select Edit, Delete**

With all the clips selected, choose **Edit**, **Delete** to remove all the tracks from the timeline.

 Set a Picture Clip's Duration

Before You Begin

✔ **22** Import Still Pictures into Movie Maker

✔ **34** Display a Clip's Properties

See Also

→ **48** Add a Soundtrack to Your Video

→ **69** Transition from Clip to Clip

Picture duration—The length of time a picture clip remains onscreen before the next clip plays. The picture duration applies only to picture clips. Video clip length is determined by the clip's playback time.

The **Picture duration** setting determines the duration for which clips play. If you change the **Picture duration** setting, subsequent clips change, but the ones already on the timeline do not.

Whether your project contains one or more picture clips, the clip's *picture duration* determines how long the clip remains on the screen during playback before the next clip begins its playback.

Movie Maker uses a default picture duration setting of five seconds. You can change this default setting by opening the **Options** dialog box and clicking the **Advanced** tab. In addition to setting the overall project's duration, you can set the duration for individual picture clips so that they remain on the screen for a longer or shorter amount of time than the others.

1 **Select Tools, Options**

From the main menu, choose **Tools**, **Options** to open the **Options** dialog box. This dialog box contains the settings for your work with Movie Maker.

2 **Click the Advanced Tab**

In the **Options** dialog box, click the **Advanced** tab. The default **Picture duration** setting is located on this tab of information.

3 **Click to Change Duration**

Click the up arrow next to the **Picture duration** field to increase the number of seconds each picture appears. Click the down arrow to decrease the number of seconds each picture appears.

Tools

AutoMovie...
Titles and Credits...

Video Effects
Video Transitions

Create Clips
Take Picture from Preview
Narrate Timeline...
Audio Levels

New Collection Folder

Options...

2 **Click the Advanced Tab**

Options   ? X

General   Advanced

General options
Default author:

Temporary storage:
C:\Documents and Settings\Greg Perry\Local Setti   Browse...

☐ Open last project on startup
☑ Save AutoRecover info every: 10   minutes
☑ Download codecs automatically

Reset Warning Dialogs

Click this button to see any previously hidden warning messages.
Warning messages are hidden when you select the "Do not show
this dialog again" check box.

Clear All Passwords and User Names

Click this button to clear any passwords and user names entered
into Windows Movie Maker.

Restore All Defaults

OK   Cancel

3 **Click to Change Duration**

Options   ? X

General   Advanced

Default durations
A default duration will be assigned to each picture or transition when
it is added to the storyboard or timeline.

Picture duration: 5   seconds
Transition duration: 1.25   seconds

Video properties
The video properties specify how video is captured and movies are
saved.

Video format: ⦿ NTSC   ○ PAL
Aspect ratio: ⦿ 4:3   ○ 16:9

Learn more about video settings.

E-mail
Maximum file size for sending a movie as an attachment in an e-mail
message.

1   MB

Restore All Defaults

OK   Cancel

1 **Select Tools, Options**

4 **Click OK**

4 **Click OK**

When you've specified the duration for which each picture clip will display, click **OK**. The **Options** dialog box closes and Movie Maker uses this **Picture duration** setting for all remaining picture clips you place on the storyboard/timeline.

40 **Repeat a Clip**

Often you'll find yourself wanting to use the same clip in two or more places in your project. You might want to loop through the same scene two or more times. Perhaps you want to emphasize a scene by repeating it with a different audio track. Such methods are useful, for example, when you show a dynamic replay in which your proud slugger got to third base with a single hit in last season's Little League softball championship. When you repeat a clip, you might want to add special effects, such as showing it in slow motion (**see** **67** **Put Your Video in Slow Motion**).

Before You Begin

✔ **36** Place a Clip on the Timeline

See Also

→ **43** Combine Multiple Clips into One

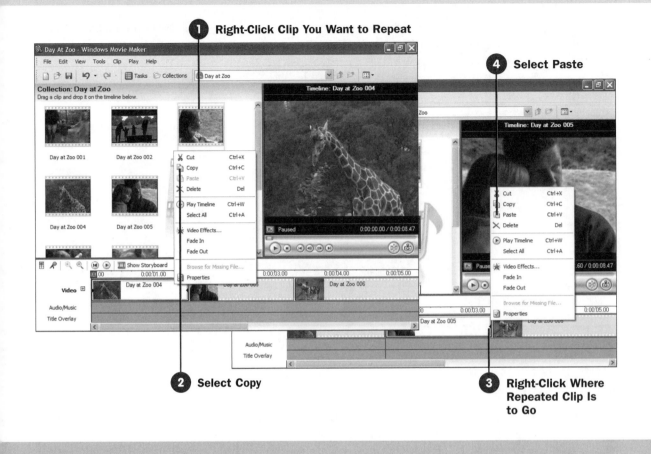

1 Right-Click Clip You Want to Repeat

4 Select Paste

2 Select Copy

3 Right-Click Where Repeated Clip Is to Go

To repeat a clip that you've already placed on the timeline, you can drag the clip once again from the **Contents** pane to the timeline. However, copying and pasting it as explained in these instructions is often simpler. When you decide that you want to repeat a clip, you might have already scrolled through to other areas of the **Contents** window, and locating the clip in the **Contents** window to drag to the timeline again would be more work than the copy-and-paste method.

① Right-Click the Clip You Want to Repeat

In the timeline, right-click the clip you want to repeat. The context menu appears.

TIP

You can repeat multiple clips by selecting more than one before copying and pasting them elsewhere on the storyboard/timeline. Press **Ctrl** as you click to select multiple clips in the timeline, and then right-click any of the selected clips.

Select Copy

From the context menu, select **Copy**. Movie Maker copies the clip to the **Clipboard**. As an alternative to using the context menu, you can select the clip and then press **Ctrl+C** to copy the clip to the **Clipboard**.

③ **Right-Click Where the Repeated Clip Is to Go**

Right-click the line between two clips, which is where your inserted clip will go.

④ **Select Paste**

Select **Paste** from the context menu to insert the clip or clips you copied into the timeline. As an alternative to using the context menu, you can click to position the insertion point and then press **Ctrl+V** to paste the clip.

41 Take a Picture from a Clip

Although you can import pictures into Movie Maker, Movie Maker can also capture pictures from any frame within a video clip. To prepare to capture the picture from the video, all you have to do is pause the clip on the frame you want to make into a picture.

 Click to Select Clip

Click to select the clip that holds the frame you want to capture as a picture.

 Click Play

Click the **Play** button; Movie Maker begins playing the selected clip.

 Click to Pause

Click the **Play** button once again to pause at the frame you want to save as a picture. You do not have to pause exactly on the actual frame—just get as close as you can.

Before You Begin

✔ 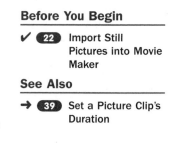 **22** Import Still Pictures into Movie Maker

See Also

→ **39** Set a Picture Clip's Duration

 TIP

You can move the seek bar under the video viewing screen to move through the video frames until you locate the frame you want to make into a picture instead of playing to that position.

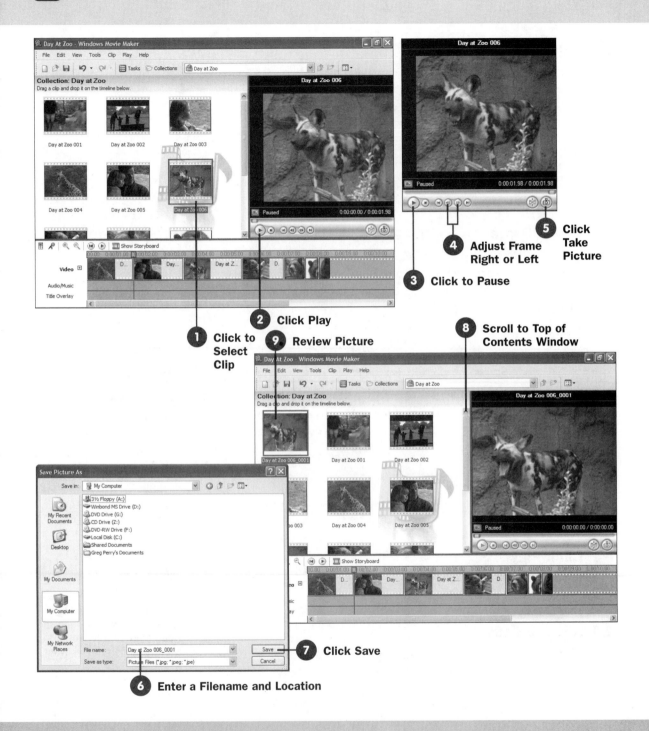

1 Click to Select Clip

2 Click Play

3 Click to Pause

4 Adjust Frame Right or Left

5 Click Take Picture

6 Enter a Filename and Location

7 Click Save

8 Scroll to Top of Contents Window

9 Review Picture

Adjust Frame Right or Left

Click the **Previous Frame** or **Next Frame** button to locate the specific frame you want to use for the picture. **Previous Frame** and **Next Frame** step through your video one frame at a time.

 Click Take Picture

Click the **Take Picture** button. Movie Maker displays a dialog box where you can enter the picture's file information.

 Enter a Filename and Location

Type a filename for the picture clip you are about to create. Movie Maker assigns the **.jpg** extension to all picture clip filenames. If you first want to select a specific folder to place the clip, click **Browse** and locate the folder you want to use.

 Click Save

When you've entered the filename and storage location, click **Save**. Movie Maker places the picture, sorted by filename, at the start of the **Contents** window.

8 **Scroll to Top of Contents Window**

Scroll to view the clips at the top of the **Contents** window and look for the newly created picture clip. Remember that you cannot rearrange clips within the **Contents** window. The **Contents** window has nothing to do with the timeline or the sequence of your project. The **Contents** window simply holds all the clips available for use in your video.

9 **Review Picture**

Look at the picture to determine whether it's acceptable to you. If you do not want the picture clip, you can delete it (**see** **30** **Delete Clips from the Storyboard**) and take a picture of another clip.

 NOTE

Movie Maker places all picture clips at the start of the **Contents** window, sorted alphabetically by filename.

TIP

You can use graphics editing software, such as Adobe Photoshop, to enhance the picture clip before using it in your Movie Maker project.

42 Split a Clip into Multiple Clips

Before You Begin

✔ **29** Add Clips to The Storyboard

✔ **35** About the Timeline and Storyboard

See Also

→ **43** Combine Multiple Clips into One

→ **44** Set Trim Points

 TIP

Insert a scene transition inside a clip by splitting the clip into two clips first and then inserting the transition between them.

NOTE

You can split a picture clip into two separate picture clips on the storyboard or the timeline. If the clip contains both audio and video, both the audio and video are split together.

 TIP

You can move the seek bar under the video viewing screen to move through the video frames until you locate the frame you want to make into a picture instead of playing to that position.

Large clips are less manageable than smaller ones. Although the number of clips grows the smaller they are, several clips give you more freedom in the arrangement of your final video than a single, large clip.

Sometimes you might want to remove the first or last portion of a clip or to divide a long clip into two or more shorter clips. Movie Maker can split a clip into two smaller clips, which you can then continue to split into even smaller clips if necessary. Movie Maker does not require the split to occur in the clip's middle frame; you can split one clip into two clips wherever you want to make the split.

1 **Click to Select a Clip**

Select the clip you want to split. You can click a clip in the **Contents** window or a clip in the storyboard/timeline.

2 **Click Play**

Click the **Play** button; Movie Maker begins playing the selected clip.

3 **Click Pause**

Click again to pause the frame where you want to split the clip. You do not have to pause exactly on the actual frame, just get as close as you can.

4 **Adjust Frame Right or Left**

Click **Previous Frame** or **Next Frame** to locate the specific frame where you want to split the clip. **Previous Frame** and **Next Frame** step through your video one frame at a time.

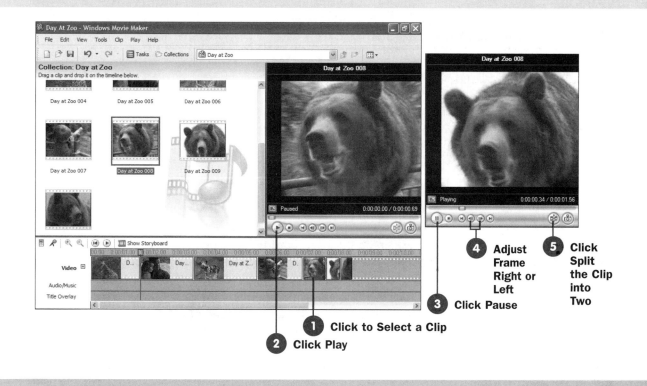

4 Adjust Frame Right or Left

5 Click Split the Clip into Two

3 Click Pause

1 Click to Select a Clip

2 Click Play

5 Click Split the Clip into Two

Click the **Split the Clip into Two** button, located in the lower-right corner of the monitor. Movie Maker splits the single clip into two clips at the frame you selected in step 4. If you split the clip from the **Contents** window, Movie Maker creates a new **Contents** window clip and gives the new clip the same name as the original full clip with an index number in parentheses. In other words, a clip named **BallGame_Homerun 008** would be split into two clips, the first one with the original name **BallGame_Homerun 008**, and the second one named **BallGame_Homerun 008 (1)**. When you save your project, the split clip is saved along with the rest of the clips.

43 Combine Multiple Clips into One

Before You Begin

✔ **29** Add Clips to the Storyboard

✔ **42** Split a Clip into Multiple Clips

See Also

→ **45** Nudge a Clip to Adjust Its Start Time

NOTE

If you combine clips on the storyboard/timeline, the clips are not combined in the **Contents** window. If you combine clips in the **Contents** window, they are not combined on the storyboard/timeline if the separate clips were there before the combination operation.

If you want to combine two or more clips into one, you can. The only requirement is that the clips are contiguous—that is, next to each other in the **Contents** pane, storyboard, or timeline. The single clip that results will have no break or indication where the combination operation occurred; it will appear that the clip was always a single clip once combined.

You cannot combine clips that are noncontiguous, such as the first and final clip in a multiclip video, unless you move those clips together.

The name assigned to the combined clip is the same name as the first, left-most clip on the storyboard/timeline before you combined the clips. All remaining clips in the project retain their original names. Movie Maker truly combines the clips; you cannot split a clip where you combined it from other clips without going through the manual process of splitting the clip into its original parts (**see** **42** **Split a Clip into Multiple Clips**). Actually, you can select **Edit**, **Undo Combine** (or press **Ctrl+Z**) to reverse the combination operation, as long as you perform the **Edit**, **Undo Combine** command within the same editing session. If you've performed other commands since you combined the clips, click the down arrow on the toolbar's **Undo** button to scroll through the list of items to undo and select the **Combine** entry.

1 **Click the First Clip**

Click to select the first clip. The first clip to be combined must be the left-most clip of all the clips you want to combine. You can select the clip in the **Contents** window or on the storyboard/timeline.

2 **Hold Ctrl and Click Additional Clips**

Press and hold the **Ctrl** key as you click to select the other clips to combine into a single clip. Remember that the subsequent clips must be contiguous to each other and to the first clip.

3 **Select Clip, Combine**

From the main menu, choose **Clip**, **Combine**. You can also press **Ctrl+M** to combine the selected clips. Movie Maker combines the clips into one single clip. The name assigned to the combined clip is the same name as the first, left-most clip you selected in step 1.

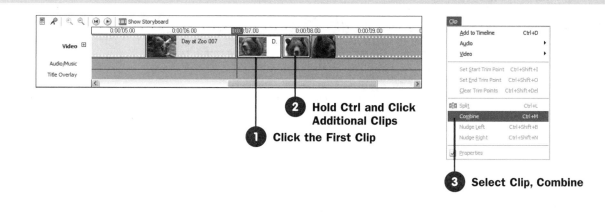

2 Hold Ctrl and Click Additional Clips

1 Click the First Clip

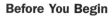

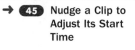

3 Select Clip, Combine

---

44 Set Trim Points

Trim, trim, and then trim some more if you want your video to retain the audience's attention. The subject is often not enough to keep people's interest; you, the director, are in charge of keeping the video's pace and changing scenes and camera angles as much as possible to keep the camera from sitting too long on the same subject.

The term *trim* is slightly misleading in Movie Maker vernacular. When you trim a clip, you trim the start time or the ending time (or both). Movie Maker will not play any part of the clip that you've trimmed off. Yet, the clip still retains its original content and length. If you later move or clear a trim point, the video and audio in the trimmed portions will reappear.

The primary reason you trim a clip is to adjust its start or ending time. Therefore, trimming shortens the playback of that clip. The first trim point is called the *start trim point*; if you want to shorten where the clip ends, you'll set an *end trim point*.

After you've trimmed a clip, you can easily change the start or end trim point, or clear the trim points altogether. You can trim clips only on the timeline; therefore, you must display the timeline before you can trim any clip. The clip you want to trim must reside on the timeline. The **Audio** track is automatically trimmed as you trim the **Video** track. You can trim clips on the **Transition**, **Audio/Music**, and **Title Overlay** tracks, as well as clips on the **Video** track.

Before You Begin

✔ **33** Watch a Clip

✔ **37** Zoom a Timeline Clip

See Also

→ **45** Nudge a Clip to Adjust Its Start Time

🔍 KEY TERM

Trim—To shorten a portion of a clip by positioning a trim point so that Movie Maker starts playing or stops playing the clip at that point.

🖐 NOTE

You cannot lengthen an untrimmed clip unless you combine the clip with another one.

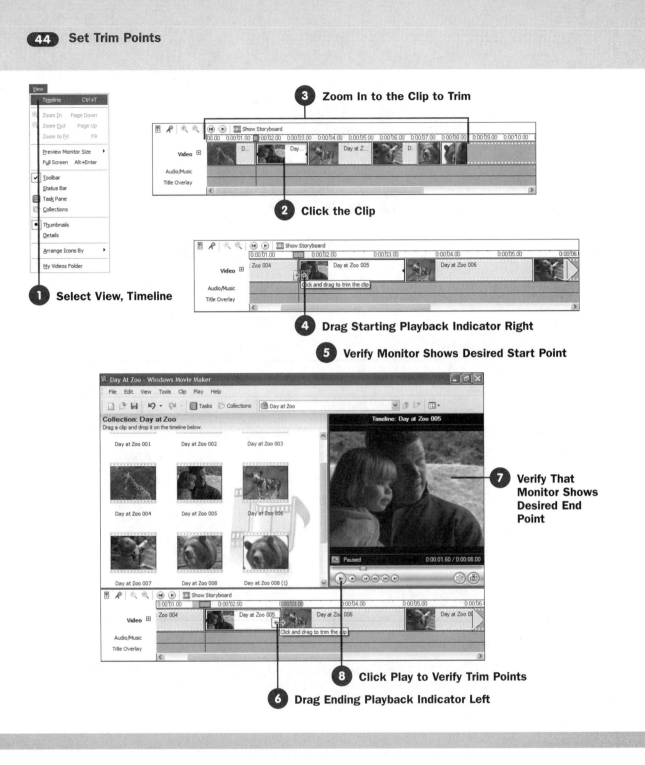

3 Zoom In to the Clip to Trim

2 Click the Clip

1 Select View, Timeline

4 Drag Starting Playback Indicator Right

5 Verify Monitor Shows Desired Start Point

7 Verify That Monitor Shows Desired End Point

8 Click Play to Verify Trim Points

6 Drag Ending Playback Indicator Left

 Select View, Timeline

Choose **View, Timeline** from the main menu or click the **Show Timeline** button. If the timeline is already displayed, you do not have to perform this step.

 Click the Clip

You must select a clip on the timeline before you can adjust its trim points.

 Zoom In to the Clip to Trim

It helps to increase the timeline's clip width so that you can more easily adjust the trim points. Press **PageDown** to zoom in to the timeline.

4 **Drag Starting Playback Indicator Right**

Position the mouse pointer over the *starting playback indicator* (the left edge of the clip). The mouse pointer changes to a red, double-headed arrow, indicating that you can adjust the trim point by clicking and dragging with your mouse. Drag the starting playback indicator to the right to move the starting point of the clip further "into" the clip.

5 **Verify That Monitor Shows Desired Start Point**

Sometimes it's difficult to drag the trim points to the exact frame where you want the clip to start or stop playing. Therefore, after you get close to the desired frame, you can click **Next Frame** or **Previous Frame** until the **Monitor** displays the frame where you want to place a trim point. Then select **Clip**, **Set Start Trim Point** to set the start trim point.

6 **Drag Ending Playback Indicator Left**

If you want to trim where the clip ends, adjust its end trim point. Position the mouse pointer over the *ending playback indicator* (the right edge of the clip). The mouse pointer changes to a red, double-headed arrow. Drag the ending playback indicator to the left to move the end point of the clip further "into" the clip.

 **KEY TERMS**

Start trim point—Determines where the clip begins playback.

End trim point—Determines where the clip stops playback.

 **NOTE**

You can trim only one selected clip at a time; you cannot trim multiple clips that you select as a group.

KEY TERMS

Starting playback indicator—A selected clip's left edge on the timeline.

Ending playback indicator—A selected clip's right edge on the timeline.

7 Verify That Monitor Shows Desired End Point

Use the **Monitor's Next Frame** and **Previous Frame** buttons to display the frame where you want to place the trim point and choose **Clip**, **Set End Trim Point**. You want to verify that the monitor shows your desired end point for the clip. After you've positioned the end trim point, the clip on the timeline adjusts to its new length set by the trim points. If you drag to change the trim points later (or remove them altogether by selecting **Clip**, **Clear Trim Points**), the timeline clip's width changes once again to reflect the clip's playback length relative to surrounding clips on the timeline.

8 Click Play to Verify Trim Points

Click the **Play** button; the **Monitor** plays the selected clip only from the starting trim point to the ending trim point. By clicking **Play** to watch the playback, you can verify that your trim points are accurate.

Nudge a Clip to Adjust Its Start Time

Before You Begin

✔ **33** Watch a Clip

✔ **36** Place a Clip on the Timeline

See Also

→ **69** Transition from Clip to Clip

From the timeline, you can change the start point of a **Video**, **Audio/Music**, or **Title Overlay** clip slightly by nudging the start of the clip to the left or right. Nudging the clip moves the beginning of the clip to the left or right; all clips to the right of the nudged clip are also affected by this movement.

If you left-nudge a clip that immediately follows another clip, the nudged clip's beginning overlaps the previous clip's conclusion. This creates a kind of ghosted transition, which you can use as the basis for adding Movie Maker's special transition effects.

1 Click to Select a Clip

You must select a clip on the timeline's **Video** track, **Audio/Music** track, or **Title Overlay** track. When you nudge a video clip, its corresponding audio clip moves with it.

2 Select Clip, Nudge Left

From the main menu, choose **Clip**, **Nudge Left**. Alternatively, press **Ctrl+Shift+B** to nudge the clip to the left.

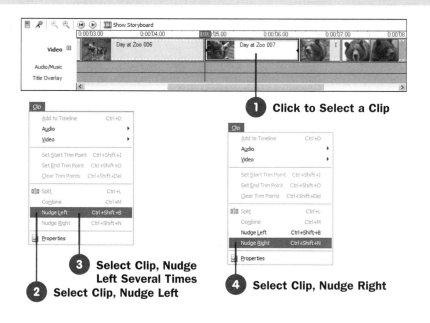

1 Click to Select a Clip

3 Select Clip, Nudge
Left Several Times

2 Select Clip, Nudge Left

4 Select Clip, Nudge Right

3 Select Clip, Nudge Left Several Times

Repeat step 2 several times to move the clip so that it overshadows the end of the preceding clip in the timeline. You might want to select both clips and click **Play** to see the effects of the second clip being nudged into the first one.

4 Select Clip, Nudge Right

From the main menu, choose **Clip**, **Nudge Right**. Movie Maker reverses the nudge and begins to move the clip back to the right.

 NOTE

You cannot nudge the start of a clip to the right if you have not yet nudged it to the left. In other words, Movie Maker will not leave an empty gap on the timeline between two clips. In addition, you cannot nudge a clip's right edge (its end point), and you should have no reason to do so.

7

Working with Sound and Music

IN THIS CHAPTER

NOTE

Keep in mind that the Audio track includes the audio that's imported along with your video. The Audio/Music track includes additional audio clips you add to your project.

Hollywood understands the need for an effective soundtrack and so should you. A good soundtrack often goes unnoticed throughout a movie. The soundtrack helps accentuate the action or prepare the audience for a slower scene. The soundtrack can bring the audience into a chase, or take them away from conflict as the camera follows suit.

A soundtrack comprises sounds, music, voice, and narration. As a Movie Maker producer, you can add a soundtrack with any and all of these elements to your own movies. The timeline's Audio and Audio/Music tracks will be your focus as you work with your movie's sound.

46 About Movie Maker Audio

Before You Begin

✔ **7** About Making Audio a Priority

See Also

→ **47** About Importing Existing Digital Files

→ **48** Add a Soundtrack to Your Video

 TIP

If you cannot see the Audio track, click the plus sign next to the timeline's Video track labeled **Video**. Clicking the plus sign displays both the Audio track and the Transition track, and the plus changes to a minus sign. Clicking the minus sign once again hides the Audio and Transition tracks to save screen space.

The two timeline tracks related to your movie's audio are the Audio track and the Audio/Music track. When you import a video into the **Collections** pane, any audio associated with that video is imported at the same time. This audio will remain sequenced to the video it complements. In other words, if you import a birthday party video in which the crowd sings "Happy Birthday," the movie's Audio track will hold the singing of the song at the proper place in the video. You cannot modify the timing of such audio; the audio remains in synch with the video if you import the video and audio together in this way. If you delete any audio clips from the Audio track, Movie Maker deletes the corresponding video clip also.

The Audio/Music track holds audio not necessarily synched to your video when you first import or record the video. You can freely move, add, and delete audio clips from the Audio/Music track without affecting the Video track in any way.

Movie Maker offers you complete control over your movie's audio by allowing you to perform the following actions:

- **Narration**—You can synchronize music or voice narration to action taking place within your movie.

- **Audio Level Adjustment**—You can adjust audio levels for balance when playing back audio and video from both the Audio and Audio/Music tracks.

- **Audio Effects**—You can adjust audio to offer effects such as a fade-out from your movie's closing credits or a complete mute of the soundtrack at a specific point.

- **Audio Clip Volume**—You can adjust the volume on any and all Audio track or Audio/Music track clips in your movie.

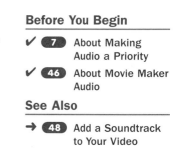

Set Audio Levels

Narrate the Timeline

Click to Hide Audio and Transition Tracks

Audio Track

Audio/Music track

All audio and video work together, in sequence, as shown by their tracks on the timeline.

> **NOTE**
>
> Sometimes you'll need to adjust volume levels simply to fix a problem in the original video footage. For example, if the camera's microphone was too close to the sound source in raw video footage you import into Movie Maker, you'll adjust the volume level down for that clip to maintain consistency with the volume levels in the rest of your movie.

47 About Importing Existing Digital Files

Movie Maker supports the import of audio files that have the following filename extensions: **.aif**, **.aifc**, **.aiff**, **.asf**, **.au**, **.mp2**, **.mp3**, **.mpa**, **.snd**, **.wav**, and **.wma**. Of these 11 types, **.mp3** (called MPEG), **.wav** (called *wave*), and **.wma** (from Windows Media Player) are by far the most common.

Before You Begin

✔ **7** About Making Audio a Priority

✔ **46** About Movie Maker Audio

See Also

→ **48** Add a Soundtrack to Your Video

TIP

At first, Movie Maker seems to limit you by not letting you move or rename audio files you import. By keeping the file on the disk (as opposed to the alternative of copying the file's contents directly into your project) you can change the imported audio file, and that change will automatically appear in your project without requiring you to import the file once again.

NOTE

Because Movie Maker creates no copy of your audio file, if you delete an audio clip in your **Contents** pane, the audio file still remains on your disk unchanged.

As with imported video content, when Movie Maker imports audio files, the files appear in your **Collections** pane. Actually, a representation of the audio file appears in your **Collections** pane.

Movie Maker never makes a copy of your imported audio file—it only links to that file from your **Collections** pane. Therefore, you cannot move, rename, or delete an audio file after you've imported it into your collection; otherwise, Movie Maker won't be able to locate the file. If you move the file to another location, you will have to import the audio file once again into your project's collection.

Microsoft created Movie Maker to adhere to digital rights management encoding. Therefore, if your audio file is protected in some way by digital rights management, you will be unable to import the audio file into your project. For more information about digital rights management, see **21** **Import Video into Movie Maker**.

48 Add a Soundtrack to Your Video

Before You Begin

✔ **7** About Making Audio a Priority

✔ **35** About the Timeline and Storyboard

See Also

→ **49** About Improving Your Soundtrack's Quality

→ **51** Create Narration Outside Movie Maker

Adding a soundtrack (as opposed to using the audio that comes with imported video) gives you control over your movie's audio. You cannot edit or delete audio that you import with video. When you import audio into your collection and then drag audio clips to the timeline's Audio/Music track, that audio synchronizes with the video on the timeline, but it isn't attached to it. In other words, you can add more audio clips, delete audio clips, or rearrange audio on the Audio/Music track without affecting the Video track in any way.

As this task demonstrates, importing an audio file into your Audio/Music track is easier than importing video. All you must do is ensure that the audio is in the proper format required by Movie Maker. (See Chapter 1, "Start Here," for a review of Movie Maker's file types.)

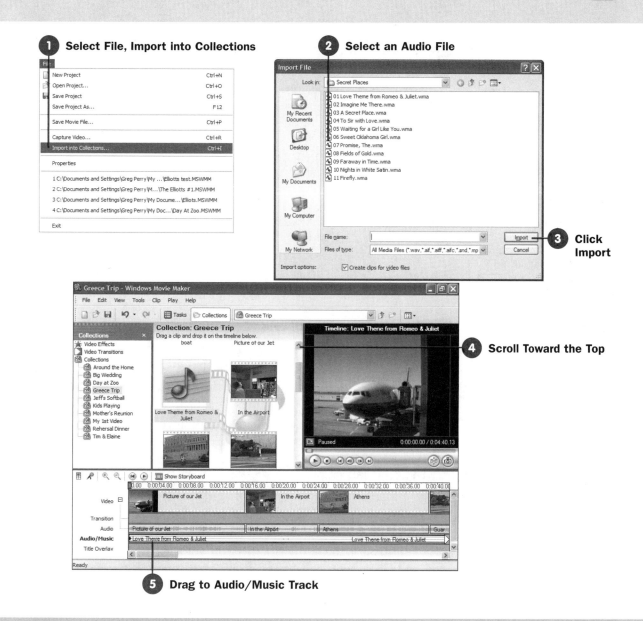

1 Select File, Import into Collections

2 Select an Audio File

3 Click Import

4 Scroll Toward the Top

5 Drag to Audio/Music Track

NOTE

If you import a video with sound into your project, and then you import audio onto the project's Audio/Music track, you will hear both audio tracks play when you play the movie, and both audio tracks will appear in the final movie that you save later. Unless you want both soundtracks competing with each other, you should either use the audio that you import with the video exclusively by muting the audio when importing video (see **21** **Import Video into Movie Maker**) and adding a soundtrack later to the Audio/Music track, or adjust both audio levels to work with one another (see **54** **Adjust Audio Levels**).

TIP

If you plan to add an opening or closing musical score to your movie, or add special audio effects throughout your movie, you might want to keep the original audio when importing your video, and then just add the audio effects to the Audio/Music track later. Such use of both audio tracks would complement, not compete, with each other.

TIP

Import multiple audio files at once by holding the **Ctrl** key while you click each audio file.

① Select File, Import into Collections

Begin the import process by selecting **Import into Collections** from the **File** menu. You will be importing one or more audio clips into your **Collections** pane, where you can then drag one or more of those clips to your **Contents** pane for inclusion in your movie.

② Select an Audio File

Locate the audio file you want to import and click to select it.

③ Click Import

When you click **Import**, Movie Maker imports all the selected audio files into your **Collections** pane and stores them there as clips, with each clip sharing the same name as the filename (without the filename extension).

④ Scroll Toward the Top

To see your imported audio clip, you must scroll toward the top of your project's **Contents** pane, if the **Contents** pane is not already scrolled to that point. Movie Maker places imported audio clips toward the top of the **Contents** pane.

The location of the imported audio clips in your **Contents** pane has nothing to do with their location in your movie. Only when you drag an audio clip to the timeline's Audio/Music track does the clip's location have any bearing on your movie.

⑤ Drag to Audio/Music Track

Drag the audio clips you want added to your video to the Audio/Music track. You can then rearrange them, delete them, or add more audio clips on the Audio/Music track, just as you do with other kinds of clips.

49 About Improving Your Soundtrack's Quality

When you record audio for your movie, be sure to pay attention to its quality and content as much as you pay attention to your video's quality and content. Too often, users of digital video cameras focus on the lighting and finding the best shot, but fail to pay close attention to the video's sound. The result is a good-looking video that is not enjoyable because of poor sound quality.

Microsoft warns against *ambient noise*, and suggests that you soften hard surfaces close to your video if possible by turning off electrical equipment such as computers and other devices that can add a hum to a video's audio. Be sure to also turn off air conditioners or heaters to keep your microphone from adding their sound to your video's background.

If you visit a recording studio, you will see that the walls often have curtains on them. The curtains reduce ambient noise that might reflect off the hard walls.

If you record music for a movie, use a direct cable between the stereo playing the music source and your computer instead of recording with a microphone, so you get the best recorded sound without any danger of picking up ambient noise. Connect a cable from your stereo's line out to your computer's line-in jack. Depending on your hardware, you might need to obtain an adapter or cable with the proper connections to run two output jacks from your stereo to your computer sound card's single line-in jack.

If you use your camera's microphone and cannot control the sounds around where you're shooting the video, perhaps the sound actually accentuates your movie. For example, if your microphone picks up birds flying overhead on the beach, the birdcalls might help give your video a realistic feel. Be careful when recording voices on the beach, however, because the waves share a sound range similar to the human voice, and often will detract from your speaker's voice dramatically.

Before You Begin

✔ **7** About Making Audio a Priority

See Also

→ **47** About Importing Existing Digital Files

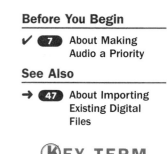

KEY TERM

Ambient noise—Unwanted noise that can creep into your video, such as traffic, air conditioner motors, and echoes off walls, windows, and even your camera.

50 About Movie Narration

Before You Begin

✔ **7** About Making
Audio a Priority

✔ **46** About Movie Maker
Audio

See Also

→ **52** Add Narration to
Your Movie

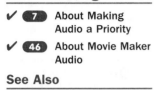

Narration—Voicing over a
video to provide a description, tell a story, or introduce scenes and events.

You can record narration
either outside Movie Maker
(see **51** Create
Narration Outside Movie
Maker) or from within
Movie Maker. If you record
narration within Movie
Maker, you can watch the
video as you record the
narration, and Movie Maker
will keep the video and narration properly synchro-
nized when you play back
the movie.

Movie Maker supports *narration* so that you can add a voice track on
top or in place of your video's Audio track. Perhaps you want to produce
an instructional video that teaches viewers how to buy and sell items
online. You might want to capture the video from a computer screen-
based video recording program and then add the narration that guides
the viewer through the steps taken later. You might also add narration
on top of video that already has a soundtrack recorded with it. For
example, if your video contains people talking, you might want to add
narration to the beginning that tells who is doing the speaking.

Click to See Audio Track

Audio/Music Track ——

Narration Also Appears Here

*The Audio and Audio/Music tracks hold your movie's sounds, sound-
track, and any narration you want to use.*

Your movie can contain still pictures. For example, you might want to
focus on a single shot and explain what is going on through narration.
You can take a picture from any video clip (**see** **41** **Take a Picture
from a Clip**), adjust its duration to keep that picture on the screen for a

while, and then add narration so that your audience will hear you describe what is happening in the picture.

If your movie is composed entirely of still pictures, your movie will actually be a slideshow. Music and narration will help engage your audience in a way that the old family slideshows before the 1990s never could.

51 Create Narration Outside Movie Maker

Most computers have supported multimedia (graphics, sound, and video) since the early 1990s, and several recording programs have appeared on the market that help you create and edit a recording, such as you would do with a microphone when you record narration for a video.

Sound Recorder is a bare-bones recording program that comes free with every copy of Microsoft Windows. Sound Recorder is designed to take input from your microphone (plugged into your sound card's microphone jack) and digitize the sound to digital audio that your computer can play. Sound Recorder creates wave files, which are sound files with the **.WAV** filename extension. Movie Maker reads wave files easily, so you can import narration that you've recorded with Sound Recorder into Movie Maker.

1 Click Start Button

From your Windows desktop, click your Windows **Start** button to open your **Windows** menu.

2 Select All Programs, Accessories, Entertainment, Sound Recorder

From the **Windows** menu, select **All Programs**, **Accessories**, **Entertainment**, **Sound Recorder** to start the Sound Recorder program. (Your Windows **Start** menu might not contain the same amount of items as the one in the figure.)

Before You Begin

✔ **50** About Movie Narration

See Also

→ **52** Add Narration to Your Movie

 **NOTE**

When discussing *narration* and Movie Maker together, one usually thinks of the narration that you can record from within Movie Maker itself (see **52** Add Narration to Your Movie). Yet you will not always be able to do this. Perhaps you don't have a quality microphone, and you must use a friend's computer to make your narration recording. Sometimes the source material you read from to create narration will be at a location separate from your Movie Maker computer. Therefore, you need to have some way to create a recording using a microphone outside of Movie Maker. Windows includes the free Sound Recorder program, and this task explains its use.

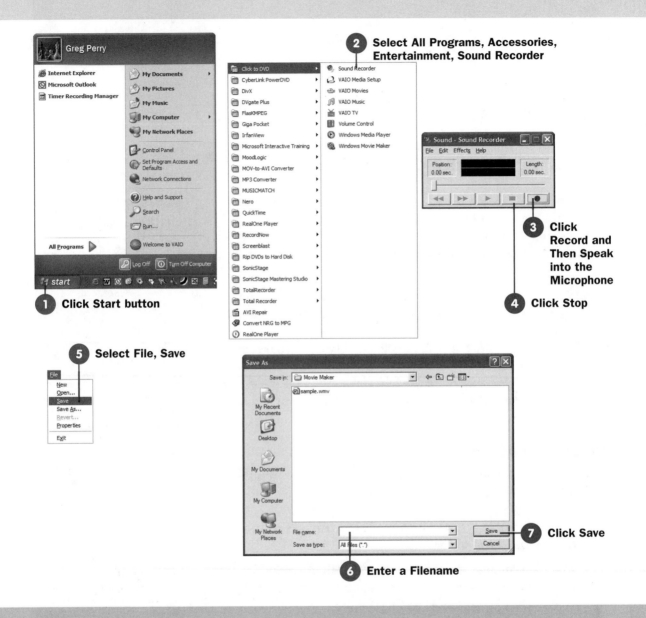

2 Select All Programs, Accessories, Entertainment, Sound Recorder

3 Click Record and Then Speak into the Microphone

4 Click Stop

1 Click Start button

5 Select File, Save

6 Enter a Filename

7 Click Save

3 **Click Record and Then Speak into the Microphone**

When you're ready to speak into your microphone, click the Sound Recorder's **Record** button (the red button at the right of the program's bottom area) and speak into the microphone. As Sound

Recorder records your voice, the sound wave pattern appears in the Sound Recorder's central view port.

 Click Stop

Click Sound Recorder's **Stop** button when you finish speaking.

 Select File, Save

Select **Save** from Sound Recorder's **File** menu to open the **Save As** dialog box.

 Enter a Filename

Type the name that you want Sound Recorder to use for the recording filename.

 Click Save

When you click **Save**, Sound Recorder saves your narration onto your disk in a wave file that Movie Maker can easily import.

TIP

By recording several short audio clips instead of one long clip, you can easily re-record over a mistake by re-recording the clip where you made the mistake. If you record one long narration and mess up toward the end, you will have to re-record the entire narration or use a sound editing program to replace the unwanted material.

---

52 **Add Narration to Your Movie**

To synchronize your narration exactly to your video, use Movie Maker's built-in narration recording feature.

When you begin to record narration, Movie Maker plays the video on your timeline so you can speak as you watch the action. As you speak, Movie Maker records your voice, and also records where your words coincide with the video. Upon finishing, you will save the narration, and Movie Maker adds it to the Audio/Music track. When you play back the movie, you will hear your narration.

1 **Click Show Timeline**

Movie Maker supports narration creation only from the timeline, so click **Show Timeline** to display the timeline if the storyboard is showing.

Before You Begin

✔ **50** About Movie Narration

✔ **51** Create Narration Outside Movie Maker

See Also

➜ **53** Adjust Advanced Narration Options

TIP

If you want to capture video from a source such as a video camera and that video contains unwanted sound, drag the **Input Level** control all the way down on the **Video Capture** dialog box (the dialog box you see when you first begin capturing a video) to mute the input volume.

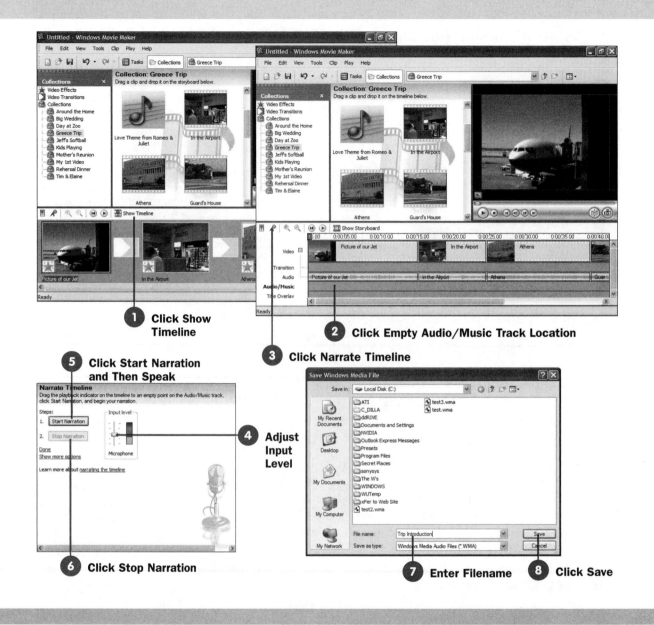

① Click Show Timeline

② Click Empty Audio/Music Track Location

③ Click Narrate Timeline

⑤ Click Start Narration and Then Speak

④ Adjust Input Level

⑥ Click Stop Narration

⑦ Enter Filename

⑧ Click Save

② Click Empty Audio/Music Track Location

You must tell Movie Maker where your narration should appear. You don't have to narrate the entire video; you can narrate only pieces of it. Click on an empty Audio/Music track location where you want to start the narration on the timeline's time interval to inform Movie Maker where on the Audio/Music track you want to begin the narration.

 Click Narrate Timeline

Click the microphone on the timeline's toolbar to display the **Narrate Timeline** dialog box.

 Adjust Input Level

Speak into your microphone and test the input volume level. If the level is too high or too low, drag the **Input Level** slider control to ensure that the input volume is as loud as possible without showing the red warning color at the top of the volume level. As you speak, your voice should fall within the green area to maintain proper volume.

 Click Start Narration and Then Speak

When you click the **Start Narration** button, Movie Maker begins the recording of your narration, so watch the **Monitor** pane and narrate over the video.

 Click Stop Narration

Click the **Stop Narration** button. Movie Maker opens the **Save As** dialog box so you can save the narration in a file.

 Enter Filename

Type the filename you want to save the narration in. Movie Maker saves the narration as a Windows Media Audio file with the filename extension .**WMA**.

8 **Click Save**

When you click **Save**, Movie Maker saves the audio file. The narration will appear as an audio clip at the top of your **Contents** pane.

 NOTE

As you record the narration, you will hear any sound that you imported with the video that appears on the Audio track. You can speak around or over the video's audio, but you cannot replace any audio on the Audio track.

 TIP

Movie Maker supports several advanced narration options (see **53** Adjust Advanced Narration Options).

 NOTE

You can continue to narrate parts of your movie by repeating steps 3 through 8. When you are finished adding narration, click the **Done** option in the **Narrate Timeline** dialog box to stop narrating and return to Movie Maker's regular screens.

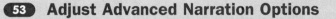

53 **Adjust Advanced Narration Options**

Before You Begin

✔ **50** About Movie
Narration

✔ **52** Add Narration to
Your Movie

See Also

→ **54** Adjust Audio Levels

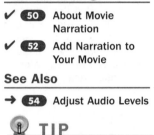

TIP

As you record narration, the
Narrate Timeline dialog box
displays the total amount
of narration time you've
recorded.

TIP

Did you know you can add
music to your video even if
you've already added narration? Just drag the imported music clip to the end of
the Audio/Music track (following your narration).
Then just drag the music
clip to the left over your
narration, and the music
will play as your narration
speaks!

You can select and change several advanced narration options. The
default values often suffice for most narration needs, but the advanced
options are there when you need to adjust them.

If you have multiple input devices that you record from (such as a tape
player plugged into your sound card's line-in jack and a microphone),
you can select the one you want to use for a specific narration session.
In addition, you can limit the amount of timeline space used during a
narration recording session to ensure that you don't run over another
recording later on the Audio/Music track.

1 Click Show More Options

Movie Maker normally does not show the advanced narration
options, but you can show them by clicking the option labeled
Show More Options.

2 Select Audio Device

If you have multiple audio devices, select the device you want to
use for the narration from the **Audio Device** list.

3 Select Audio Input Source

Select the source you want to use, such as microphone or line-in
jack on your audio card, from the **Audio Input Source** list.

4 Click to Limit Recording Space

If your Audio/Music track already has content on it, you might not
want your narration to overwrite this content. For example, perhaps you've added music to the beginning and end of your video.
You can ensure that Movie Maker stops recording narration if it
runs into another audio clip on the Audio/Music track by clicking
the option labeled **Limit Narration to Available Free Space on
Audio/Music Track**.

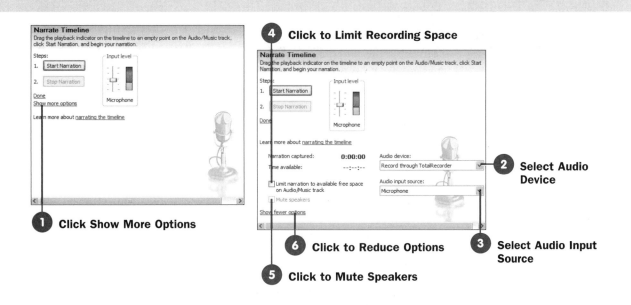

Click to Limit Recording Space

Click Show More Options

Select Audio Device

Click to Reduce Options

Select Audio Input Source

Click to Mute Speakers

5 **Click to Mute Speakers**

Your computer might be playing back audio from an online radio station, or perhaps you are playing a music CD in the background while you work. If you click the **Mute Speakers** option, Movie Maker mutes your computer's speakers until you uncheck this option, so the audio does not interfere with the narration that you are recording.

6 **Click to Reduce Options**

If you have no need for the advanced options, you can hide them by clicking the option labeled **Show Fewer Options**.

54 Adjust Audio Levels

Before You Begin

✔ **46** About Movie Maker Audio

✔ **48** Add a Soundtrack to Your Video

See Also

→ **56** Change the Movie's Volume

As you know, your movie can contain two audio tracks: the Audio track that contains the audio included with the video you imported or captured into your project, and the audio on the Audio/Music track that you added separately.

The two audio tracks often play at the same time, as would be the case if you added music that was to play beneath a voice speaking in the movie. The only potential problem you can run up against with two audio tracks is that the volume on each track might compete with one another. Movie Maker enables you to adjust the volume levels of the audio tracks so that one is dominant and the other remains in the background.

① Select Tools, Audio Levels

To inform Movie Maker that you want to adjust the relative volume between the two audio tracks, select **Audio Levels** from the **Tools** menu to display the **Audio Levels** dialog box.

② Drag the Slider

Drag the slider toward the **Audio From Video** option if you want to increase the volume of the video's original audio track. Drag the slider toward the **Audio/Music** option if you want to increase the volume of the audio you added to the Audio/Music track. As you increase the volume of one track, Movie Maker also decreases the volume of the other track accordingly.

③ Click to Close

Click the **Close** button to close the **Audio Levels** dialog box and return to Movie Maker with your audio levels adjusted to your liking.

TIP

To completely mute one of the audio tracks, slide the **Audio From Video** slider control all the way in the direction of the other audio track. If, therefore, you slide the **Audio From Video** slider all the way to the **Audio/Music** side, any audio from the Audio track is muted and will not play.

NOTE

During playback within Movie Maker, the audio from the Audio track might begin to play even when you've slid the **Audio From Video** slider control all the way to the **Audio/Music** track. The playback will not occur in your final movie, however, that you eventually create in Movie Maker (see **85** Start the Save Movie Wizard).

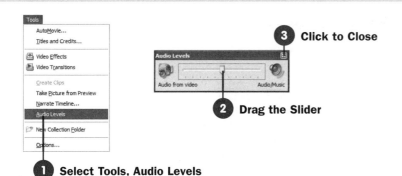

3 Click to Close

2 Drag the Slider

1 Select Tools, Audio Levels

55 **Add Sound Effects to Your Movie**

Creating sound effects is more of a craft that you learn by doing, not by reading about it. Many of Hollywood's sound effect engineers were hired for blockbuster movies only after years of apprenticeship working for others in the field.

This task focuses on adding sound effects that you've already recorded or obtained from other sources.

Adding sound effects requires only that you locate the place on the timeline where the sound is to go (you might need to increase the timeline's interval setting; **see** **37** **Zoom a Timeline Clip** for help with this) and add the sound to the Audio/Music track on the timeline.

1 **Zoom into Timeline**

If you need to zoom into the timeline to place the sound effect more accurately, press **PageDown** until the time interval is small enough that you can see the location you want to place the sound effect.

2 **Click Target Location**

If you did not locate the sound effect's insertion point by playing the timeline, and you can accurately locate the time interval where you want to insert the sound effect, click the time interval where you want the sound effect to go. The timeline's status line will appear at that location.

Before You Begin

✔ **48** Add a Soundtrack to Your Video

See Also

➔ **56** Change the Movie's Volume

 TIP

Several Web sites offer free and inexpensive sound effects—http://www. A1FreeSoundEffects. com/ provides several hundred. Be sure to purchase royalty-free sound effects if you plan to use them in movies you produce to sell, such as training videos.

NOTE

This task assumes you've imported the needed sound effects into your **Collections** pane before you begin. If you have not imported the sound effects, see **47** **About Importing Existing Digital Files** if you need help doing so.

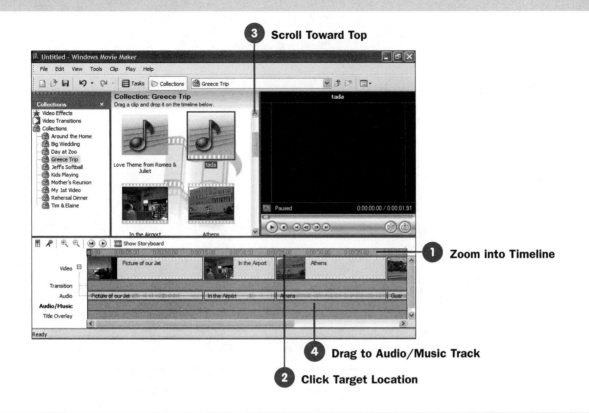

③ **Scroll Toward Top**

① Zoom into Timeline

④ Drag to Audio/Music Track

② Click Target Location

NOTE

You can play the timeline and pause the playback at the point where you want to place the sound effect. Click the **Monitor** pane's **Next Frame** or **Previous Frame** buttons to locate the exact position where your sound effect is to go.

③ Scroll Toward Top

Scroll to the top portion of your **Contents** pane where sound clips are located.

④ Drag to Audio/Music Track

Drag the sound effect clip to the timeline's Audio/Music track. When you get close to the insertion point, release your mouse button. The sound effect will now rest on the timeline's Audio/Music track. If you need to move the clip slightly left or right, nudge the clip left or right a frame at a time (**see** **45** **Nudge a Clip to Adjust its Start Time**).

56 Change the Movie's Volume

You can change the volume of a single clip or a group of selected clips. You can even change the volume of an entire movie by selecting all the clips and then adjusting the volume. You'll want to change the entire movie's volume if it's generally too loud or too soft when you play back the movie. You'll want to adjust the volume of individual clips if some are too low in relation to surrounding clips. You don't want your audience to keep working the volume control just to hear your movie at an adequate level.

You can adjust the volume of an audio clip on the Audio track or adjust the volume of an audio clip on the Audio/Music timeline. Volume adjustment is one of the few things you can do to the Audio track without affecting the video track, which is synchronized with the Audio track. (If you delete a clip from the Audio track, the video clip associated with it leaves the Video track at the same time.)

Movie Maker gives you three options for adjusting volume:

- Raise or lower a clip's volume

- Mute the clip's volume completely

- Reset the clip's volume to its original level

 Right-Click Clip

Locate the clip you want to adjust. The clip may reside on the Audio track or on the Audio/Music track. Right-click over the track to display the menu.

 Select Volume

Select **Volume** from the menu to display the **Adjust Clip Volume** dialog box.

 Drag Left to Decrease

Drag the volume's slider control left if you want to decrease the clip's volume.

4 **Drag Right to Increase**

Drag the volume's slider control right if you want to increase the clip's volume.

Before You Begin

✔ **46** About Movie Maker Audio

✔ **48** Add a Soundtrack to Your Video

✔ **54** Adjust Audio Levels

See Also

➜ **57** Fade In and Fade Out Your Soundtrack

 **NOTE**

The volume changes on the clip's playback, but the actual clip volume inside the clip's file does not change. Therefore, you might insert the same sound effect multiple places in your movie and lower the volume in one place and raise the volume in another.

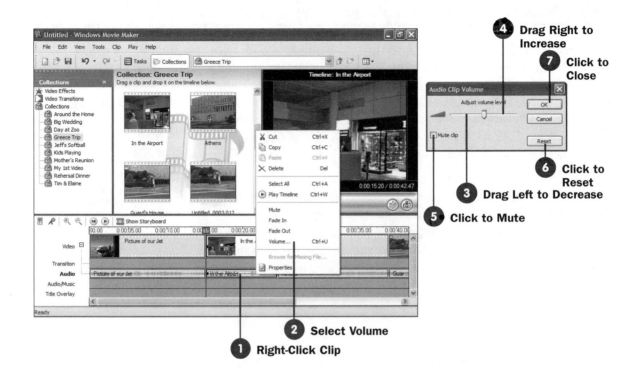

Drag Right to
Increase

Click to
Close

Click to
Reset

Drag Left to Decrease

Click to Mute

Select Volume

Right-Click Clip

5 Click to Mute

Click the **Mute clip** option to silence the clip's playback volume completely. If an audio clip also appears on the other audio track, only the clip you right-clicked is muted.

6 Click to Reset

If you want to reset a clip's volume back to its original level, click the **Reset** button.

7 Click to Close

Click the **OK** button to apply whatever volume changes you requested for the clip.

57 Fade In and Fade Out Your Soundtrack

If you want a clip to begin at a low volume and gradually rise to full volume, you need to fade in the clip. Movie Maker spends two-thirds of a second on the fade sound effect, so it takes almost a full second for the sound to rise from low volume to full volume. You can also fade out a clip's volume.

The fade-in and fade-out effects have a bearing on how split or combined audio clips behave. If you fade in or fade out a clip, you split that clip into two clips, and both of the split clips will also fade in or fade out. If, however, you combine two separate clips, Movie Maker applies the fade-in and fade-out effects of the first clip to the combined clip.

1 Right-Click Clip

Locate the clip to which you want to apply a fade effect and right-click it.

2 Select Fade In

Select the **Fade In** option to apply the fading effect to the beginning of the clip.

3 Right-Click Clip

Once again, right-click the clip to which you want to apply a fading effect.

4 Select Fade Out

Select the **Fade Out** option to apply the fading effect to the end of the clip.

Before You Begin

✔ **46** About Movie Maker Audio

✔ **48** Add a Soundtrack to Your Video

✔ **54** Adjust Audio Levels

See Also

→ **58** About Finding Audio Content on the Web

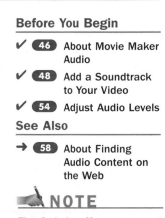**NOTE**

The fade-in effect occurs at the start of a clip, and the fade-out effect occurs at the end of a clip.

NOTE

No visible sign appears when you fade in or fade out a clip. The only way you can tell whether you've set a fading effect for a clip is to right-click the clip and see whether one or both of the fade options are selected.

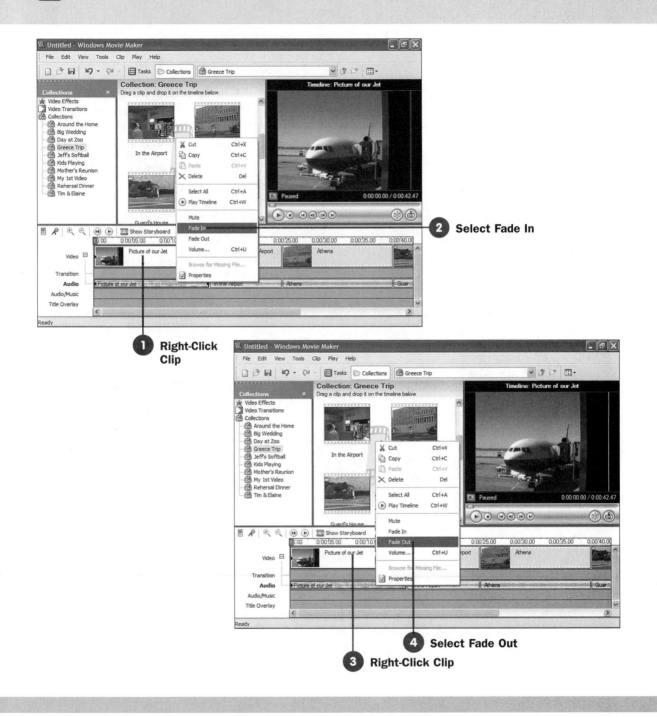

2 Select Fade In

1 Right-Click Clip

4 Select Fade Out

3 Right-Click Clip

58 **About Finding Audio Content on the Web**

The Internet is full of audio content from all over the world that you can listen to, download, edit, and redistribute—although you cannot do all those things with all online audio files. Given the publicity in recent years about MP3 file sharing, you surely know many audio files are copyrighted for specific use. Rarely do you ever actually own an audio file that you download. Instead of owning the file, usually you only own a license to use it in some way. Be sure to read the fine print on the site where you download to discern what you are allowed to do with the file.

Several sites offer *royalty-free* audio content. Such content is great for soundtrack music that you can add to the opening of your videos, to place as a low-volume score during some scenes, and to end your movie while you roll credits (**see** **78** **Add End Credits**).

A search on the Internet for "royalty-free audio" will turn up sites that offer downloadable audio content as well as video content available on CD-ROM and DVD that you can order. Generally, you will pay a higher one-time fee if you plan to distribute your video professionally than if you purchase audio content for home and private use.

More and more audio files will begin appearing on the Web with digital rights management (DRM) features included. Depending on who offers the file, and the rights the owner allows you to have based on how you acquired it (bought or copied), the DRM features will determine what you can do with them. If Movie Maker refuses to import an audio file you downloaded from the Internet, even though that file plays perfectly in Windows Media Player, the file probably has DRM controls that prevent you from editing or using the audio inside another video.

If you have *newsgroup* access, you can often find audio files uploaded for others to see and use categorized by subject. Search through newsgroups that have **multimedia** or **sounds** or **music** in their name for possible videos you can download and use. Use Outlook Express, bundled with Windows, to access newsgroups after you learn from your Internet service provider (ISP) how to set up newsgroup access.

Before You Begin

✔ **46** About Movie Maker Audio

See Also

→ **94** Download the Movie Maker Creativity Fun Pack

 **KEY TERM**

Royalty-free—A label that indicates you can own a license to use a file any way you want, or that you are free to use the file in a specific, predefined way.

 **KEY TERM**

Newsgroups—Electronic bulletin boards, categorized by name and function, where users upload and download messages and files.

Different Pricing Levels

Sound Effects Available

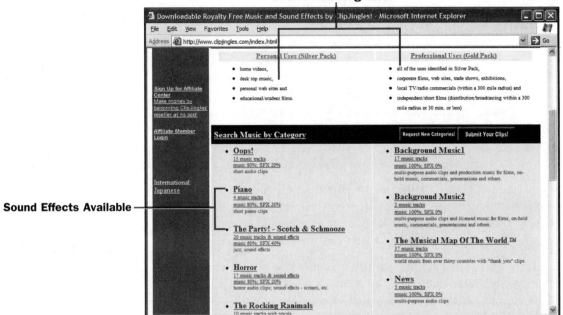

Sites such as ClipJingles.com offer royalty-free audio content that you pay for once and use in your videos.

8

Simplifying Movie Creation with AutoMovie

IN THIS CHAPTER:

One of Movie Maker's most interesting and unique features is *AutoMovie*. Instead of requiring you to select clips, drag them to the storyboard/timeline, add transitions, and save the movie, AutoMovie does all this for you. Surprisingly, AutoMovie does a credible job at guessing how it should generate your resulting movie, and can even add background music and generate a movie based on a preselected style you choose.

When you instruct Movie Maker to create your movie automatically with AutoMovie, you can control the following elements and AutoMovie does the rest:

- **Editing style**—After you enter a style, AutoMovie creates your movie based on your selection. For example, if you select the **Sports Highlights** style, AutoMovie puts your clips together in a collage of fast pans and zooms to generate excitement in the movie it creates.

- **Movie title**—AutoMovie adds text you specify to the start of the movie, introducing the playback.

- **Audio** or **background music**—AutoMovie adds background music you select to the movie it generates. You can control the audio level between the two audio tracks, just as you can control audio levels in the movies you produce without AutoMovie (**see 54 Adjust Audio Levels**).

59 About AutoMovie

Before You Begin

✔ **29** Add Clips to the Storyboard

See Also

→ **64** Finalize Your AutoMovie

One way to make a movie with Movie Maker is to follow these steps:

1. Drag clips to the storyboard/timeline.

2. Add transitions between clips to direct the style of movie you want to make (fast-paced, slow and easy, or whatever tone you want your movie to portray).

3. Add a beginning title to introduce your movie.

4. Select a background musical score, add the score to the movie, and adjust the volume level.

5. Add titles and credits.

6. Save the movie.

Instead of following each of those steps, you could do this:

1. Let AutoMovie do all the work!

From the two previous lists, AutoMovie appears to save you a lot of work—and it does. You do maintain one advantage in not using AutoMovie, however: You maintain more control over your movie's details. In many cases, you simply cannot allow AutoMovie to create your movie because you must control the way too many details play out, such as when you need to adjust clip lengths, add special sound effects, fade in or out of certain clips, and add special effects to certain scenes. When you want a straightforward movie from your clips, though, especially if that movie falls within one of AutoMovie's predefined styles, you will find that AutoMovie's speed advantage more than makes up for the lack of control over all details of your project.

Editing Styles ——

Title Options ——

Audio Options ——

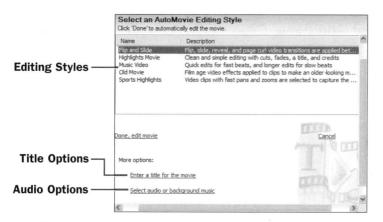

AutoMovie provides numerous style, title, and audio options to choose from to control the tone of the generated movie.

60 Select AutoMovie's Clips

Your **Collection** pane contains lots of video and audio clips, and depending on how much raw footage you might have imported into your project, it probably contains far more clips than you want to appear in your final movie.

Before You Begin

✔ **36** Place a Clip on the Timeline

See Also

→ **59** About AutoMovie

NOTE

AutoMovie requires that you select more than 30 seconds of clips. If you select one or more clips that consume fewer than 30 seconds of total playback time, AutoMovie will stop and issue an error message stating that an AutoMovie-generated movie must exceed 30 seconds.

TIP

You can lasso multiple clips by clicking and holding the left mouse button on the first clip and dragging your mouse down through the remaining clips you want to go in your movie. As you drag your mouse, Movie Maker highlights all the clips in the selection that your "lasso" surrounds.

NOTE

Make sure no clips appear on your timeline before you drag any AutoMovie clips there. If any clips appear there, Movie Maker places its generated AutoMovie at the end of your timeline, and if you save your project as a video, the opening clips will appear before your AutoMovie starts playing.

AutoMovie cannot read your mind and know exactly which set of clips you want in your final movie, so you must select the clips you want AutoMovie to use when generating your movie. After selecting all the clips you want to add, you drag those clips to the timeline before requesting AutoMovie's help. AutoMovie then looks at the clips and creates your movie based on AutoMovie options you've selected, such as the AutoMovie style (see **61** Select an AutoMovie Style).

1 **Scroll to Top**

Scroll to the top of your **Contents** pane to see the start of your clips.

2 **Select a Clip**

Click to select a clip from your **Contents** pane. This is the first clip that you want to appear in your movie.

3 **Select Additional Clips**

Hold your **Ctrl** key and click on additional clips to select multiple clips.

4 **Drag to Storyboard/Timeline**

Drag your selected clips to your storyboard or timeline. Drag additional clips if you need to.

5 **Select Tools, AutoMovie**

Select **AutoMovie** from the **Tools** menu to start the AutoMovie wizard. You can now begin the task of generating a movie automatically using the AutoMovie tools.

If the **Task** pane appears on your screen (from the **View**, **Task Pane** menu option), you can start AutoMovie by clicking the **Task** pane's **Make an AutoMovie** option.

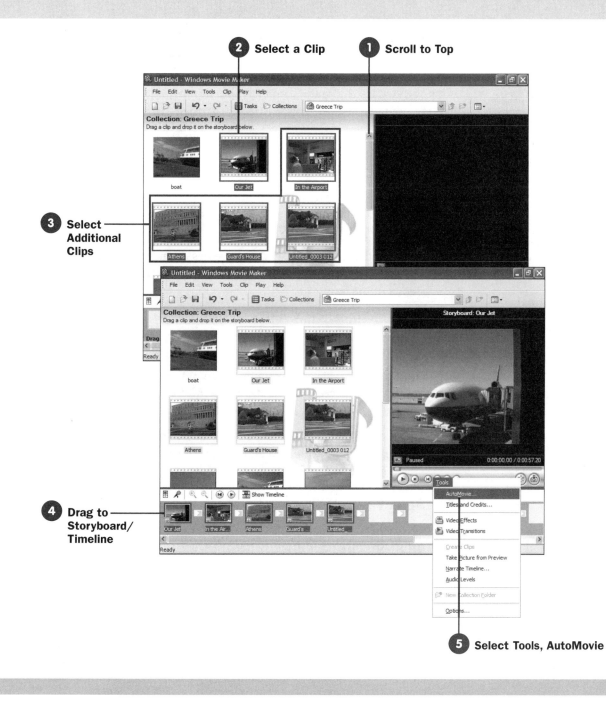

2 Select a Clip

1 Scroll to Top

3 Select Additional Clips

4 Drag to Storyboard/ Timeline

5 Select Tools, AutoMovie

61 **Select an AutoMovie Style**

Before You Begin

✔ **59** About AutoMovie

See Also

→ **64** Finalize Your AutoMovie

✎ NOTE

When you select a style, you are selecting the way AutoMovie plays your video and transitions from clip to clip.

Not all AutoMovies play the same, or even play in the same style. It's not just the video and audio content that changes, but also the speed and tone of the movie.

AutoMovie can generate a movie based on your selected clips. The following styles are available to help AutoMovie generate the style of movie your production requires:

- **Flip and Slide**—Movie Maker applies the following transitions between clips: flip, slide, reveal, and page curl (**see** **69** **Transition from Clip to Clip**).

- **Highlights Movie**—Movie Maker creates a kinder, gentler movie with cuts and fades between clips, a title at the beginning, and credits at the end.

- **Music Video**—Movie Maker turns your movie into a music video, adding quick edits for fast-paced clips and long edits for slower clips based on the audio track's beat.

- **Old Movie**—Movie Maker produces an old-time movie by adding effects that age your video (**see** **68** **Make Your Movies Look Vintage**).

- **Sports Highlights**—Movie Maker adds excitement to your movie with an exploding title and end credits that wrap around your video, including fast pans and zooms between clips.

1 **Select Tools, AutoMovie**

After you've dragged your selected clips to the timeline, select **AutoMovie** from the **Tools** menu.

2 **Select a Style**

Click to select one of the AutoMovie styles. Movie Maker will apply your selected style to the generated movie. You are now ready to finish the AutoMovie's titles and soundtrack.

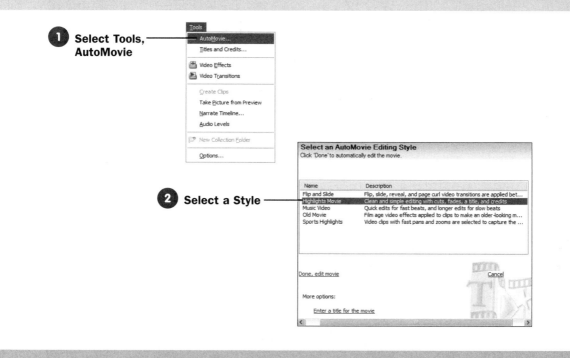

1 Select Tools,
AutoMovie

2 Select a Style

---

62 Refine AutoMovie's Soundtrack

The audio you add to the background for AutoMovie can be a music soundtrack, or any other kind of audio you want to use. The audio appears in your **Collections** pane if you import the audio file there. Even if you have not imported the audio into your collection, you can still tell AutoMovie to use a file located on your disk or across your network, as long as you have access to the file.

Given that you are familiar with your clips' soundtrack, as well as any background audio you select for AutoMovie to use, AutoMovie requests that you adjust the volume levels between the Audio track and the Audio/Music track so one doesn't override the other. In other words, if your clips use a lot of people speaking, their words will take precedence over any background music you've added to the AutoMovie. In that case, you would add more volume to the Audio track and take away volume from the Audio/Music track where AutoMovie will place your background sound.

Before You Begin

✔ **60** Select AutoMovie's
Clips

See Also

→ **61** Select an
AutoMovie Style

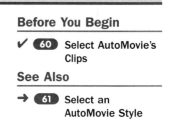

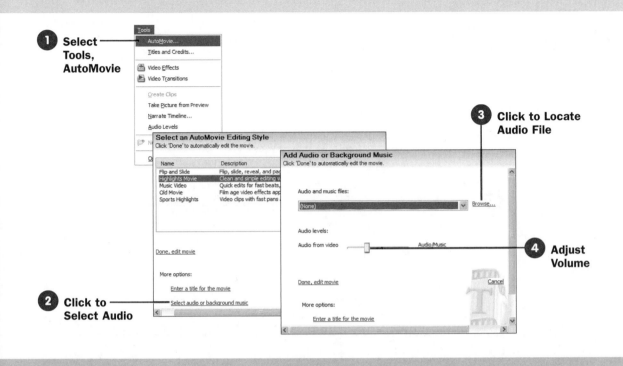

① **Select Tools, AutoMovie**

③ **Click to Locate Audio File**

④ **Adjust Volume**

② **Click to Select Audio**

Remember that after AutoMovie uses an audio clip or file for the soundtrack, you cannot move, rename, or delete that soundtrack if you want to use your current project to build an AutoMovie of a different style later. In a final movie file you create, unlike a Movie Maker project, Movie Maker merges the actual audio file into the final movie file, so you can always move, rename, or delete an audio file after your video is made and you are pleased with the results (see **85** Start the Save Movie Wizard).

① **Select Tools, AutoMovie**

After you've dragged your selected clips to the timeline, select **AutoMovie** from the **Tools** menu.

② **Click to Select Audio**

If you have already imported an audio file into your **Collections** pane, click the down arrow to select an audio clip from the list labeled **Audio and music files**. You can only select one audio file for your soundtrack, and Movie Maker will loop the file throughout the movie.

③ **Click to Locate Audio File**

If you have not imported your audio file into your **Collections** pane, you can still add an audio file to your AutoMovie. Click the **Browse** option and select an audio file to use for your movie. The audio file must play longer than 30 seconds or AutoMovie will not accept the file for use in your AutoMovie.

If you have used AutoMovie previously, AutoMovie tries to use the same audio file when you make additional movies. If you do not want to add a soundtrack to the additional movies, select **(None)** from the audio clips list. If you don't, AutoMovie uses the same soundtrack in your current movie.

④ Adjust Volume

Drag the **Audio levels** slider left or right to give more volume emphasis to either the audio included with your video, or the soundtrack audio you imported in step 3. You are now ready to finish the AutoMovie's titles and complete the AutoMovie.

63 Add Titles to Your AutoMovie

Your AutoMovie can have a title and ending credits. The text you enter is used for both an opening title and an ending title before the credits roll. The text fades in all at once before fading out at the beginning of your movie, then scrolls up from the bottom at the end.

If you enter more than four lines of text, Movie Maker displays all the lines (up to seven total) for the movie title, but when the AutoMovie ends, Movie Maker plays only the first four lines and then displays a **Directed By** tagline.

① Select Tools, AutoMovie

After you've dragged your selected clips to the timeline, select **AutoMovie** from the **Tools** menu.

② Click for the Title Dialog Box

Click the option labeled **Enter a title for a movie** to display a text box where you can enter your title's text.

③ Type Title

Type the title you want for your AutoMovie. Remember to keep the title to seven lines or less, and also remember that the first four lines will appear as the first scrolling credit at the end of your movie. Generally, if you limit your text to four lines or less, the title works best both at the front and back of your AutoMovie. You are now ready to complete the AutoMovie.

Before You Begin

✔ **60** Select AutoMovie's Clips

✔ **61** Select an AutoMovie Style

✔ **62** Refine AutoMovie's Soundtrack

See Also

→ **64** Finalize Your AutoMovie

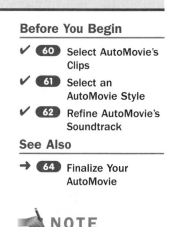

NOTE

Be sure to add your name to the **Author** field in your movie's **Properties** dialog box (available from **File**, **Properties**). AutoMovie uses the **Author** field for the director's name at the end of the AutoMovie.

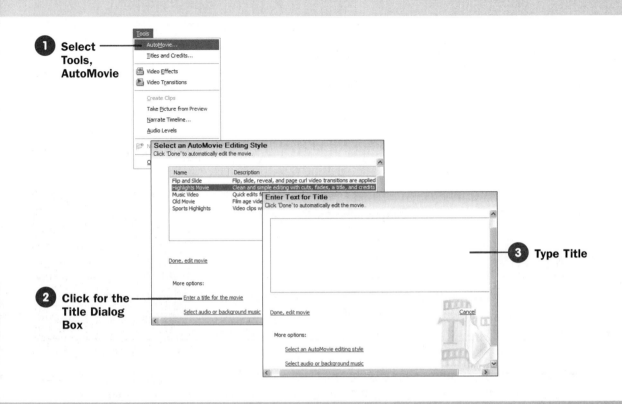

1 Select Tools, AutoMovie

2 Click for the Title Dialog Box

3 Type Title

---

64 Finalize Your AutoMovie

Before You Begin

✔ **61** Select an AutoMovie Style

✔ **62** Refine AutoMovie's Soundtrack

✔ **63** Add Titles to Your AutoMovie

See Also

→ **85** Start the Save Movie Wizard

This is the easy part of the AutoMovie process! Just finalize your AutoMovie and wait while Movie Maker generates the movie according to your specifications.

As a review, here are the steps that lead up to finalizing your AutoMovie:

1. Select clips to place in the AutoMovie.

2. Drag the clips to your timeline.

3. Select **Tools**, **AutoMovie** to start the AutoMovie process.

4. Choose an AutoMovie style.

5. Select background audio.

6. Add text for the title and credits.

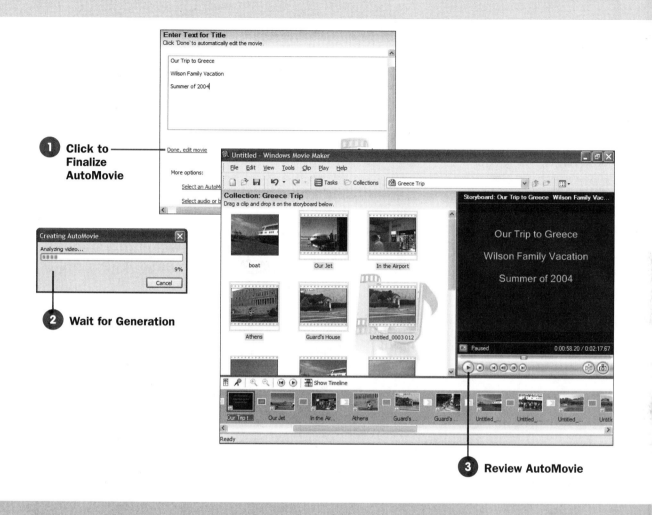

① **Click to Finalize AutoMovie**

② **Wait for Generation**

③ **Review AutoMovie**

After you've prepared AutoMovie by following these steps, you only need to finalize your movie and wait for Movie Maker to generate the results. Depending on the speed of your computer and the length of the clips you told AutoMovie to use, the generation might take from a few seconds to several minutes. After AutoMovie finishes, watch your video before creating a movie file. If the AutoMovie isn't exactly what you expected, all the AutoMovie options (such as the title and so on) will still be set, and you can make adjustments as necessary to get the movie you really want.

NOTE

If you made a mistake setting AutoMovie options, such as adding a nonexistent audio file for the background or choosing AutoMovie clips that play for fewer than 30 seconds, AutoMovie displays an error window here. Correct the problem and start over at step 1 to generate your AutoMovie.

① Click to Finalize AutoMovie

After you've prepared AutoMovie by setting the clips, style, background audio, and title, click the option labeled **Done, edit movie** to finalize your AutoMovie.

② Wait for Generation

Wait for AutoMovie to generate the video. AutoMovie's progress bar shows you the status of the movie's generation.

③ Review AutoMovie

Click the Monitor pane's **Play** button to play the AutoMovie. Keep in mind that your movie has not been saved to disk yet—you still must save the movie (**see 85 Start the Save Movie Wizard**) if you like the results of the playback.

PART V

Working with Special Effects

IN THIS PART:

9

Adding Pizzazz to Movie Maker Movies

IN THIS CHAPTER

 **TIP**

Too many special effects distract an audience from the movie. Your content is far more important than the special effects you add to the content. That's why special effects are called "special"; use them to accent the content and to bring an audience more into your movie.

KEY TERM

Transition—The way a movie moves from one clip to another, with the tail of the earlier clip twirling, folding, exploding, fading, or in some manner changing into the next clip.

Movie Maker enables you to spruce up your videos by adding special effects. You can add special effects to single or multiple clips. To compound the excitement, you can add more than one special effect to the same set of clips, and Movie Maker applies each effect sequentially as the movie plays.

Movie Maker's special effects include *transitions*. Transitions can help move your audience from clip to clip. The tone of the underlying movie determines what kind of transition is best at the time. Actually, all clips transition from one clip to the next, but unless you specify a transition effect, the first clip's final frame ends and the next clip's earliest frame begins playing without any visual effect occurring, except for the clip change.

In addition to transitions, Movie Maker's special effects will change the way single clips or the entire movie plays. You can make your movie look old, turn gray, fade to white, fade from white, play upside down, and a host of other effects. The truly amazing thing about Movie Maker's special effects is how easy they are to apply. You simply drag a special effect from the **Contents** pane to whatever clip (or clips) you want to apply the special effects to and Movie Maker does the rest.

65 Add a Special Effect to a Clip

Before You Begin

✔ 35 About the Timeline and Storyboard

✔ 36 Place a Clip on the Timeline

See Also

→ 66 Manage and Delete Special Effects

 **KEY TERM**

Video effects—Movie Maker's term for special effects you add to change the way a clip or movie plays back.

Movie Maker's special effects (called *video effects* in Movie Maker) might surprise you. You can turn a plain movie into one laden with effects with just a few mouse clicks and drags.

Select **Tools**, **Video Effects** to see all the effects available to you. Double-click any special effect to see, in your **Monitor** pane, what that effect produces.

Keep in mind that you can apply Movie Maker's special effects to all kinds of clips:

- Video clips
- Still picture clips
- Titles and credits

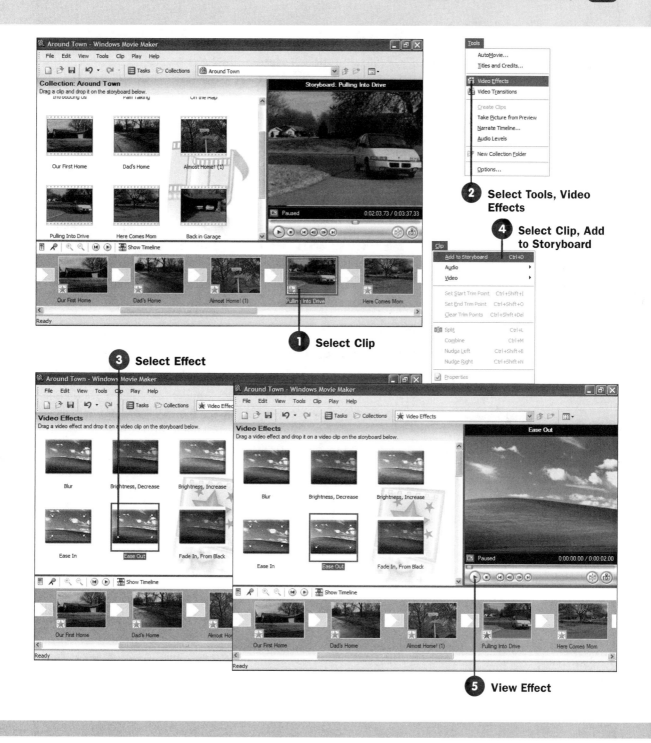

2 Select Tools, Video Effects

4 Select Clip, Add to Storyboard

1 Select Clip

3 Select Effect

5 View Effect

When you apply a special effect to a clip, the special effect appears on both clips if you split that clip into two clips. If you combine two clips, the combined clip takes on the special effects of the first clip. Movie Maker indicates that a special effect applies to a clip by putting a square icon in the clip's thumbnail with a blue star inside the box.

① Select Clip

Click to select the clip on which you want to apply a special effect.

② Select Tools, Video Effects

You can display all available special effects in the **Contents** pane by selecting **Video Effects** from the **Tools** menu.

③ Select Effect

Click to select whatever special effect you want to apply to your selected clip.

④ Select Clip, Add to Storyboard

To apply the effect, select **Add to Storyboard** from the **Clip** menu. A boxed icon with a blue star inside appears on the storyboard's clip indicating that a video effect is attached to that clip. If you rest your mouse pointer over the clip's effect icon, the name of the effect you applied to that clip will show.

⑤ View Effect

The effect appears on the storyboard's thumbnail image for the clip. If you add multiple effects for the clip, two blue stars appear in the square effects icon indicating that multiple effects are attached to the clip.

 TIP

You can drag the effect to the timeline or storyboard clip to apply the effect instead of using the **Clip** menu. If the timeline is compressed so that the clips are thin, you will need to zoom into the timeline more closely (**see** **Zoom a Timeline Clip**) to ensure that you place the effect on the desired clip.

Manage and Delete Special Effects

Before You Begin

✔ **65** Add a Special Effect to a Clip

See Also

→ **69** Transition from Clip to Clip

When you apply more than one video effect to the same clip, Movie Maker generates the effects in order as the movie plays. The effects do not occur at the same time.

Given that you can apply multiple effects to a single clip, you need a way to manage them so that you can add and remove effects. Movie Maker offers a way to see all available effects and all effects that you've already applied to a clip in one dialog box. From this **Add or Remove Video Effects** dialog box, you can easily manage multiple special effects.

 Locate Clip with Multiple Effects

Click to select a clip on your storyboard/timeline that contains multiple effects. You can tell by the square special effects icon that multiple effects are applied if two stars appear in the icon's box.

 Right-Click the Clip

Right-click the clip to display a menu.

 Select Video Effects

Select **Video Effects** from the menu. The **Add or Remove Video Effects** dialog box appears. All available special effects appear in the dialog box's left list under **Available effects**, and all the effects already applied to the clip appear in the dialog box's right list under **Displayed effects**.

4 **Select Effect**

To remove an effect from the clip, select that effect from the right list.

5 **Click Remove**

When you click the **Remove** button, Movie Maker removes that effect from the clip. All other effects remain on the clip.

6 **Select Effect**

To add a new effect to the clip, click to select the effect from the dialog box's left list.

7 **Click Add**

When you click the **Add** button, Movie Maker adds the effect to the clip and the effect appears at the top of the **Displayed effects** list.

 TIP

To change a clip's special effect from one effect to another, remove the effect and add the one you prefer.

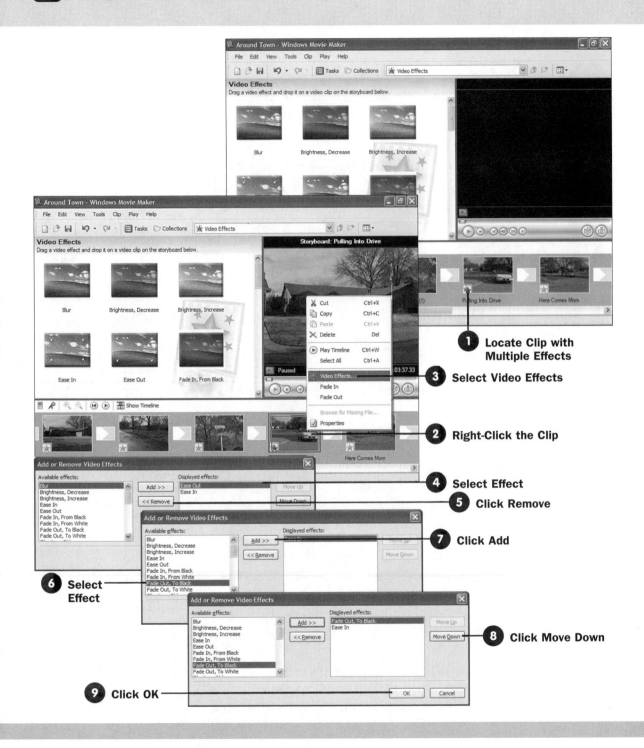

1. Locate Clip with Multiple Effects

3. Select Video Effects

2. Right-Click the Clip

4. Select Effect

5. Click Remove

7. Click Add

6. Select Effect

8. Click Move Down

9. Click OK

Click Move Down

You won't always want the effects to be generated in the sequence you added them. You can move any effect up or down in the list by clicking the **Move Down** or **Move Up** button. The effect's position within the **Displayed effects** list changes to reflect its new position.

 Click OK

When you're done, click the **OK** button. The **Add or Remove Video Effects** dialog box disappears and the clip updates with its new effects.

 Put Your Video in Slow Motion

One way to see Movie Maker special effects in action is to slow down your movie. With special effects, you can put one or more clips into slow motion. Doing so enables you to see exactly how to apply effects across clips so that an entire video conforms to the effect.

When you put movie clips into slow motion, the audio slows down as well. Your audio becomes full of *s-l-o-w*, *d-r-a-w-n-o-u-t s-p-e-e-c-h* to match the slow, drawn-out action on the screen.

 Select Tools, Video Effects

Display the available video effects by selecting **Video Effects** from the **Tools** menu. The special effects will appear in the **Contents** pane.

2 Scroll to Slow Down, Half

Locate the slow motion special effect which is called **Slow Down, Half**, by scrolling your **Contents** pane until that effect appears. This video effect will slow down any clip you apply it to by 50%.

 Drag to Clip

Drag the special effect thumbnail image to the clip on which you want to apply the effect. Notice the **Video Effect** icon that now appears on the clip. Click **Play** to watch and hear the slow motion.

Before You Begin

✔ **65** Add a Special Effect to a Clip

See Also

→ **66** Manage and Delete Special Effects

 TIP

Speed up your video to double-time by applying the **Speed Up, Double** video effect.

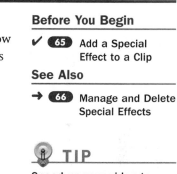 **TIP**

Double-click any effect to see what it does. The **Monitor** pane will show a preview of the effect.

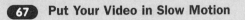

1 Select Tools, Video Effects

2 Scroll to Slow Down, Half

3 Drag to Clip

68 Make Your Movie Look Vintage

Movie Maker provides three special effects that age your movie to make it look old, older, and very old. These three effects produce the following results:

- **Film Age, Old**—Turns your clip grainy, as though it's been played a few too many times in the movie theater.

- **Film Age, Older**—Adds a deteriorating effect to the clip to make it look old and almost damaged. The clip jumps as it plays and appears to skip frames now and then.

- **Film Age, Oldest**—Turns the clip into fuzzy, black-and-white aged footage that seems to have come from the earliest days of film.

Consider using the aging special effects when you film dream sequences of long ago times, or perhaps when you provide a flashback from the current time period. As with any special effect, you can overdo the aged look—but when you need to add years to your video's action, there is hardly a better way to do so than by applying these **Film Age** special effects.

1 Select Tools, Video Effects

Display the available video effects by selecting **Video Effects** from the **Tools** menu. The special effects will appear in the **Contents** pane.

2 Scroll to Film Age, Older

Locate one of the three aging effects, such as **Film Age, Older**, by scrolling your **Contents** pane until you see the aging effects.

3 Double-Click the Thumbnail Image

Double-click the aging effect's thumbnail image to see how the effect plays on your monitor. If you want more aging or less, select one of the other **Film Age** effects.

4 Drag to Clip

Drag the aging special effect thumbnail image to the clip to which you want to apply the effect. Notice the **Video Effect** icon that now appears on the clip. Click **Play** to review the effect on the clip.

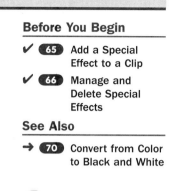

Before You Begin

✔ **65** Add a Special Effect to a Clip

✔ **66** Manage and Delete Special Effects

See Also

→ **70** Convert from Color to Black and White

 TIP

Movie Maker will not change the audio when you apply an aging special effect to a clip. You should either mute the clip's volume during the aged playback or use a bad recording of your audio so the audio doesn't belie the film's aged effect. You can record your audio file onto a cheap tape recorder and then record back to your computer via the computer's microphone to help reduce the audio's quality.

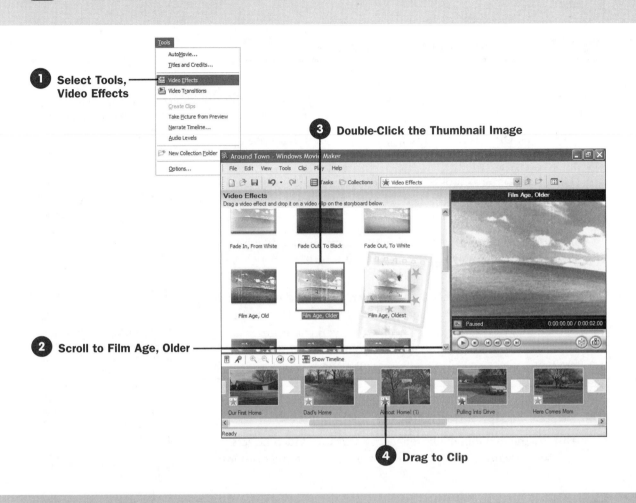

1 Select Tools, Video Effects

2 Scroll to Film Age, Older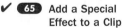

3 Double-Click the Thumbnail Image

4 Drag to Clip

---

69 Transition from Clip to Clip

Before You Begin

✔ **65** Add a Special Effect to a Clip

See Also

→ **71** Copy Effects from One Place to Another

When one clip finishes and another begins, the second clip will **straight cut** from the previous clip. Perhaps a scene changes from an inside shot to an outside shot. The first clip shows the action indoors, and the second begins playing and immediately shows the action outdoors. By adding a video transition between the clips, Movie Maker **cross-fades** the clips during playback. The clips will then show a gradual transfer from one clip to the next as the first clip fades into the second one using a transition pattern that you select.

Depending on the clips and the tone of your movie at the point of the transition, you might want to extend the transition's duration or slow it down. The shorter of the two clips around the transition determines the maximum duration time length you can apply. No transition can extend beyond the playback time of the shortest clip in the pair.

You can control the way one clip transitions to another clip. The transition begins playing as the first clip ends and continues to its conclusion as the next clip begins playing. Movie Maker offers a plethora of transition effects from page-turning transitions or swirls, scatters, explosions, and fades. Both the storyboard and the timeline indicate transitions. The storyboard shows a transition by placing the transition's thumbnail image between two clips. The timeline shows a transition by placing it on the **Transition** track when you add the transition between two tracks.

 1 Select Tools, Options

Adjust the default video transition duration by selecting **Options** from the **Tools** menu.

 2 Click Advanced

Click the **Advanced** tab to display the **Default durations** page.

3 Adjust Default Duration

Click the up or down arrows next to the **Transition duration** value to increase or decrease the default time value of the transition effect.

4 Click OK

Click **OK** to close the **Options** dialog box.

 5 Click Show Storyboard

You can more easily see transitions from the storyboard even though the timeline has its own **Transition** track. The timeline's tracks can get squeezed if you have zoomed out too far. You might be able to see a transition's effect better by working from the storyboard. Therefore, click the **Show Storyboard** button to change from the timeline to the storyboard if your movie's timeline is showing.

KEY TERM

Straight cut—The playing of two clips without any noticeable delay or effect occurring when the first clip changes to the next.

Cross-fade—The playing of two clips with a fading-out of the first clip while the next clip fades in at the same time, usually with some pattern such as a swirl effect, and with the second clip completely taking over at the last moment of the transition.

NOTE

If you place a video transition between two picture clips or between a picture and a video clip, the transition will still occur when the playback leaves the picture clip to enter the next clip.

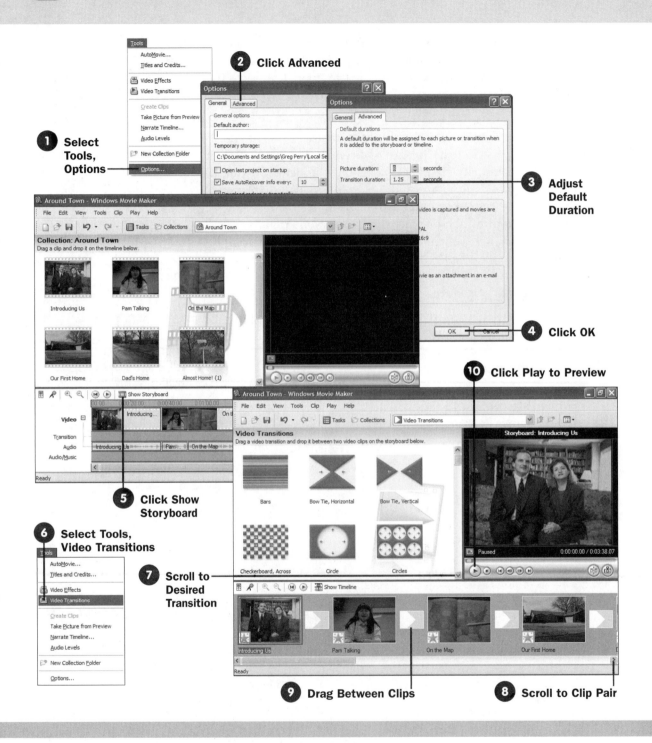

Select Tools, Video Transitions

Display the video transitions available to you by selecting **Video Transitions** from the **Tools** menu.

 Scroll to Desired Transition

Click the **Contents** pane's scrollbar to review all the available transitions.

 Scroll to Clip Pair

Scroll to the pair of clips between which you want to insert the transition.

9 **Drag Between Clips**

Drag the transition to the space between two clips on the storyboard.

10 **Click Play to Preview**

See how the transition occurs from the first clip to the second one by clicking the **Play** button in your **Monitor** pane. The movie will continue playing to its conclusion if you don't click **Stop** when you're done reviewing the transition.

TIP

Double-click any transition in your **Contents** pane to see a preview of that transition effect in the **Monitor** pane.

TIP

To remove a video transition from your movie, right-click the transition on your timeline/storyboard and select **Delete** from the menu.

TIP

You can add transition effects between titles and credits, too. See **79** Add Special Effects to Titles and Credits.

Convert from Color to Black and White

In today's world, it seems as though a movie or picture has to be in color to be cool. The famous black-and-white photographer Ansel Adams would definitely beg to differ, and if you've seen a Federico Fellini film, you would never agree to let it be colorized.

Black-and-white films and pictures have their place in the entertainment world, and Movie Maker offers a special effect labeled **Grayscale** that enables you to convert pictures and video clips to *grayscale*. You can age a scene by converting it to grayscale without adding the graininess that Movie Maker's **Film Age** special effects create.

1 **Select Tools, Video Effects**

Display the available video effects by selecting **Video Effects** from the **Tools** menu. The special effects will appear in the **Contents** pane.

Before You Begin

✔ **65** Add a Special Effect to a Clip

✔ **66** Manage and Delete Special Effects

See Also

→ **71** Copy Effects from One Place to Another

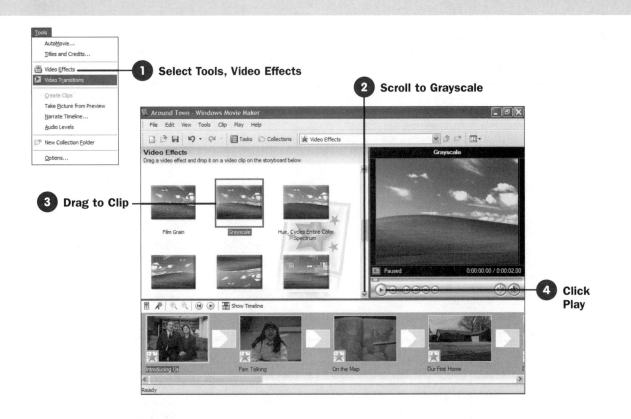

① Select Tools, Video Effects

② Scroll to Grayscale

③ Drag to Clip

④ Click Play

⚲EY TERM

Grayscale—The color description of a film or picture that shows various shades of gray and white without any other color. Often, a grayscale image or movie is called a black-and-white production, but such productions typically use grayscale and not a strictly limited black-and-white monochrome color scheme.

② Scroll to Grayscale

Locate the **Grayscale** special effect by scrolling your **Contents** pane until you find the **Grayscale** entry.

③ Drag to Clip

Drag the **Grayscale** effect to the clip you want to apply it to. Make sure the clip's video effect icon appears on the clip's thumbnail.

④ Click Play

Click **Play** to review the grayscale effect of the clip.

71 Copy Effects from One Place to Another

Throughout this chapter, numerous tasks explain how to add various special effects to your clips. You can add one effect or multiple effects to clips.

If you need to apply the same video effect to more than one clip, the job gets to be tedious if you add the effects to each clip in your movie. A much more efficient way to apply multiple special effects to multiple clips is to use the Windows clipboard to copy and paste the effects where you want them. After you copy a set of special effects to the **Windows** clipboard, you can easily paste those effects into multiple clips on the storyboard.

 Click Show Storyboard

Display the storyboard if it is not currently showing by clicking the **Show Storyboard** button atop the timeline.

 Drag Effect to Clip

Locate a special effect that you want to apply to multiple clips. Drag the effect to the first clip that is to receive the effect. Notice the special effect's icon changes to reflect the fact that clip has a video effect attached.

 Drag Effect to Clip

Drag a second video effect to the same clip. Watch once again as the effect's icon changes to show multiple effects are now applied to the clip.

 Click Effect Icon

Click the effect's icon on the clip.

 Select Edit, Copy

From the **Edit** menu, choose the **Copy** option. You can also press **Ctrl+C** to choose this option. All special effects applied to the underlying clip go to the **Windows** clipboard.

Before You Begin

✔ **65** Add a Special Effect to a Clip

See Also

→ **79** Add Special Effects to Titles and Credits

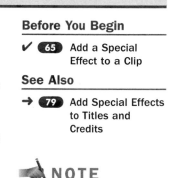

NOTE

Unfortunately, you cannot select more than one timeline or storyboard clip and then drag a special effect to all those selected clips at the same time. If you attempt to do this, Movie Maker adds the effect only to the clip you are pointing to when you release your mouse button after you complete the dragging of the effect to the story-board/timeline.

NOTE

When copying effects to the **Windows** clipboard, be sure you click the effect's icon, and not on the clip anywhere outside the effects icon. If you click the clip, the clip and not the effect will go to the **Windows** clipboard.

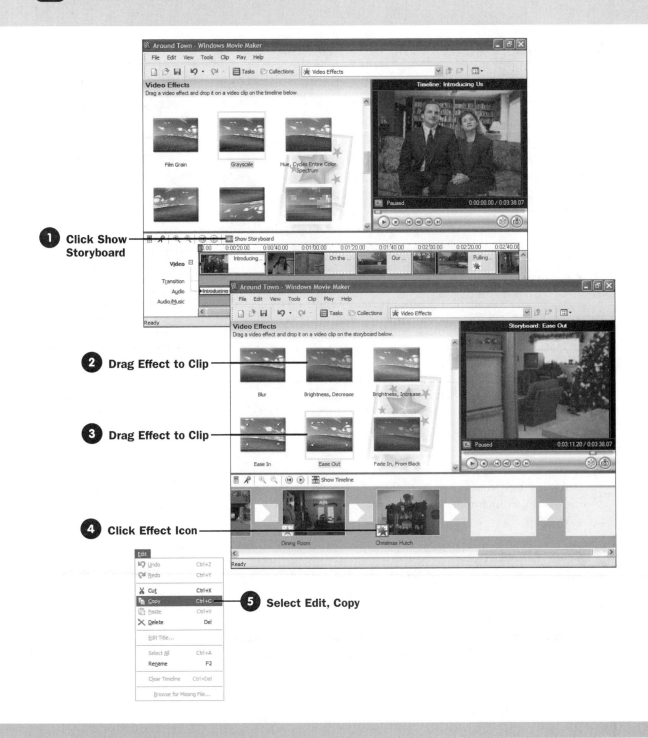

1 Click Show Storyboard

2 Drag Effect to Clip

3 Drag Effect to Clip

4 Click Effect Icon

5 Select Edit, Copy

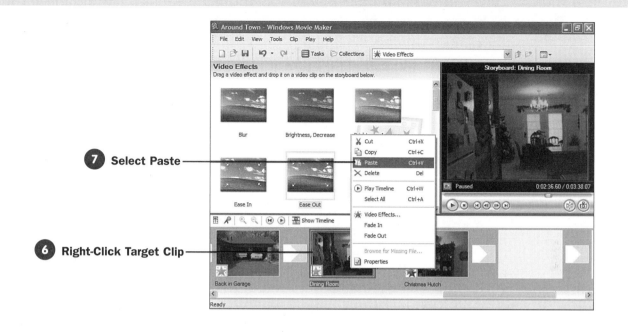

7 Select Paste

6 Right-Click Target Clip

6 Right-Click Target Clip

Locate the clip onto which you want to apply the effects. You might have to scroll the storyboard to locate the proper clip if it's not currently in view. Right-click the clip to display a menu.

7 Select Paste

When you select **Paste** from the menu (or press **Ctrl+V**), Movie Maker pastes the effects onto the target clip. The effects all travel in the order and duration they appeared on the original clip. If desired, continue selecting additional clips and pasting effects; the effects are still copied onto your **Windows** clipboard even though you've already pasted them once.

NOTE

Even if you select multiple clips before choosing **Paste**, Movie Maker will only insert the special effects from the **Windows** clipboard onto the clip your mouse pointer is pointing to at the time you paste the effects.

10

Using Titles and Credits

IN THIS CHAPTER:

KEY TERMS

Titles—The name of your movie, the names of the cast and crew, and anything else you might want to tell your audience before your movie begins comprise the title.

Credits—Descriptions of who did what at the end of a movie, such as the production staff, as well as a repeat of the stars and head people. Typically, credits scroll from the bottom to the top of the screen.

NOTE

Titles and credits are the movie maker's notes to the audience members telling them what to expect and who did all the work.

Titles and *credits* serve to introduce your movie to your audience and to tell them who was responsible for it after they finish watching.

Your titles and credits always appear in text that fades in and out or scrolls onto the screen. Movie Maker gives you full control over the special effects used as the titles and credits appear and disappear. In addition, you can select the style of text you want used, such as the font and color.

Titles and credits can sometimes serve to distinguish quickly shot and edited videos from more professional work that you spend time and effort creating and editing. Movie Maker offers a large number of special effects and styles for your movie's titles and credits. You'll want to ensure that the style of titles and credits match the mood of your movie. Don't add flashy titles and credits to a low-key movie, but do spruce up your titles and credits when your movie is fast-paced and exciting.

---

72 ## About Titles and Credits

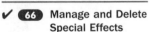
Before You Begin

✔ **66** Manage and Delete Special Effects

See Also

→ **73** Create Movie Titles

KEY TERM

Overlay title—Text that appears on a clip that can be used to explain the current action, translate foreign speech, or to label a certain locale being shown.

Your titles can appear in several places throughout your movie, as the following list describes:

- **Title appears at the beginning of movie**—Add a title at the beginning to show the audience the movie's title, as well as introductory text that might be necessary to explain what is about to take place in the movie, as might be needed for training videos.

- **Title appears before a selected clip**—Previews a clip in some way, perhaps to describe the passing of time or to explain a procedure that is about to be taught.

- **Title appears on a selected clip**—These *overlay titles* display when a clip begins. You can use overlay titles for subtitles when a foreign language appears in the clip. Overlay titles appear on the timeline's Overlay title track.

- **Title appears after selected clip**—May be used to introduce an upcoming scene in the next clip.

- **Credits at the end of your movie**—When they appear at the end of a movie, titles are called *credits* and serve to wrap up details of the movie (such as a "Where they are now" biography of movie characters) and to display names and production companies used in the making of the movie.

Ending credits tell the audience who should take credit (or blame) for the movie they just watched.

Many feel that adding titles and credits to short home movies such as parties might not be worth the effort. In reality, such movies often beg for titles, because years later, when your family watches past events, they'll always want to know when it took place, who is that woman talking to Aunt Terri, and how old were the kids when we went to the country fair? How many times have you looked at old pictures that had no names or date written on the back and wondered about such questions? Movie Maker simplifies the job of adding titles, and you should plan to add some kind of titles to virtually every movie you make.

 **Create Movie Titles**

Before You Begin

✔ **72** About Titles and Credits

See Also

→ **79** Add Special Effects to Titles and Credits

→ **80** Freeze a Video Frame

 TIP

If you want to apply the title before, on, or following a specific clip, click to select the clip on the timeline before continuing.

 NOTE

If you're adding credits to the end of your movie, you'll have several secondary text fields to enter for all the credits you want to add (see **78** Add End Credits).

No matter where you want to place your titles, the procedure is the same. You first determine where you want the title to appear (such as before the movie or following a clip), select that location on the timeline, and type the title's text. Movie Maker typically offers two fields in which to type your titles: a primary text field, or *title* field, and a secondary text field, or *subtitle* field. When the title appears, the title field's text will display on top of the subtitle and in a larger font.

1 **Click to Show Timeline**

Show the timeline by clicking the **Show Timeline** button if your storyboard currently appears.

2 **Select Tools, Titles and Credits**

To add titles or credits, select **Titles and Credits** from the **Tools** menu.

3 **Determine Where Title Goes**

Select where you want the title to appear by clicking one of the location options in the **Where do you want to add a title?** dialog box.

4 **Type Primary Text**

Type the title text in the top field. As you type, Movie Maker displays the text in the **Monitor** pane for your review.

5 **Type Secondary Text**

Type the subtitle text in the bottom field. As you type, Movie Maker displays the subtitle in the **Monitor** pane for your review.

6 **Click to Change Font**

If you want to change the font size, color, or format, click **Change the text font and color** to display the **Select Title Font and Color** dialog box.

7 **Select Font**

Click to open the **Font** list and select a different font.

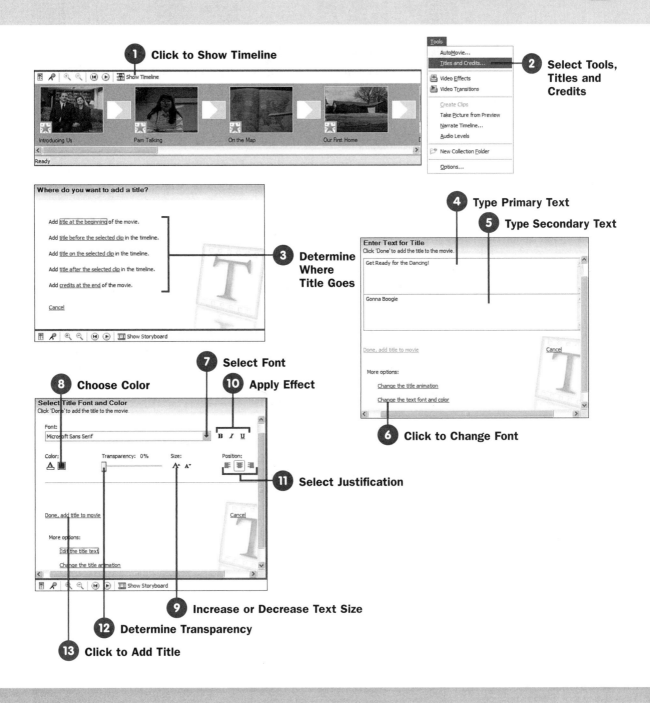

1 Click to Show Timeline

2 Select Tools, Titles and Credits

3 Determine Where Title Goes

4 Type Primary Text

5 Type Secondary Text

6 Click to Change Font

7 Select Font

8 Choose Color

9 Increase or Decrease Text Size

10 Apply Effect

11 Select Justification

12 Determine Transparency

13 Click to Add Title

Choose Color

Click to open the **Color** dialog box, from which you can select a color for the text. Click **OK** to close the **Color** dialog box after you choose a color.

 Increase or Decrease Text Size

To increase or decrease the text size, click one of the **Size** options.

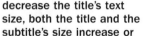 **Apply Effect**

Click one of the **bold**, **italic**, or **underline** options to apply that effect to the text. The effect applies to both the title and the subtitle text and as you click an effect, the **Monitor** pane updates to reflect the results.

⑪ **Select Justification**

Movie Maker will left-align, center, or right-align your text when you click one of the **Position** options. The default is centered text, and rarely will you need to change from this default position.

⑫ **Determine Transparency**

Titles can appear on top clips as title overlays. Usually, your title text will overwrite the clip's video that appears beneath it. You can make your text transparent and adjust the level of transparency by dragging the **Transparency** slider control left or right.

⑬ **Click to Add Title**

Click **Done, add title to movie** to add the title to your movie.

NOTE

When you increase or decrease the title's text size, both the title and the subtitle's size increase or decrease. You cannot change the size of the title (or subtitle) by itself.

 Add a Title to the Start of Your Movie

Before You Begin

✔ ⑦② **About Titles and Credits**

✔ ⑦③ **Create Movie Titles**

See Also

→ ⑦⑨ **Add Special Effects to Titles and Credits**

The location of your titles determines how you apply them and where they appear on the timeline. If you want to add a title at the beginning of your movie, as you might with a movie title and opening credits, the title appears differently depending on whether you view the storyboard or timeline:

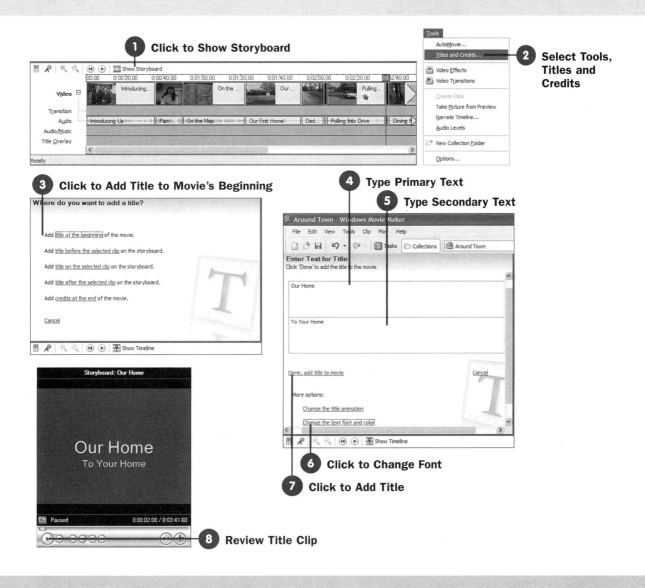

1 Click to Show Storyboard

2 Select Tools, Titles and Credits

3 Click to Add Title to Movie's Beginning

4 Type Primary Text

5 Type Secondary Text

6 Click to Change Font

7 Click to Add Title

8 Review Title Clip

- **Storyboard**—A title before your movie appears as the storyboard's first clip

- **Timeline**—A title before your movie appears as the first clip on the timeline's Video track

Click to Show Storyboard

Click the **Show Storyboard** button to display the storyboard if the timeline currently appears. Beginning titles are often easier to review on the storyboard than on the timeline.

 Select Tools, Titles and Credits

Start the title process by selecting **Titles and Credits** from the **Tools** menu.

 **Click to Add Title to Movie's Beginning**

Because you want to add the title to the beginning of the movie, click **Add title at the beginning of the movie**. Movie Maker opens the **Enter Text for Title** dialog box.

4 Type Primary Text

Type the title's primary text that appears as a title above any subtitle text you enter.

5 Type Secondary Text

Type the title's secondary text that appears as a subtitle beneath the title.

6 Click to Change Font

Click the **Change the text font and color** option if you want to modify the text style or color (**see** **73** **Create Movie Titles**).

 TIP

Drag the line that divides the storyboard from the **Contents** pane toward the top of your screen to increase the size of the storyboard clips if you have difficulty reading all the text on the storyboard's first clip.

7 Click to Add Title

Place the title at the beginning of your movie by clicking the option labeled **Done, add title to movie**.

8 Review Title Clip

The title appears at the start of your storyboard. The title and subtitle show in the first clip. You can click to select the title clip and preview the title in the **Monitor** pane.

75 Add a Title Before a Clip

The location of your titles determines how you apply them and where they appear on the timeline. If you want to add a title to the beginning of a clip, perhaps to introduce a new scene, the title appears differently depending on whether you view the storyboard or timeline:

- **Storyboard**—A title before the selected clip appears before your selected clip

- **Timeline**—A title before the selected clip appears before your selected clip on the timeline's Video track

Before You Begin

✔ **72** About Titles and Credits

✔ **73** Create Movie Titles

See Also

➜ **79** Add Special Effects to Titles and Credits

1 **Click to Show Storyboard**

Click the **Show Storyboard** button to display the storyboard if the timeline currently appears. Titles before clips are often easier to review on the storyboard than on the timeline.

2 **Click Clip**

Click to select the clip that your title will precede.

3 **Select Tools, Titles and Credits**

Start the title process by selecting **Titles and Credits** from the **Tools** menu.

4 **Click to Add Title to Clip's Beginning**

Because you want to add the title to the beginning of a clip, click **Add title before the selected clip on the storyboard**. Movie Maker opens the **Enter Text for Title** dialog box.

5 **Type Primary Text**

Type the title's primary text that appears as a title above any sub-title text you enter.

6 **Type Secondary Text**

Type the title's secondary text that appears as a subtitle beneath the title.

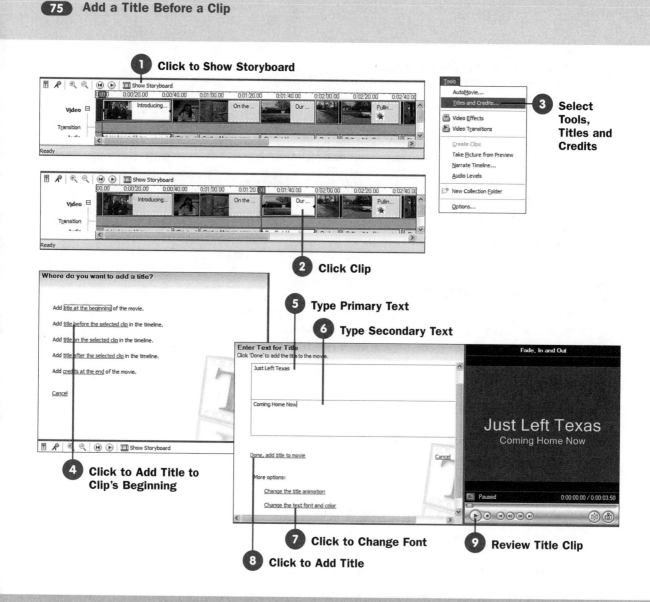

1 Click to Show Storyboard

3 Select Tools, Titles and Credits

2 Click Clip

5 Type Primary Text

6 Type Secondary Text

4 Click to Add Title to Clip's Beginning

7 Click to Change Font

8 Click to Add Title

9 Review Title Clip

7 Click to Change Font

Click the **Change the text font and color** option if you want to modify the text style or color (see **73** **Create Movie Titles**).

Click to Add Title

Place the title at the beginning of the selected clip by clicking the option labeled **Done, add title to movie**.

 Review Title Clip

The title appears in your storyboard before your selected clip. You can click to select the title clip and preview the title in the **Monitor** pane.

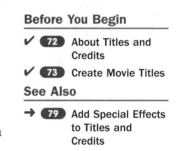

TIP

Drag the line that divides the storyboard from the **Contents** pane toward the top of your screen to increase the size of the storyboard clips if you have difficulty reading all the text on the storyboard's first clip.

76 Put a Title on a Clip

The location of your titles determines how you apply them and where they appear on the timeline. If you want to place a title on a particular clip, you are placing a title overlay on the clip to be shown while the clip plays (as opposed to showing the title in a clip before the scene plays). You can use a title overlay on top of a clip to translate a foreign language being spoken or to provide background to the scene.

You can only place title overlays on clips with the timeline showing. You cannot place a title on a clip with the storyboard showing. The title appears on the timeline's Title Overlay track.

Before You Begin

✔ **72** About Titles and Credits

✔ **73** Create Movie Titles

See Also

→ **79** Add Special Effects to Titles and Credits

 Click to Show Timeline

Click the **Show Timeline** button to display the timeline if the storyboard currently appears. You can only place titles on clips with the timeline showing.

2 Click Clip

Click to select the clip on which you want to place the title.

3 Select Tools, Titles and Credits

Start the title process by selecting **Titles and Credits** from the **Tools** menu.

4 Click to Add Overlay Title to Clip

Because you want to place the title on the clip, click **Add title on selected clip in the storyboard**. Movie Maker opens the **Enter Text for Title** dialog box.

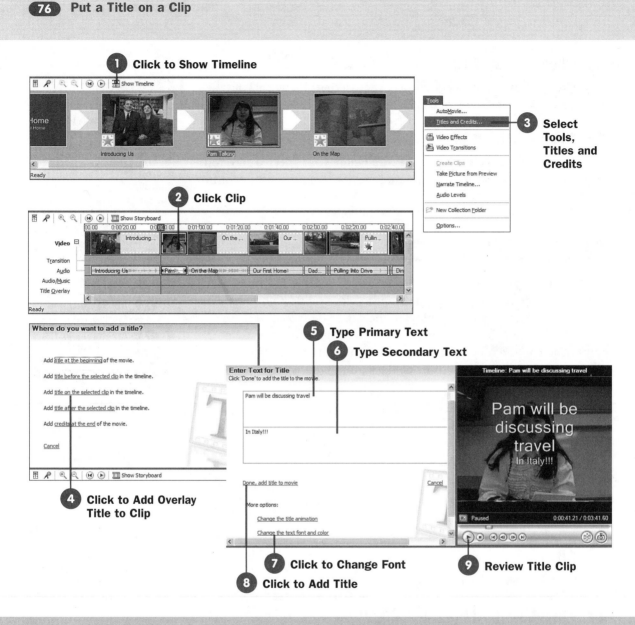

1 Click to Show Timeline

3 Select Tools, Titles and Credits

2 Click Clip

5 Type Primary Text

6 Type Secondary Text

4 Click to Add Overlay Title to Clip

7 Click to Change Font

8 Click to Add Title

9 Review Title Clip

5 **Type Primary Text**

Type the title's primary text that appears as a title above any sub-title text you enter.

Type Secondary Text

Type the title's secondary text that appears as a subtitle beneath the title.

 Click to Change Font

Click the **Change the text font and color** option if you want to modify the text style or color (**see 73 Create Movie Titles**).

8 **Click to Add Title**

Place the title on the selected clip by clicking the option labeled **Done, add title to movie**.

9 **Review Title Clip**

The title appears on your timeline's Title Overlay track in line with its clip. You can click to select the clip and preview the clip's title in the **Monitor** pane.

NOTE

The **Monitor** pane shows a picture under the title that you preview. If you're adding a title before or after the clip, the **Monitor** pane shows only a blue background. If you adjust the title's transparency (**see 73 Create Movie Titles**), you will be able to preview how the transparency contrasts to the underlying clip in the **Monitor** pane.

**TIP**

Drag the line that divides the timeline from the **Contents** pane toward the top of your screen to increase the size of the timeline tracks if you have difficulty seeing the Overlay Title track.

---

77 **Add a Title After a Clip**

The location of your titles determines how you apply them and where they appear on the timeline. If you want to add a title after a clip, perhaps to review the current clip or to introduce the next scene, the title appears differently depending on whether you view the storyboard or timeline:

- **Storyboard**—A title after the selected clip appears after your selected clip

- **Timeline**—A title after the selected clip appears after your selected clip on the timeline's Video track

1 **Click to Show Storyboard**

Click the **Show Storyboard** button to display the storyboard if the timeline currently appears.

Before You Begin

✔ **72** About Titles and Credits

✔ **73** Create Movie Titles

See Also

→ **79** Add Special Effects to Titles and Credits

TIP

Titles that follow clips are often easier to review on the storyboard than on the timeline.

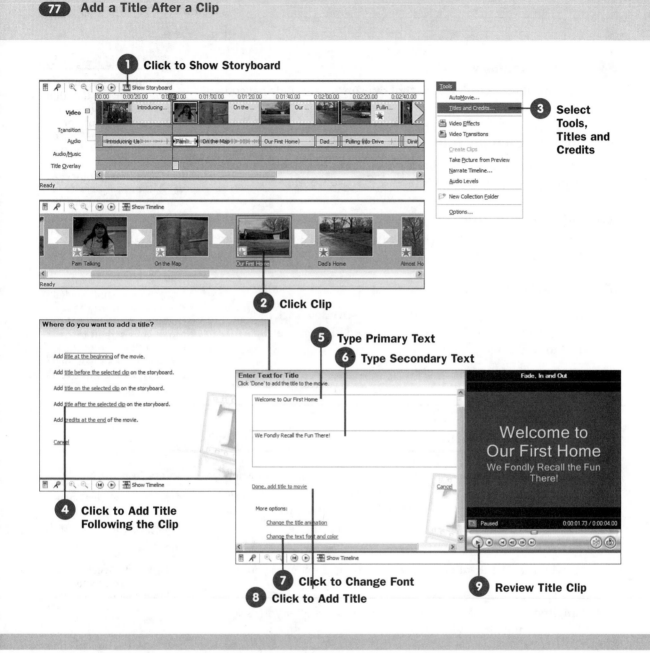

① Click to Show Storyboard

③ Select Tools, Titles and Credits

② Click Clip

⑤ Type Primary Text

⑥ Type Secondary Text

④ Click to Add Title Following the Clip

⑦ Click to Change Font

⑧ Click to Add Title

⑨ Review Title Clip

 Click Clip

Click to select the clip that your title will precede.

Select Tools, Titles and Credits

Start the title process by selecting **Titles and Credits** from the **Tools** menu.

 Click to Add Title Following the Clip

Because you want to add the title to the end of the movie, click **Add title after the selected clip on the storyboard**. Movie Maker opens the **Enter Text for Title** dialog box.

 Type Primary Text

Type the title's primary text that appears as a title above any sub-title text you enter.

 Type Secondary Text

Type the title's secondary text that appears as a subtitle beneath the title.

 Click to Change Font

Click the **Change the text font and color** option if you want to modify the text style or color (**see 73 Create Movie Titles**).

 Click to Add Title

Place the title after the selected clip by clicking the option labeled **Done, add title to movie**.

9 **Review Title Clip**

The title appears in your storyboard following your selected clip. You can click to select the title clip and preview the title in the **Monitor** pane.

TIP

Drag the line that divides the storyboard from the **Contents** pane toward the top of your screen to increase the size of the storyboard clips if you have difficulty reading all the text on the storyboard's first clip.

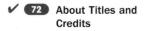 **Add End Credits**

Before You Begin

✔ **72** About Titles and Credits

✔ **73** Create Movie Titles

See Also

→ **79** Add Special Effects to Titles and Credits

Credits are titles that conclude your movie. The credits scroll from the bottom of the screen to the top in a rolling format until all credits have displayed.

The ending credits appear differently depending on whether you view the storyboard or timeline:

- **Storyboard**—Credits appear as the final clip on your storyboard
- **Timeline**—Credits appear as the final clip on the timeline's Video track

 NOTE

The text-entry area for your credits looks different from the text-entry area for other titles. Movie Maker gives you three places to enter text. The top field is for your first closing credit, which often will say nothing more than **The End**. The remaining fields work in pairs, with each left field's text appearing smaller than the field on the right. You could, for example, type **Director** in one field on the left and then type your name in the field to the right. Your name will display in a larger size than the **Director** title.

🖉 **TIP**

If you want all credit text to display in the same font size, ignore either the left or the right column when entering your text.

1 **Click to Show Storyboard**

Click the **Show Storyboard** button to display the storyboard if the timeline currently appears. Credits are often easier to review on the storyboard than on the timeline.

2 **Select Tools, Titles and Credits**

Start the credit process by selecting **Titles and Credits** from the **Tools** menu.

3 **Click to Add Credits to End of Movie**

Because you want to add the credits to the end of the movie, click **Add credits at the end of the movie**. Movie Maker opens the **Enter Text for Title** dialog box.

4 **Type Closing Text**

Type the end credit's primary text at the top of the text-entry area. This will be the first credit your audience sees.

5 **Type Text Pairs**

Type the remaining text in pairs knowing that text you type in the left column will be smaller and appear before text you type in the right column.

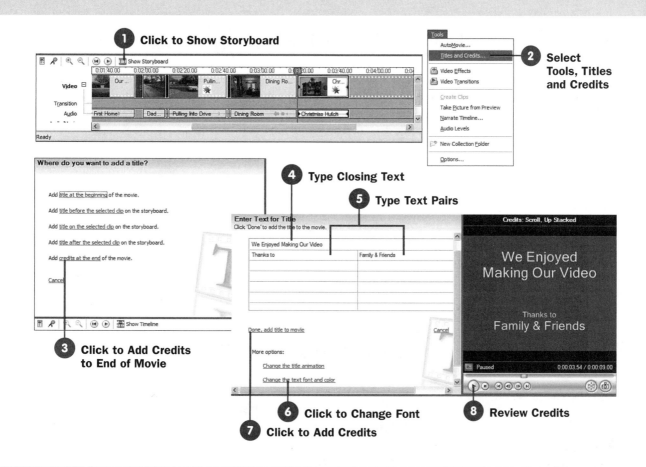

1 Click to Show Storyboard

2 Select Tools, Titles and Credits

3 Click to Add Credits to End of Movie

4 Type Closing Text

5 Type Text Pairs

6 Click to Change Font

7 Click to Add Credits

8 Review Credits

6 Click to Change Font

Click the **Change the text font and color** option if you want to modify the text style or color (**see** **73** Create Movie Titles).

7 Click to Add Credits

Place the credits at the end of your movie by clicking the option labeled **Done, add title to movie**.

8 Review Credits

The credits appear at the end of your storyboard. Click to select the credits and preview them in the **Monitor** pane.

 TIP

Drag the line that divides the storyboard from the **Contents** pane toward the top of your screen to increase the size of the storyboard clips if you have difficulty reading all the text on the storyboard's credit clip.

79 Add Special Effects to Titles and Credits

Before You Begin

✔ **73** Create Movie Titles

See Also

→ **81** Preview Your Final Movie

NOTE

Movie Maker limits your titles to about 35 characters in length, per line, depending on the font you select. If your title is long, you might need to modify the font so it fits.

NOTE

Movie Maker supports three categories of titles and credits. The default title category is **Titles, Two Lines**, which shows two lines of text. You can select a different category, such as **Titles, One Line**, which provides a single line for your titles. The **Credits** category contains animations for closing credits (although you can use this category for titles if you want to). Within each category are several kinds of animation effects you can choose that determine how the title or credit text appears and disappears on the screen.

Why settle for default titles and credit effects when you can dazzle your audience with special effects-laden titles and credits? Of course, you should use your good judgment. Add special effects when they enhance and don't detract from your movie. If your movie is fast-paced with lots of bouncing music and quick-panned clips, you might want some dazzling effects that begin the titles and credits. If your movie ends on a soft note, you might want to keep the credits very smooth and slow.

Movie Maker offers several kinds of special effects that you can apply to titles and credits. You might want single-line or multi-lined credits, and you might want them flying onto the screen from the left or right. You have many choices when selecting effects for your opening and closing text. Selecting the effect is simple, and you can preview the effect to ensure it's what you expect.

1 **Enter Title or Credit**

Set up your title or credit (**see** **73** Create Movie Titles).

2 **Click to Animate**

To change the title's (or credit's) animation, click **Change the title animation**.

3 **Select Animation**

Scroll the animation area until you locate a style you want to use for your title or credit animation. Select the animation you want to apply to your title or credit. The animation determines how the title or credit text moves onto and from the screen during playback.

4 **Preview Animation**

Movie Maker shows a preview of your selected animation on the **Monitor** pane when you click to select an animation style.

5 **Click to Apply**

When you're done choosing an animation for your title or credit, click **Done, add title to movie** to apply the title or credit with the chosen animation to your movie.

1 Enter Title or Credit

Enter Text for Title
Click 'Done' to add the title to the movie.

3 Select Animation

Choose the Title Animation
Click 'Done' to add the title to the movie.

Driving Around Town

Going to Pick Up Pups

Name	Description
Exploding Outline	Zooms in, outline explodes off screen
Fly In, Left and Right	Flies in from left and right
Sports Scoreboard	Slides down and then up (overlay)
Newspaper	Spins and zooms in (overlay)

Credits

| Credits: Scroll, Up Stacked | Paired stacked credits scroll up |
| Credits: Zoom, In | Paired credits zoom in |

Done, add title to movie

More options:

Change the title animation

Change the text font and color

Done, add title to movie   Cancel

More options:

Edit the title text

Change the text font and color

Newspaper

Driving Around Town

Going to Pick Up Pups

Paused   0:00:01.99 / 0:00:09.00

2 Click to Animate

5 Click to Apply

4 Preview Animation

80 Freeze a Video Frame

Although a single frame is not typically considered a title or credit, there are times when you will want to use an actual picture or a frame from your movie for a title of some kind. Remember that you can display a single frame for a preset time duration during your movie's playback (see **39** Set a Picture Clip's Duration).

Using your imagination, you can come up with several ways to use a single frame as a title. Suppose you're shooting a wedding video. No matter how exciting Movie Maker's animation effects and titles are, the church's street sign with the wedding party's names and dates makes a much more effective opening title for the audience.

1 Select Tools, Options

A picture used as a title will probably need to display longer than the default picture duration. Select **Options** from the **Tools** menu to display the **Options** dialog box.

Before You Begin

✔ **41** Take a Picture from a Clip

See Also

→ **81** Preview Your Final Movie

🍵 TIP

Don't refrain from using Movie Maker's titles and credits even when you use single frames for the same purpose. An opening title might be more effective when an interesting frame from your video is used, but then you might want to scroll a few informational titles past the viewer after that opening frame.

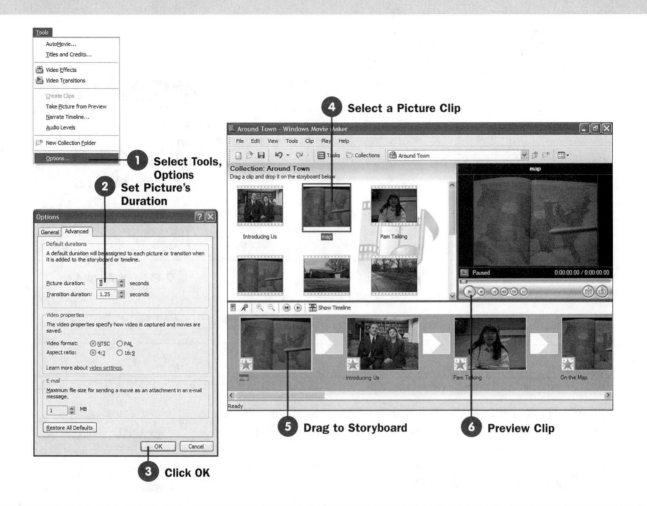

Select Tools, Options

1 Select Tools, Options

2 Set Picture's Duration

4 Select a Picture Clip

5 Drag to Storyboard

6 Preview Clip

3 Click OK

2 Set Picture's Duration

Change the **Picture Duration** to the time you want the picture to display as a title.

3 Click OK

Click the dialog box's **OK** button to apply the duration time to the next picture clip you place on the storyboard/timeline.

4 Select a Picture Clip

Locate the picture clip you want to use as the title.

5 Drag to Storyboard

Drag the clip to your storyboard where you want the title to appear. If, for example, the clip is to represent your opening title, you would drag the clip to the left end of the storyboard/timeline.

6 Preview Clip

Click **Play** to ensure that the clip plays at the proper time duration and produces the effect that you expected.

NOTE

Remember that picture clips appear at the top of your **Contents** pane. You might need to scroll the **Contents** pane up to see them.

TIP

The title's **Transparency** option is useful for placing extra text over a picture clip that you use as a title clip.

PART VI

Sharing Movies with the World

IN THIS PART:

11

Producing Your Movie

IN THIS CHAPTER:

The previous parts, chapters, and sections of this book show you how to prepare for your movie, shoot your video to capture the tone and quality you desire, and put together the raw video into a final, edited movie you want to share with others.

That's all the hard part!

Getting your production in front of others, whether you want to send out your movie via email, place the movie on a Web site, or place the movie on a CD or DVD, simply involves selecting the proper format and letting Movie Maker do most of the work.

The fact that Movie Maker does not directly write your movie to DVD does not imply that Movie Maker is limited in its output capability. Movie Maker is chock full of output formats, and you can send your movie to the following locations directly from within Movie Maker:

NOTE

Movie Maker has no capability to send your movie directly to DVD, but several products enable you to do so. In **92** About Putting Movies on DVD and **108** Produce DVDs with CD & DVD Creator, you will learn all you need to know to send your Movie Maker production to a DVD.

- **Digital video (DV) camera**—Send your movie to a digital video camera's tape for playback on a television you plug your DV camera into. If you have shot video footage on your DV camera's tape already, your Movie Maker movie will appear after that content as long as you position the tape properly.

- **Web**—Show your movies on the Web. To do this, you must use a *video hosting provider*.

- **Email**—Send your movie as an attachment from your email program, such as Microsoft Outlook.

- **CD**—Store your movie on a recordable CD that can be read by some video playback devices and most computers.

- **PocketPC**—Save your movie as a PocketPC movie. If you or others you know use the PocketPC PDA device, Movie Maker can reduce your movie's resolution down to PocketPC's required resolution settings for playback on the small PocketPC device.

KEY TERM

Video hosting provider—A Web site on which you rent space to put your movies on for others to watch.

81 Preview Your Final Movie

After you've gone through the editing process, you have in effect seen your movie over and over. Perhaps you never watched the movie straight through from the beginning to the end, but by watching all your edited clips throughout the editing process, you certainly know what's in your movie.

In spite of how much you've already seen of your production, you *must* watch your movie one more time, from the opening title to the final ending credit. Mistakes and surprises will creep into the work of the most careful movie pro. During your editing process, you could have easily deleted an extra clip or added the same clip twice to the timeline. You might also want to show the movie to friends or family before you edit it to get their feedback before you begin the final production process.

1 Click Play

After you've finished your movie's editing, click the **Monitor** pane's **Play** button to watch the entire movie from start to finish.

2 Watch Movie

Turn up the volume so you can hear your movie's soundtrack and other audio content. Sit back and watch your movie with a careful eye for flaws that you can edit out before saving the movie.

3 Press Alt+Enter to Watch Full Screen

You don't have to limit yourself to the small **Monitor** pane screen size. If you press **Alt+Enter** during playback, Movie Maker enlarges the movie to consume your entire computer monitor. You will be able to watch your movie more closely when you can see its details better in full-screen mode.

4 Press Esc to Return to Monitor Pane

If you want to return from full-screen mode to the regular Movie Maker screen, press **Esc**.

Before You Begin

✔ **31** Play Your Video on the Storyboard

✔ **33** Watch a Clip

✔ **64** Finalize Your AutoMovie

See Also

➜ **84** About Sharing Video with Others

➜ **85** Start the Save Movie Wizard

 TIP

Although Movie Maker greatly simplifies putting your movie on CD or sending it via email, you will waste time and effort as well as risk embarrassment if you send your movie to someone and the movie has flaws that a quick review could have prevented.

 TIP

If you see a mistake, stop the playback and correct the mistake right then. Your best chance of remembering to fix the flaw is right after you spot it.

 NOTE

If you find mistakes and make edits to your movie, you must once again watch the whole movie again from start to finish. New mistakes can occur during editing.

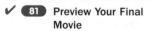

1 Click Play

2 Watch Movie

3 Press Alt+Enter to Watch Full Screen

4 Press Esc to Return to Monitor Pane

82 About Video Output Hardware

Before You Begin

✔ **81** Preview Your Final Movie

See Also

→ **83** About Output Formats

→ **84** About Sharing Video with Others

Computers are capable of playing multiple types of video and audio. The programming and hardware inside today's computers make it possible for the computer to recognize, in most cases, the kind of media you want to play. For example, when you insert an audio CD into your computer's CD drive, the computer plays the music after automatically starting your music or MP3 program. Insert a movie DVD into your computer's DVD drive, and the computer plays the movie after automatically starting your computer's DVD player. If the movie doesn't start playing right away, start your DVD playback software and select from its menus to load the movie from your DVD drive.

Noncomputer playback devices such as DVD players and DV cameras are not as forgiving, and not as multitalented. A DVD player can often play only DVD movies on DVD discs. When you store your final movie, you must know the kind of hardware the audience will have to play the movie. You cannot create a movie that will be playable on all possible devices.

After you've edited your movie and produced its final form, save your movie's project to your disk drive. Consider the project as being your movie's true source. If you create a movie CD from the project, the CD can be used to play the movie on devices that can read the CD, but don't erase your project and its associated files after you've created the CD. By keeping the movie's project, you will be able to save the movie in a different format later.

Keep this task's issues in mind as you follow subsequent tasks to save your movie in the format you require. The most important point to remember about your movie is that its true source is your movie project, and not the media to which you save your final movie.

NOTE

Some DVD players do play MP3 files and audio content from CDs. Some DVD players can also play videos stored on CDs, but you should never count on your audience having that kind of DVD player. If you store your movie on a CD, you must expect your audience to watch your movie on a computer that can read the movie on the CD.

NOTE

If you do not save your project, you will have lost all clips and tracks from your movie. The movie on the CD (or whatever media you save to, including an email attachment) is not segmented into clips and transition tracks that you can keep track of later. The media, such as the CD, will hold only a single movie file in a format such as **WMV**, which Movie Maker can no longer edit using tracks and clips.

83 About Output Formats

Although your project can consist of many video and audio files, your final saved movie is a single file. Movie Maker combines all of the movie's video, sound, transitions, titles, and credits into the movie file. The source location of all the project files is no longer tied to anything in the movie file. In other words, you do not need to worry about moving or renaming any content that went into the movie, because moving or renaming source content files has no effect on the final saved movie's playback.

Before You Begin

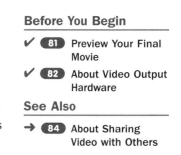

✔ **81** Preview Your Final Movie

✔ **82** About Video Output Hardware

See Also

→ **84** About Sharing Video with Others

Everything the movie needs is stored in the movie file. The movie file can be quite large, depending on the quality of the movie file. Movie Maker saves your movie using a variety of qualities. The quality is primarily determined by these factors:

KEY TERM

Bits—Small data values that, when combined, describe the sound and video of your movie.

KEY TERM

Pixel—Stands for *picture element*, and is the smallest dot available on a monitor.

- **Bit rate**—The number of informational *bits* played in a second during the movie's playback. The higher the bit rate, the better your movie looks.

- **Display size**—The size, in *pixels*, of your movie's playback screen size. The display size is given as the number of pixels wide and the number of pixels tall your movie comprises. The more pixels used, the better your movie looks at larger sizes.

- **Aspect ratio**—The relation of the width to the height of your movie's playback. On playback devices that do not offer a wide screen, such as the PocketPC, your movie requires a different aspect ratio from a larger device designed for movies such as a high-definition television. An aspect ration of 16:9 means the movie's width-to-height ratio is 16-to-9, so the width is almost twice the length of the movie's height.

- **Frames per second**—The number of movie frames that will play back per second. The higher the number of frames that play each second, the smoother and better your movie will play back.

Although it supports 18 output qualities, Movie Maker is still surprisingly limited on the kind of movie files it can create. Movie Maker supports only the following two movie file formats:

- **WMV**—The Windows Media Video format playable by the Windows Media Player and also by some non-Microsoft video playback programs and hardware.

- **AVI**—The Audio-Video Interleave format required by digital video cameras you send your movie to and is playable by virtually all video playback programs available today.

Of the 18 movie-saving resolutions Movie Maker offers, 17 are different resolutions and qualities of the WMV format, and one is the AVI format. Obviously, as Microsoft is the creator of Movie Maker, it's biased toward favoring its own file format, the WMV file format used by Windows Media Player. The WMV format compresses video files well while maintaining high quality. Unfortunately, WMV is not a standard recognized by all other video-related software, notably most *DVD burner programs* on the market today.

KEY TERM

DVD burner programs—A program you need, in addition to Movie Maker, that will write your movie to a DVD so the movie is playable on a DVD player.

84 About Sharing Video with Others

After you've assembled your clips, added transitions, added sound effects, created titles and end credits, and produced your movie, it's time to get that movie in front of other people! Movie Maker makes it simple to share your movie with others.

Movie Maker provides a variety of options to get your movie into your friends' hands. Here are the primary ways you can do just that:

- **Save the movie to your computer**—You can save your final movie to your own computer. Doing so ensures that you can watch the movie at any time. Also, you then can copy the movie file to a CD or use DVD-burning software to put the movie on DVD media. In addition, if you work on a network, others on your network can see the movie as long as you give them access to the disk and folder where the movie resides. Perhaps you're waiting to buy a new DVD burner. You can finalize your movie now, save the movie to your own computer, and then save the movie when the DVD burner arrives.

- **Save the movie to a CD**—Movie Maker uses Windows XP's integrated support for burning CDs to copy movies directly to CDs.

- **Send the movie in an email message**—Save your movie as an email attachment and send the email to friends and family.

Before You Begin

✔ **81** Preview Your Final Movie

✔ **82** About Video Output Hardware

See Also

→ **85** Start the Save Movie Wizard

TIP

Today's blank DVD media is fairly inexpensive, so if you produce a DVD movie and want to make edits (using the movie's project file), you have not wasted a lot of money if you discard the first DVD you make. Watch for rebates around the holidays, because many computer and electronic stores offer large rebates on blank CDs and DVDs to lure you into the store to buy other items.

NOTES

CDs hold only about 650 megabytes, so if your movie consumes more disk space than that, you must save it to a DVD or keep it on a hard disk for playback later. If you want to send your entire movie to a CD and the movie will not fit, you can select a lower movie quality so the saved movie consumes less space. Unfortunately, this means you probably cannot use the AVI format, except for short videos.

Keep your movies under one megabyte, as many email systems limit the attachment size to that size. In addition, keep your movie file small using a low quality if the email recipient uses dial-up Internet access.

TIP

As you'll see as you master DVD-burning programs such as Roxio's CD & DVD Creator (see **108** **Produce DVDs with CD & DVD Creator**), most DVD-burning software programs enable you to create a menu for scene selection. With such a menu, you can also add additional content to your movie, such as a bloopers video, that your audience can access by selecting the right menu choice.

- **Send the movie to the Web**—After you sign up with a video hosting provider (see **89** **Select a Video Hosting Provider**), you'll have a place on the Internet to send your movie for others to watch at their leisure.

- **Send the movie to a DVD**—To store your Movie Maker movie to a DVD, you must first save your movie onto your hard disk, exit Movie Maker, start your DVD-burning software, and follow the DVD-burning program's instructions. You'll get a glimpse at simple DVD-burning software named MyDVD in task **92** **About Putting Movies on DVD** and the final chapter of this book demonstrates several programs such as Adobe's Premiere Pro (see **110** **About Editing Professionally with Adobe Premiere Pro**).

- **Send the movie to a DV camera**—If your digital video camera is connected to your computer (typically by a FireWire cable), you can save the movie to the tape in the camera for playback on a television you later connect to the DV camera.

85 Start the Save Movie Wizard

No matter where you want to send your final movie, the steps you take to save the movie are similar. Movie Maker's Save Movie Wizard walks you through the saving process.

When you select the target for your movie, such as a DV camera or a CD, the Save Movie Wizard changes somewhat to reflect your choice. For example, if you want to send your movie as an email, Movie Maker does not give you a quality choice. Instead, Movie Maker selects a low-resolution movie quality to keep the size of the movie attachment on the email as small as possible.

1 Review Movie

Click the **Monitor** pane's **Play** button to watch your movie. Make sure the movie is final and ready to be produced.

2 Select File, Save Movie File

If the movie is final, select **Save Movie File** from the **File** menu. You will be presented with several destinations for your movie.

3 Select Movie Output

Click to select the location where you want to place the movie. Your choice determines what Movie Maker prompts you for next.

4 Click Next

Click the **Next** button to enter a filename and location for your saved movie.

Before You Begin

✔ **81** Preview Your Final Movie

See Also

→ **86** Send Your Movie to Your Disk

 NOTE

The sole purpose of this task is to familiarize you with the Save Movie Wizard. This wizard walks you through the process of saving your movie to one of the output destinations. The tasks that follow provide a more specific application of the Save Movie Wizard.

 NOTE

The rest of the Save Movie Wizard varies depending on your output destination. For example, Movie Maker will ask for a filename and location if you send your movie to a file on your computer. If, instead, you elect to save your movie to a CD drive, Movie Maker automatically begins writing the movie to your CD (assuming you have a blank recordable CD in your drive).

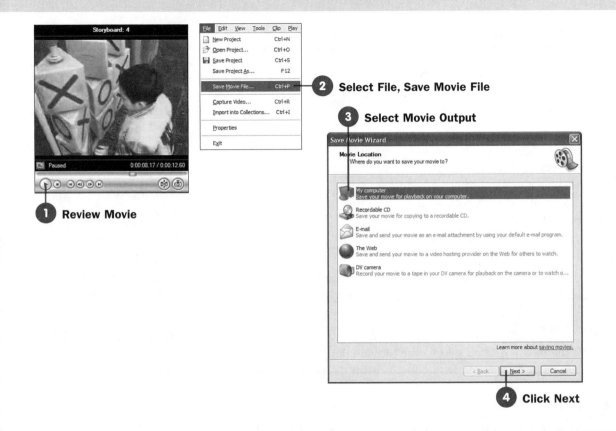

2 Select File, Save Movie File

3 Select Movie Output

4 Click Next

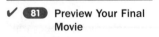

1 Review Movie

---

86 Send Your Movie to Your Disk

Before You Begin

✔ **81** Preview Your Final Movie

See Also

→ **85** Start the Save Movie Wizard

When you want to save your movie to your computer, Movie Maker asks for the target filename and location for the saved file. The saved movie file is a complete movie and you have no need to keep source files around if you truly do not need them. Remember, however, that you cannot easily edit the movie without the project file's source clips, sounds, and transitions.

Saving your movie to your computer gives you the most flexibility. You can save the file in one of the higher quality formats and later transfer one of those formats to a CD, DVD, or another computer on your network.

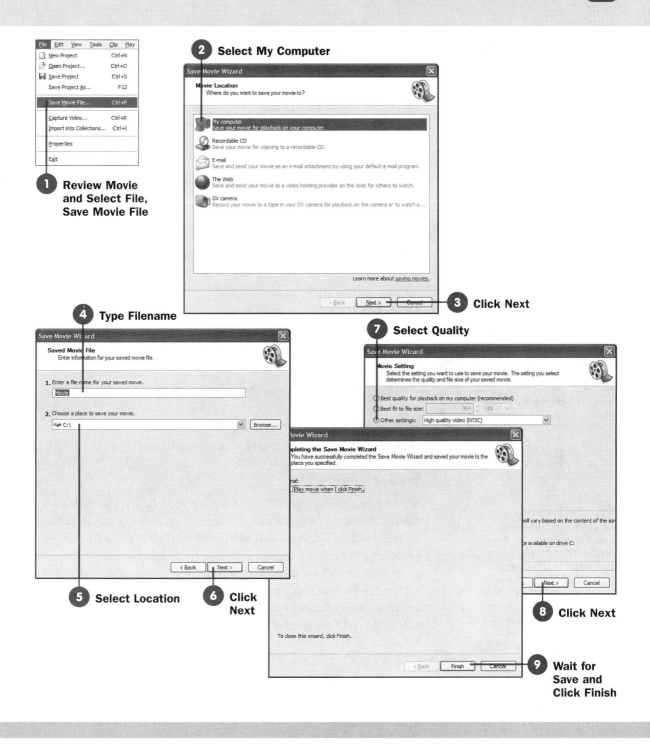

1 Review Movie and Select File, Save Movie File

2 Select My Computer

3 Click Next

4 Type Filename

5 Select Location

6 Click Next

7 Select Quality

8 Click Next

9 Wait for Save and Click Finish

NOTE

Movie Maker's saved movie files can be quite large. Unless you have plenty of storage space, you might not want to keep a copy of all movies you make on your computer. Consider getting an external backup drive, such as an external FireWire hard drive, on which to place all your saved movies. The movies then won't consume disk space you need for your computer's operating system, application programs, and data.

TIP

If you routinely display the **Task** pane (using **View**, **Task Pane**), you can skip right to step 5 by clicking the **Task** pane option labeled **Save to my computer**.

TIP

As you select different quality settings, the **Save Movie Wizard** dialog box updates the file statistics in the lower left-hand corner to tell you the file type, bit rate, display size, aspect ratio, and frames per second that matches your selected quality (see **83** About Output Formats).

1 Review Movie and Select File, Save Movie File

Click the **Monitor** pane's **Play** button to watch your movie. Make sure the movie is final and ready to be produced. If the movie is final, select **Save Movie File** from the **File** menu. You will be presented with several destinations for your movie.

2 Select My Computer

Click **My Computer** at the top of the dialog box to send your movie to a file on your computer.

3 Click Next

Click the **Next** button to enter a filename and location for your saved movie.

4 Type Filename

Type a filename for your movie's destination file.

5 Select Location

Select a location where you want the saved movie file to appear.

6 Click Next

Click the **Next** button to continue saving the movie.

7 Select Quality

Movie Maker automatically selects the option labeled **Best quality for playback on my computer**, but you can override the default by clicking **Show more choices**. If you select **Best fit to file size**, you can enter the maximum disk space you want the movie to consume, and Movie Maker determines the best quality that will fit within the limited disk space you enter. If you select **Other settings**, Movie Maker lets you scroll through a drop-down list to choose from the entire variety of quality settings available.

8 Click Next

After selecting the best quality choice, click the **Next** button to begin the save.

9 **Wait for Save and Click Finish**

Movie Maker updates the Save Movie Wizard with the saved file's process. Depending on your selected quality and your movie's length, the saving could take only a few seconds or several minutes. When the save completes, you can click **Finish** to return to Movie Maker. If you want to see your movie play before you return to Movie Maker, select the option labeled **Play movie when I click Finish**.

87 Save Your Movie to a CD

Just about anybody can play your movie if you put your movie on a CD, because just about everybody has a Windows-based computer these days. As long as they have a computer, the chances are good they can play your CD. Windows Media Player plays Movie Maker movies with ease, and it comes with all versions of Windows.

Depending on the length of your movie, you might not be able to maintain the highest quality possible simply because a CD holds only about 650 megabytes of storage. An hour-long movie of average quality might consume close to 800 megabytes of storage, so you'll need to adjust your quality until you can store your movie onto a CD.

Movie Maker saves your movie to the CD using Microsoft's *HiMAT (High Performance Media Access Technology)* technology. By using HiMAT, Movie Maker ensures that your CD-based movie is playable on as many devices as possible.

1 **Review Movie and Select File, Save Movie File**

Click the **Monitor** pane's **Play** button to watch your movie. Make sure the movie is final and ready to be produced. If the movie is final, select **Save Movie File** from the **File** menu. You will be presented with several destinations for your movie.

2 **Select Recordable CD**

Select the **Recordable CD** option from the wizard screen.

3 **Click Next**

Click **Next** to enter filename information for the movie.

Before You Begin

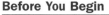 ✔ **84** About Sharing Video with Others

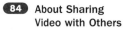 **NOTE**

Insert a blank, recordable CD into your CD drive before starting the Save Movie Wizard. If you start the wizard without a blank CD, Movie Maker issues an error on the wizard's second screen.

KEY TERM

HiMAT (High Performance Media Access Technology)—A storage method that is now recognized by many end-user consumer devices, including some DVD players.

 NOTE

If you have not inserted a blank, recordable CD into your CD drive, Movie Maker will issue an error and refuse to continue until you insert the CD.

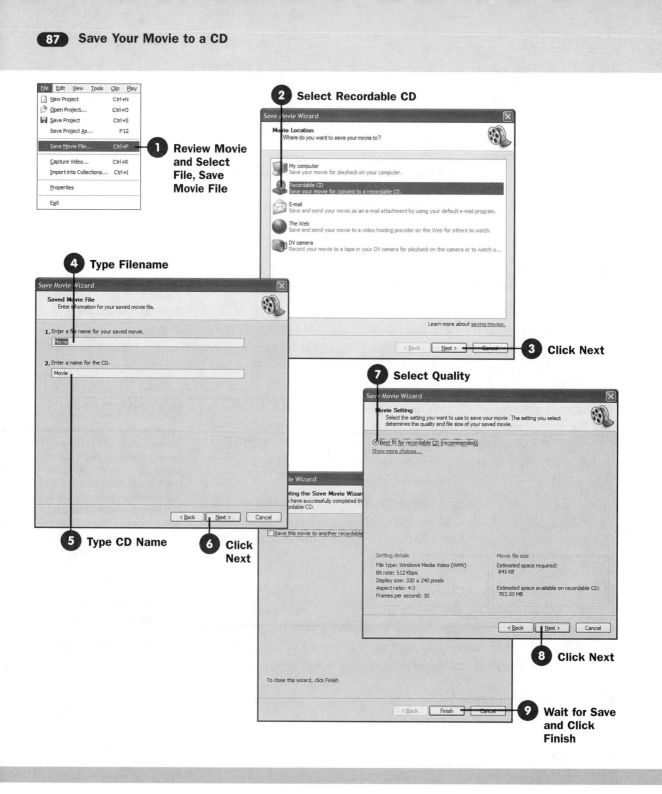

2 Select Recordable CD

1 Review Movie and Select File, Save Movie File

4 Type Filename

3 Click Next

7 Select Quality

5 Type CD Name

6 Click Next

8 Click Next

9 Wait for Save and Click Finish

Type Filename

Type a filename for your movie. Movie Maker will store the movie on the CD under that name.

 Type CD Name

Type a name for your CD, up to 16 characters. If your movie name (in step 5) is under 17 characters, you can probably give the CD the same name as the movie file.

 Click Next

Click the **Next** button to continue.

 Select Quality

The best quality setting will be the default setting labeled **Best fit for recordable CD**. Unless you have an overriding reason to deviate from this default, leave this setting alone.

 Click Next

Click the **Next** button to begin saving the movie onto your recordable CD.

9 **Wait for Save and Click Finish**

Movie Maker displays the saving process while you wait. Depending on your CD's speed and the movie's size and quality, the save could take from a minute to an hour. At the end of the saving process, Movie Maker will eject your CD from the drive. During the save process, you will see the **Microsoft HiMAT technology** icon on the page indicating that your movie will be compatible with other HiMAT devices and players. Click **Finish** to return to the Movie Maker screen. If you first click the option labeled **Save the movie to another recordable CD**, Movie Maker prompts you to insert another blank CD so you can save the movie once again.

 TIP

If you routinely display the **Task** pane (using **View**, **Task Pane**), you can skip right to step 5 by clicking the **Task** pane option labeled **Save to CD**.

TIP

If your movie is extremely short, you can select a higher quality than Movie Maker's default. To do so, click the **Show more choices** option. If you deviate from the default by selecting this option, use the second option labeled **Best fit for file size** and adjust the size to 650MB or less to ensure you get the best movie possible on the CD.

88   Send Your Movie Using Email

Before You Begin

✔ 84   About Sharing
          Video with Others

See Also

→ 90   Publish Your Movie
         on the Web

Sharing movies is perhaps the most fun aspect of digital video production. With today's Internet-connected computers, you can put your movie into the hands of friends in Italy as easily as you can send your movie to your next-door neighbor. Movie Maker enables you to send your movies through email to your recipients from within Movie Maker. As long as you have an email program on your computer such as Microsoft Outlook or Outlook Express, Movie Maker will locate the email system and handle the interface from within Movie Maker.

After you prepare a movie for sending over email, you can send your movie to one or multiple recipients. Movie Maker opens a new email message window and automatically attaches the movie to the email. After you finish entering the recipient information and type a subject and message line, you only need to click the email message's **Send** button to send your movie to your audience.

1   Review Movie and Select File, Save Movie File

Click the **Monitor** pane's **Play** button to watch your movie. Make sure the movie is final and ready to be produced. If the movie is final, select **Save Movie File** from the **File** menu. You will be presented with several destinations for your movie.

2   Select E-mail

Select the option labeled **E-mail** to tell Movie Maker you want to send the movie as an email attachment using your default email program, such as Microsoft Outlook.

3   Click Next and Wait for Movie Compilation

Click **Next** to enter filename information for the movie. Movie Maker will compile your movie if you have yet to save it. Once saved, Movie Maker gives you the opportunity to watch your movie again or save it to your disk.

TIP

If you routinely display the **Task** pane (using **View**, **Task Pane**), you can skip right to step 5 by clicking the **Task** pane option labeled **Send in e-mail**.

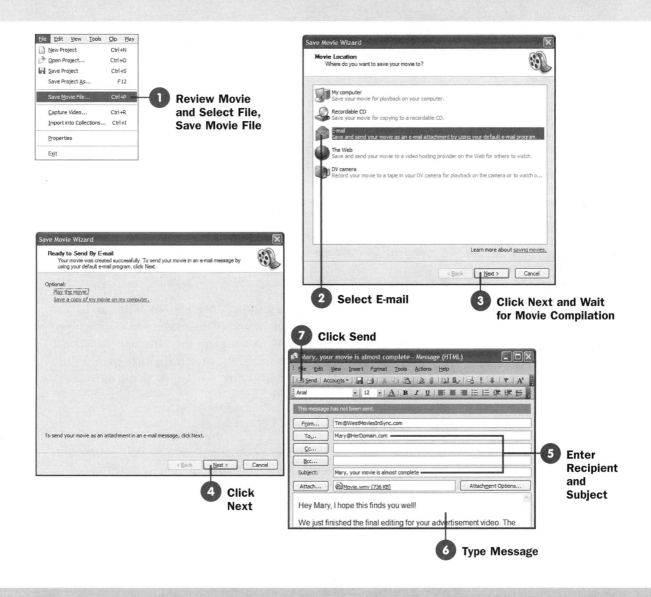

Review Movie and Select File, Save Movie File

Select E-mail

Click Next and Wait for Movie Compilation

Click Send

Click Next

Enter Recipient and Subject

Type Message

 Click Next

Click **Next** and wait a few moments while Movie Maker locates your default email program and opens a new message window. Notice that Movie Maker already attached the movie file to the message (you can locate the movie in your email message's

Attachment line, which usually appears right below the **Subject** line).

5 Enter Recipient and Subject

Type the email address or addresses (separated by semicolons if you want to send to multiple recipients) in the **To** field. Optionally, you can send a *carbon copy* or a *blind carbon copy* to more than one person. Type a meaningful subject in the **Subject** field so your recipients will have a good idea of what you are sending. For example, the subject **Judy's Birthday Video from 11/8/04** would be much more useful for such a video attachment than a title such as **Movie**. The **Movie** subject might even cause your recipients to delete the message without ever looking at it, thinking it is spam.

6 Type Message

Type a message in the large area at the bottom of the email. You might want to give a background of the movie you're attaching. You could even be creative and use this message body for your family's holiday newsletter, and the attached movie could be an annual *Happy Holidays* video from your family to the recipient's family.

7 Click Send

Click **Send** to send the movie. If you have a dial-up connection and are not currently logged into the Internet, your connection should dial and the message will go to its recipient list.

KEY TERMS

Carbon copy—Email terminology, typically designated by the **Cc** field, to recipients of an email who are not designated as the primary recipient that appears in the **To** field. The regular recipient in the **To** field will see that a copy was also sent to the **Cc** field's email address.

Blind carbon copy—Email terminology, typically designated by the **Bcc** field, to recipients of an email who are to receive a copy of the email without the primary or carbon copy recipients knowing the copy was sent.

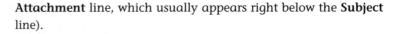

89 Select a Video Hosting Provider

Before You Begin

✔ **81** Preview Your Final Movie

✔ **84** About Sharing Video with Others

See Also

→ **90** Publish Your Movie on the Web

Many people with their own Web sites are able to perform their own *video hosting provider* service for videos they want to show on their site. Hosting your own video services often requires extra tools that you can rent or buy from your Web-hosting company so that visitors to your site can watch videos you place there. This technology is not always simple to implement. If you don't have your own Web site, or if you do but you don't want the added trouble and expense of supporting video hosting, you should rent a video hosting provider service. Such a service provides you with a simple way to place movies on the Web and give others access to those movies.

You can sign up for a video hosting provider directly from within Movie Maker. The first time you save a movie to the Web, Movie Maker gives you the opportunity to sign up for a video hosting provider.

 Select File, Save Movie File

To access the video hosting provider Web site, select **Save Movie File** from the **File** menu. You will be presented with several destinations for your movie. If you do not have a movie project loaded, go ahead and load one now so the **Save Movie File** option is available to you.

 Select The Web

Select the option labeled **The Web** to tell Movie Maker you want to send a movie to the Web. Even if you just want to sign up for a video hosting provider without sending a movie to the Web, select **The Web** and Movie Maker will eventually take you to the video hosting provider site.

 Click Next

Click **Next** to save your movie.

 Type Filename

Type a filename for the movie.

5 Click Next

Click **Next** to save your movie and display the **Internet Connection** dialog box.

6 Select Internet Connection

Select the proper Internet connection you use. If you select **Show more choices**, Movie Maker gives you the option to modify the quality of the movie.

7 Click Next and Wait for Save

Click the **Next** button and wait while Movie Maker saves your movie under the named you entered in step 4. A status bar shows the progress of the save.

 KEY TERM

Video hosting provider—A Web site that enables you to send videos so that others on the Internet can watch them.

TIP

Use a video hosting provider for your movies if the friends and family with which you want to share your movies have slow Internet connections or limited email capabilities. Instead of sending separate movies to each person by email, you only need to send an email with the location of your movie on your video hosting provider. Your friends and family then can watch the movie at their leisure.

 TIP

If you routinely display the **Task** pane (using **View**, **Task Pane**), you can skip right to step 4 by clicking the **Task** pane option labeled **Send to the Web**.

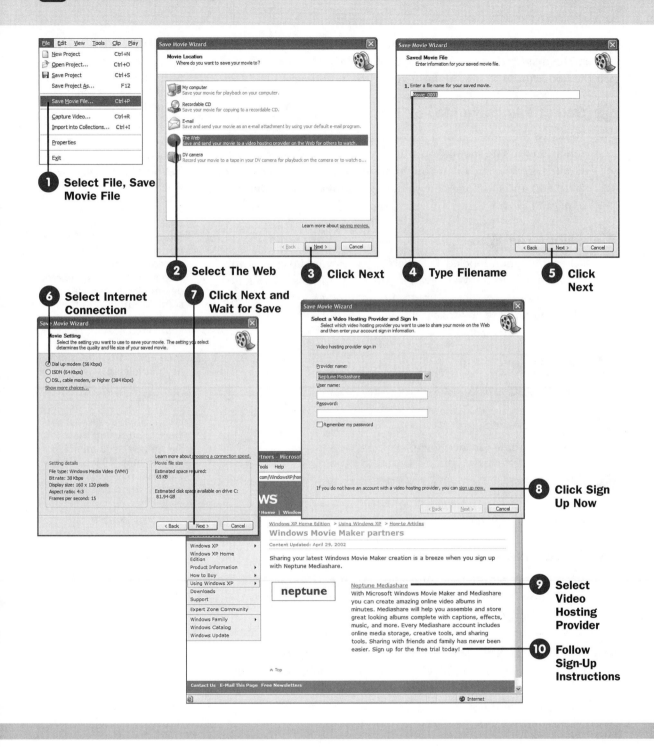

1 Select File, Save Movie File

2 Select The Web

3 Click Next

4 Type Filename

5 Click Next

6 Select Internet Connection

7 Click Next and Wait for Save

8 Click Sign Up Now

9 Select Video Hosting Provider

10 Follow Sign-Up Instructions

Click Sign Up Now

Select the **sign up now** option to go to the Internet and sign up for a video hosting provider.

 Select Video Hosting Provider

Select a video hosting provider from the one or more providers shown on the Web site.

 Follow Sign-Up Instructions

Continue surfing through the Web site and locate the type of account for which you want to sign up. Write down the user name and password you're assigned so that you can properly log on when you subsequently send your movies to the site (**see** 90 **Publish Your Movie on the Web**).

NOTE

At the time of this writing, Microsoft provides access only to the **Neptune Mediashare** site for U.S. users. Therefore, unless you use other methods to locate a video hosting site, you probably will use Neptune Mediashare.

TIP

Look for a free trial period in the sign-up options that enables you to sign up for a video hosting provider and try it a few days before you decide to pay the rental fee.

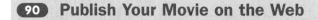 **90 Publish Your Movie on the Web**

After you sign up with a video hosting provider (**see** 89 **Select a Video Hosting Provider**), Movie Maker can send your movies to the Web for all to see. When you send your movies to the Web once instead of sending it to several users through email, you help decrease Web traffic and the congestion it causes, reduce the strain on your friends' and families' email inboxes, and help ensure that more people can successfully view your movies.

After you send your movie to your video hosting provider, you only need to send the Web address of the movie to your friends and family. With that address, they can watch your movie from any Internet connection in the world.

**Before You Begin**

✔ 81 Preview Your Final Movie

✔ 84 About Sharing Video with Others

1 **Select File, Save Movie File**

To send your movie to the Web, select **Save Movie File** from the **File** menu. You will be presented with several destinations for your movie. If you do not have a movie project loaded, go ahead and load one now so the **Save Movie File** option is available to you.

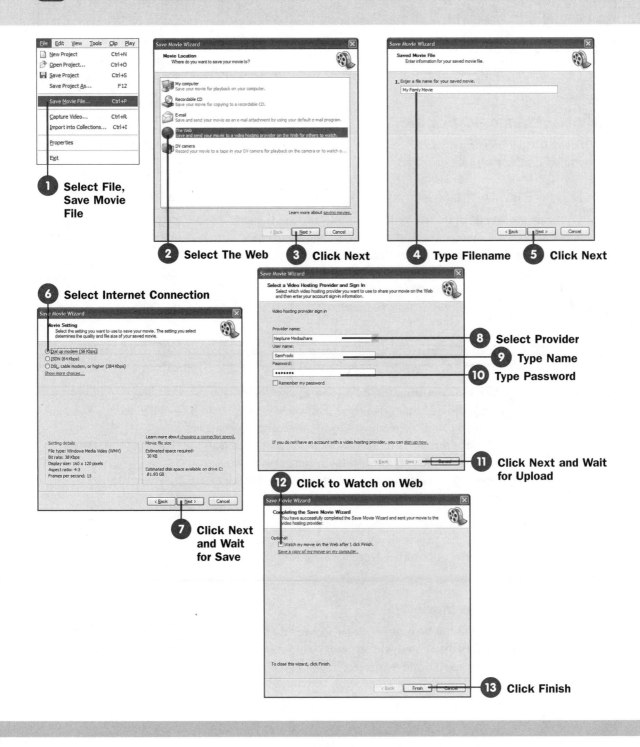

1 **Select File, Save Movie File**

2 **Select The Web** 3 **Click Next** 4 **Type Filename** 5 **Click Next**

6 **Select Internet Connection**

7 **Click Next and Wait for Save**

8 **Select Provider**

9 **Type Name**

10 **Type Password**

11 **Click Next and Wait for Upload**

12 **Click to Watch on Web**

13 **Click Finish**

Select The Web

Select the option labeled **The Web** to tell Movie Maker you want to send a movie to the Web.

 Click Next

Click **Next** to save your movie.

 Type Filename

Type a filename for the movie.

 Click Next

Click **Next** to save your movie and display the **Internet Connection** dialog box.

 Select Internet Connection

Select the Internet connection your audience typically uses. If you select **Show more choices**, Movie Maker gives you the option to modify the quality of the movie.

 Click Next and Wait for Save

Click the **Next** button and Movie Maker saves your movie. Wait while Movie Maker saves your movie under the name you entered in step 4. A status bar appears showing the progress of the save.

 Select Provider

Select your video hosting provider from the list.

 Type Name

Type your video hosting provider username in the **User name** field.

 Type Password

Type your video hosting provider password in the **Password** field.

Click Next and Wait for Upload

Click the **Next** button and Movie Maker contacts your video hosting provider, logs you in automatically using your username and

 TIP

If you routinely display the **Task** pane (using **View, Task Pane**), you can skip right to step 4 by clicking the **Task** pane option labeled **Send to the Web**.

 TIP

Click the option labeled **Remember my password** if you want Movie Maker to remember your user name and password the next time you send a movie to the Web. Do not select this option unless you are on your own computer, or others will have access to your video hosting provider.

password, and begins uploading your video to the Web site. Depending on your connection speed and movie size, the upload might take a few seconds to several minutes.

⑫ Click to Watch on Web

You can watch your movie on your video hosting site by clicking the option labeled **Watch my movie on the Web after I click Finish**. By doing so, you can verify that your friends and family will see what you want them to see and the movie will play (inside your Web browser) after the Save Movie Wizard completes.

⑬ Click Finish

Click the **Finish** button to close the wizard's dialog box and return to Movie Maker.

91 Send Your Movie to a DV Camera

Before You Begin

✔ **81** Preview Your Final Movie

✔ **82** About Video Output Hardware

NOTE

Most DV cameras connect to your computer by way of a FireWire cable. As long as your DV camera connects using a FireWire cable, Movie Maker can sense the camera's presence and write the movie to it.

NOTE

Your DV camera must be set to the VCR or VTR setting before Movie Maker can save a movie to the camera's tape (also known as *playback mode*).

If you have a digital video camera (DV camera), you can send a movie to a tape in the camera. You then can watch the movie on the DV camera or on a television you plug into the DV camera. If you have existing video on the tape before your starting point for the movie, both the previous content and your movie can reside on the tape at the same time.

Be sure to turn on your DV camera before starting this task. Movie Maker will refuse to continue with the Save Movie Wizard if you have not connected a DV camera or have not turned it on before starting the save process to the camera.

① Review Movie and Select File, Save Movie File

Click the **Monitor** pane's **Play** button to watch your movie. Make sure the movie is final and ready to be produced. If the movie is final, select **Save Movie File** from the **File** menu. You will be presented with several destinations for your movie.

② Select DV Camera

Click **DV Camera** at the bottom of the dialog box to send your movie to your digital video camera attached to your computer.

PART VI: Sharing Movies with the World

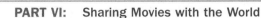

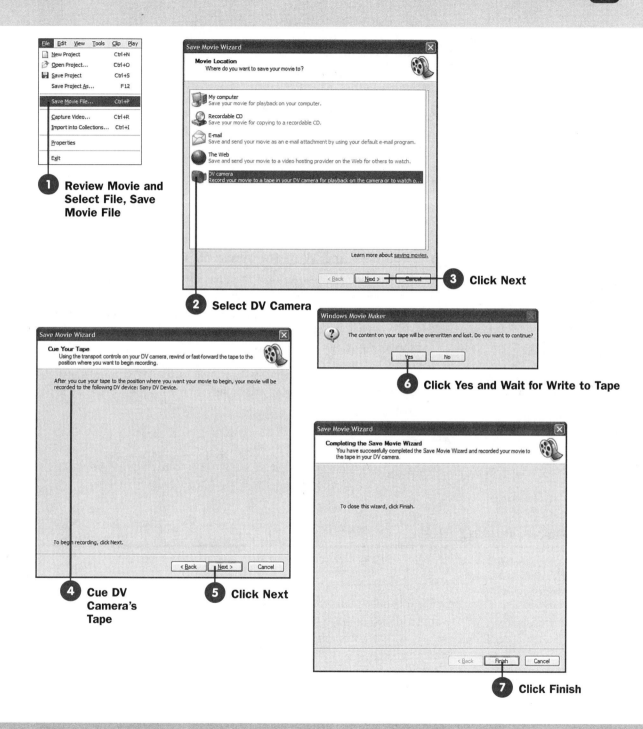

1 Review Movie and Select File, Save Movie File

2 Select DV Camera

3 Click Next

4 Cue DV Camera's Tape

5 Click Next

6 Click Yes and Wait for Write to Tape

7 Click Finish

 **Click Next**

Click **Next** to move to the camera's cueing dialog box.

NOTE

If you have multiple digital video devices connected to your computer, Movie Maker displays a list of them so that you can select the one you want to use for the movie. If you only have one DV camera connected, as will most often be the case, you won't have to select your DV camera.

 TIP

If you routinely display the **Task** pane (using **View**, **Task Pane**), you can skip right to step 5 by clicking the **Task** pane option labeled **Send to DV camera**.

④ **Cue DV Camera's Tape**

Fast forward or rewind the tape in your DV camera to the point where you want to place the movie.

⑤ **Click Next**

After your tape is cued to where you want the movie to appear, click the **Next** button to begin the recording process.

⑥ **Click Yes and Wait for Write to Tape**

Movie Maker warns you that the tape will be overwritten with your movie. Of course, that's what you want to happen. As long as you're sure you have the proper tape in your DV camera (it won't hurt to check so you don't overwrite a tape you want to keep), click the **Yes** button to start the process.

Movie Maker begins writing your movie to the DV camera's tape. A progress bar appears on your screen showing the status of the write.

⑦ **Click Finish**

After Movie Maker completes the writing to the tape in your DV camera, click the **Finish** button to return to Movie Maker.

---

92 About Putting Movies on DVD

Before You Begin

✔ **83** About Output Formats

✔ **84** About Sharing Video with Others

See Also

→ **105** Create Labels for your CDs and DVDs with DME

Sadly, one of the obvious omissions from Movie Maker is its lack of DVD-burning capabilities. Actually, Microsoft Windows XP does not contain built-in DVD-burning routines, and if Movie Maker used them, it would need to adopt a third-party DVD-burning routine that the next version of Windows may or may not adopt. Playing it safe, Microsoft is leaving the DVD-burning operation for your movies up to third-party software vendors that can do the job now.

If you need to purchase DVD-burning software to play your Movie Maker movies on DVD players, be sure the software you choose can import the Windows Media Video format (**WMV**), because that is the format Movie Maker supports best. At first, the favoring of WMV file formats might seem to limit Movie Maker. Remember, though, that Movie Maker supports the DV-AVI file format as well as 17 different quality variations of WMV files. The WMV format packs very good video and sound quality into much smaller movie files than the DV-AVI format.

The final chapter of this book demonstrates several programs that can put your movies onto DVDs and video CDs. If you have only Movie Maker at this time, you cannot place movies onto DVD. You must obtain some kind of external DVD-burning software.

The **Sonic MyDVD Plus** software is talked about quite a bit on Microsoft's Movie Maker Web site (**http://www.microsoft.com/ windowsxp/moviemaker/learnmore/dvdburn.asp**). MyDVD Plus supports Movie Maker's WMV format easily. Using MyDVD Plus to send a Movie Maker movie to a DVD requires these simple steps:

1. Save the Movie Maker movie to your hard disk using the best quality available. For the best quality with compact size, use **high quality video (large)** as opposed to DV-AVI.

2. Exit Movie Maker.

3. Start your DVD-burning program.

4. Import your saved Movie Maker movie file.

5. Edit the opening DVD title and create a DVD menu, if you desire one.

6. Insert a blank DVD into your recordable DVD drive.

7. Start the burning process.

8. Label your DVD.

NOTE

If the next version of Windows includes the rumored DVD-writing capabilities, the next version of Movie Maker will almost certainly be able to write to DVD burners as well.

Sonic MyDVD Plus creates DVDs from your Movie Maker movies.

PART VII

Adding Extras to Movie Maker

IN THIS PART:

12

Enjoying Microsoft's Free Movie Maker Fun Pack

IN THIS CHAPTER:

93 About the Movie Maker Creativity Fun Pack

94 Download the Movie Maker Creativity Fun Pack

95 Use the Fun Pack's Titles

96 Use the Fun Pack's End Credits

97 Add a Static Video Title to Your Movie

98 Grab a Fun Pack Music Sample or Music Transition

99 Select a Fun Pack Sound Effect for Your Movie

As the heart of this book demonstrates, Movie Maker is a video-editing and video-production software program that deserves respect. In spite of its price (free with Windows), Movie Maker provides extensive editing, transition, and effects capabilities to the movie maker who wants to produce quality movies.

With the release of Windows XP and the release of Movie Maker version 2 soon afterward, Microsoft somewhat blindsided the marketplace with Movie Maker. The first version of Movie Maker that came with Windows Me was rather weak, and deserved the poor reviews it got. Microsoft surprised the market with Movie Maker's second version, however, and many video producers have used Movie Maker to easily put together their video productions ever since.

In spite of its substantial feature list, Movie Maker has room for improvement and add-ons. Microsoft provides one answer for the user who wants to do more with Movie Maker by providing the Movie Maker Creativity Fun Pack, a free Movie Maker add-on that adds to Movie Maker's feature set.

TIP

The Movie Maker Creativity Fun Pack is free and available as a download from the Microsoft Web site (**see** **94** **Download the Movie Maker Creativity Fun Pack**).

---

93 About the Movie Maker Creativity Fun Pack

Before You Begin

✔ **81** Preview Your Final Movie

See Also

→ **94** Download the Movie Maker Creativity Fun Pack

The Movie Maker Creativity Fun Pack includes extras that you can add to your movie, such as

- Video titles

- Music

- Sound effects

If you only want the extra titles, or you only want the music and sound effects, you can elect to download only a partial Movie Maker Creativity Fun Pack. You might do this if you have a slow Internet connection (**see** **94** **Download the Movie Maker Creativity Fun Pack**).

Microsoft describes the quality of the fun pack's sound and music extras by stating that they come from **SoundDogs.com**, a popular sound effects Web site. The sound effects from the site have been added to popular Hollywood movies, including *Meet the Parents, Wonder Boys, As Good As It Gets, The Green Mile, Titanic, Stuart Little,* and *Jerry Maguire.*

SoundDogs.com has more than 155,000 sound effects, music clips, and samples online.

The **SoundDogs.com**-supplied music tracks include three complete songs you can use in your movies, as well as five music transitions you can use between scenes to help transition your audience from one scene to another. In addition, the Movie Maker Creativity Fun Pack includes 50 sound effects you can add to make your movie moments come alive.

The Movie Maker Creativity Fun Pack also contains several titles and end credits that add new flavors to the assortment Movie Maker already provides you. You will get countdown titles (such as a countdown to the start of the movie), a *The End* ending credit you can use, as well as several formatted blank video titles for which you can add the text. In addition, the Movie Maker Creativity Fun Pack provides several static video titles that you can use as-is or with your own titles added. These include popular holiday backgrounds and themes.

TIP

Microsoft offers several Creativity Fun Packs, such as one for Windows Media Player and one for digital photography. You can sample them all at the Creativity Fun Pack's Web site at **www.microsoft. com/WindowsXP/experiences/create** (all the Creativity Fun Packs are free for your download and use).

94 Download the Movie Maker Creativity Fun Pack

Before You Begin

✔ **93** About the Movie
Maker Creativity
Fun Pack

See Also

→ **95** Use the Fun Pack's
Titles

→ **96** Use the Fun Pack's
End Credits

→ **98** Grab a Fun Pack
Music Sample or
Music Transition

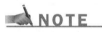NOTE

You need at least 24.83
megabytes of free disk
space to install the full
Movie Maker Creativity Fun
Pack. The titles and credits
portion of the fun pack
requires 7.39 megabytes,
and the music and sound
effects portion requires
18.37 megabytes of free
disk space.

If you've downloaded software from the Internet before, you'll find that
the installation process for the Movie Maker Creativity Fun Pack goes
rather smoothly. Even if you are unfamiliar with downloading such software online, you'll see that by following this task, you'll have no trouble
getting the Movie Maker Creativity Fun Pack off Microsoft's Web site
and onto your computer so that you can begin using the Movie Maker
Creativity Fun Pack immediately.

1 Go to Movie Maker's Home Page

Point your Web browser to the Movie Maker Home page, located
at **http://www.microsoft.com/WindowsXP/experiences/create**.

2 Click to Select Fun Pack

Click the link labeled **Windows Movie Maker 2 Fun Pack** to
move to the Movie Maker Creativity Fun Pack page.

3 Select Full or a Partial Pack

If you have a high-speed Internet connection and plenty of disk
space, select the **Full Fun Pack** option. If you want only the titles
and credits portion of the fun pack, or if you want just the music
and sound effects portion of the fun pack, click the appropriate
link.

4 Click Open, then Next after File Download

You can elect to save the fun pack installation program to your
computer and install it later. If you click **Open** now, the installation will take place now.

Depending on your Internet connection, you might have to wait
up to two hours to download the Movie Maker Creativity Fun
Pack. High-speed users such as those with DSL or a cable modem
will only need to wait a few minutes for the download to complete. When the first installation dialog box appears, click **Next** to
begin the process.

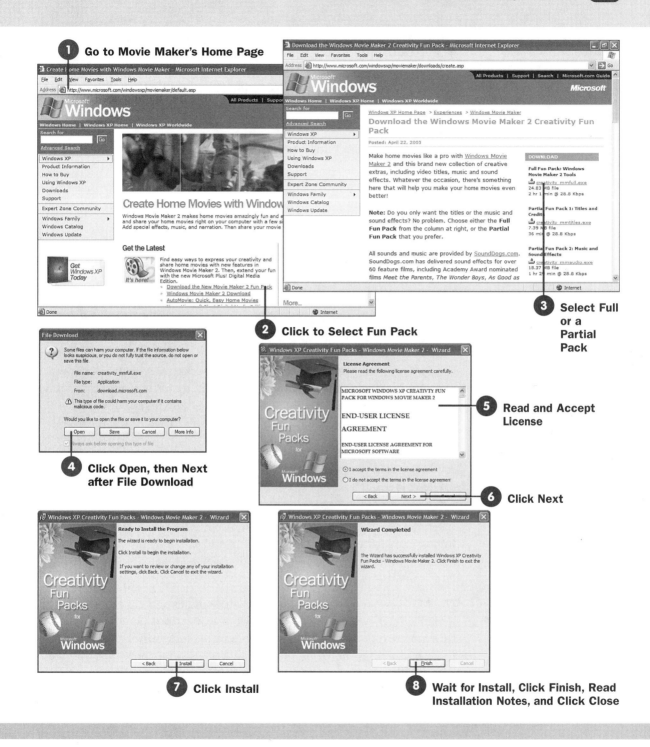

1 Go to Movie Maker's Home Page

2 Click to Select Fun Pack

3 Select Full or a Partial Pack

4 Click Open, then Next after File Download

5 Read and Accept License

6 Click Next

7 Click Install

8 Wait for Install, Click Finish, Read Installation Notes, and Click Close

5 **Read and Accept License**

The install process displays the legal license for the Movie Maker Creativity Fun Pack that you will want to read (yeah, right!).

6 **Click Next**

Click the **Next** button to continue with the installation routine.

7 **Click Install**

Click the **Install** button to start the actual installation of the Movie Maker Creativity Fun Pack onto your computer.

8 **Wait for Install, Click Finish, Read Installation Notes, and Click Close**

The installation can take several seconds or perhaps a minute or more, depending on your computer's speed. After the installation completes, click the **Finish** button to close the installation dialog box. The installation routine opens a window with fun pack installation notes. You will see that all fun packs, such as the Windows Media Player Fun Pack, appear in the notes also. Read through the notes that pertain to the Movie Maker Creativity Fun Pack. After you've looked through the notes, click the **Close** button to close the note window.

NOTE

The Movie Maker Creativity Fun Pack installs in your **My Documents** folder. Inside **My Documents**, in a folder named **My Videos**, you'll see a folder named **Creativity Fun Packs**. The four folders represent the fun pack's titles and credits, sound effects, static titles, and music tracks and transitions.

---

95 **Use the Fun Pack's Titles**

Before You Begin

✔ **93** About the Movie Maker Creativity Fun Pack

✔ **94** Download the Movie Maker Creativity Fun Pack

See Also

→ **96** Use the Fun Pack's End Credits

After you've installed the Movie Maker Creativity Fun Pack, you must import the Movie Maker Creativity Fun Pack contents into your Movie Maker collection before you can use the Movie Maker Creativity Fun Pack content in your movies.

The Movie Maker Creativity Fun Pack titles are extremely professional looking. After you import them into your **Collections** pane, look through each of them and preview them in your **Monitor** pane. You will think of the titles shown in major Hollywood productions when you see what the Movie Maker Creativity Fun Pack gives you.

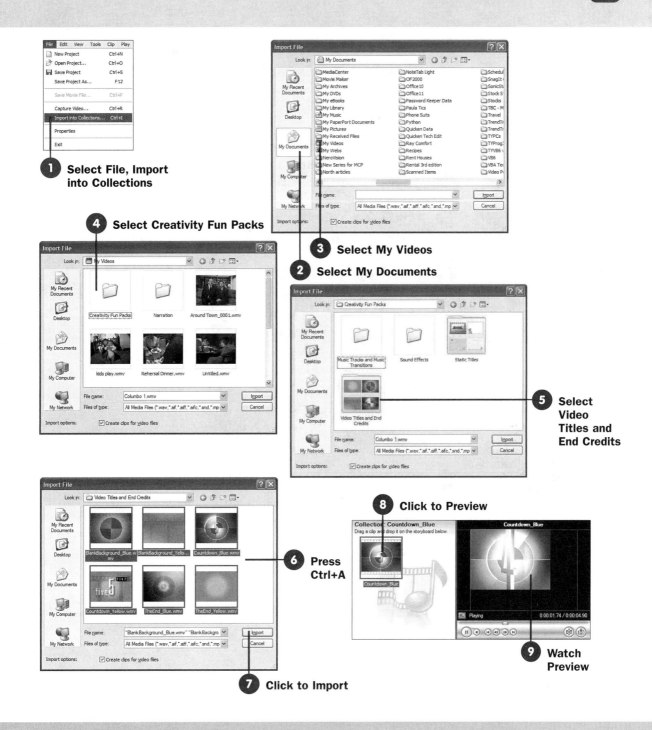

1 Select File, Import into Collections

2 Select My Documents

3 Select My Videos

4 Select Creativity Fun Packs

5 Select Video Titles and End Credits

6 Press Ctrl+A

7 Click to Import

8 Click to Preview

9 Watch Preview

1 **Select File, Import into Collections**

You must import the Movie Maker Creativity Fun Pack titles into Movie Maker before you can use the titles. Select **Import into Collections** from the **File** menu.

2 **Select My Documents**

Select the **My Documents** folder to begin browsing to the Movie Maker Creativity Fun Pack content.

3 **Select My Videos**

Select to open the **My Videos** folder.

4 **Select Creativity Fun Packs**

Select to open the **Creativity Fun Packs** folder.

5 **Select Video Titles and End Credits**

Select to open the folder named **Video Titles and End Credits**.

 TIP

The blank titles (**BlankBackground_Yellow** and **BlankBackground_Blue**) are available so that you can place your own text over these backgrounds. These backgrounds work well for opening title backgrounds because they are faint enough to allow your audience to read the text on them, but they also move and change to keep your audience's attention.

6 **Press Ctrl+A**

You'll want to import all the titles (and end credits) into your **Collections** pane. Press **Ctrl+A** to select all the titles and end credits.

7 **Click to Import**

Click the **Import** button to import the titles and end credits into Movie Maker. Movie Maker begins importing your titles and end credits. The import can take a minute or more depending on the speed of your computer.

NOTE

After you import the titles into your collection, you can drag any title to your storyboard/timeline at the start of your movie to place the title in your movie.

8 **Click to Preview**

Click on the **Countdown_Blue** title to preview it. The title's thumbnail image appears in the collection and then in the **Monitor** pane when you click the collection's thumbnail.

9 **Watch Preview**

Click the **Monitor** pane's **Play** button to see the title countdown. Doesn't that look cool?

Use the Fun Pack's End Credits

After you have installed the Movie Maker Creativity Fun Pack, you must import the Movie Maker Creativity Fun Pack contents into your Movie Maker collection before you can use the fun pack content in your movies.

The Movie Maker Creativity Fun Pack end credits are extremely professional looking. After you import them into your **Collections** pane, look through each of them and preview them in your **Monitor** pane. You will think of the end credits shown in major Hollywood productions when you see what the Movie Maker Creativity Fun Pack gives you.

Before You Begin

✔ **93** About the Movie Maker Creativity Fun Pack

✔ **94** Download the Movie Maker Creativity Fun Pack

 Select File, Import into Collections

You must import the Movie Maker Creativity Fun Pack end credits into Movie Maker before you can use the titles. Select **Import into Collections** from the **File** menu.

 Select My Documents

Select the **My Documents** folder to begin browsing to the Movie Maker Creativity Fun Pack content.

 Select My Videos

Select to open the **My Videos** folder.

 Select Creativity Fun Packs

Select to open the **Creativity Fun Packs** folder.

 Select Video Titles and End Credits

Select to open the folder named **Video Titles and End Credits**.

6 Press Ctrl+A

You'll want to import all the end credits (and titles) into your **Collections** pane. Press **Ctrl+A** to select all the titles and end credits.

TIP

If you have already imported the Movie Maker Creativity Fun Pack content into Movie Maker, you can skip to step 9 to preview the end credits you can use in your movies.

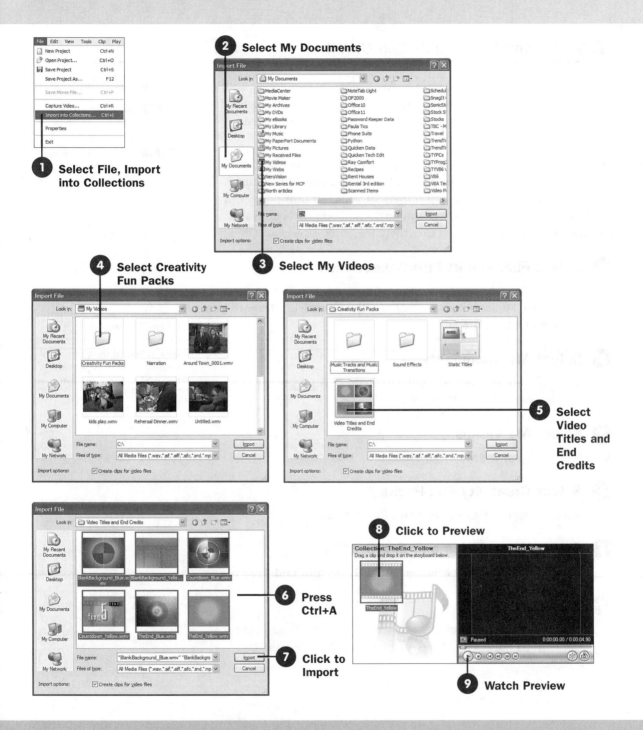

1 Select File, Import into Collections

2 Select My Documents

3 Select My Videos

4 Select Creativity Fun Packs

5 Select Video Titles and End Credits

6 Press Ctrl+A

7 Click to Import

8 Click to Preview

9 Watch Preview

Click to Import

Click the **Import** button to import the titles and end credits into Movie Maker. Movie Maker begins the importing of your titles and end credits. The import can take a minute or more depending on the speed of your computer.

8 Click to Preview

Click on the **TheEnd_Yellow** end credit to preview it. The title's thumbnail image appears in the collection and then in the **Monitor** pane when you click the collection's thumbnail.

9 Watch Preview

Click the **Monitor** pane's **Play** button to see the end credit shooting out the words, **The End**. Doesn't that look cool?

 NOTE

After you import the end credits into your collection, you can drag either end credit to your storyboard/timeline at the end of your movie to place the end credit in your movie.

---

97 Add a Static Video Title to Your Movie

After you have installed the Movie Maker Creativity Fun Pack, you must import the Movie Maker Creativity Fun Pack contents into your Movie Maker collection before you can use the Movie Maker Creativity Fun Pack content in your movies.

The Movie Maker Creativity Fun Pack static titles provide several backgrounds on which you can place text. Many of the static titles are related to holidays such as Mother's Day, so you can extend your movie's theme to the beginning or ending titles or scene, changing text that you place on the static title backgrounds.

1 Select File, Import into Collections

You must import the Movie Maker Creativity Fun Pack static titles into Movie Maker before you can use the static titles. Select **Import into Collections** from the **File** menu.

2 Select My Documents

Select the **My Documents** folder to begin browsing to the Movie Maker Creativity Fun Pack content.

Before You Begin

✔ **93** About the Movie Maker Creativity Fun Pack

✔ **94** Download the Movie Maker Creativity Fun Pack

See Also

→ **76** Put a Title on a Clip

 TIP

If you have already imported the Movie Maker Creativity Fun Pack content into Movie Maker, you can skip to step 8 to preview the static titles that you can use in your movies.

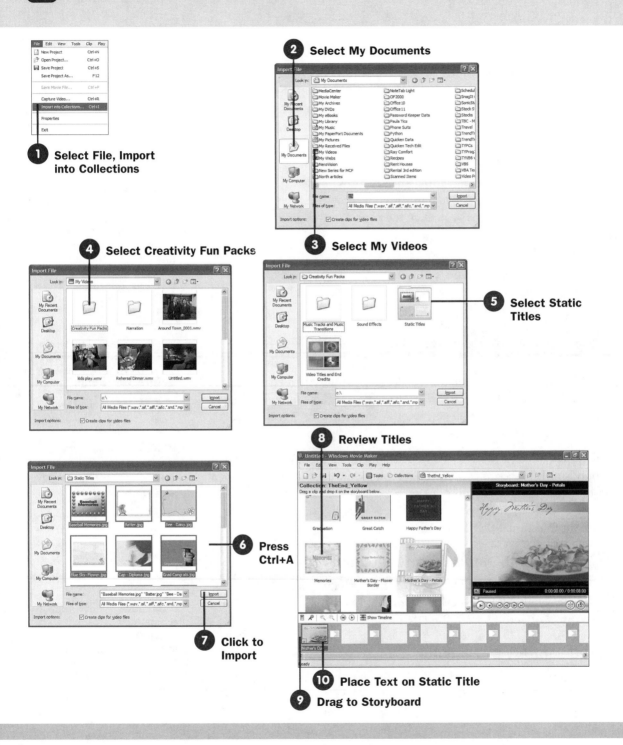

1 Select File, Import into Collections

2 Select My Documents

3 Select My Videos

4 Select Creativity Fun Packs

5 Select Static Titles

6 Press Ctrl+A

7 Click to Import

8 Review Titles

9 Drag to Storyboard

10 Place Text on Static Title

Select My Videos

Select to open the **My Videos** folder.

 Select Creativity Fun Packs

Select to open the **Creativity Fun Packs** folder.

 Select Static Titles

Select to open the folder named **Static Titles**.

 Press Ctrl+A

You'll want to import all the static titles into your **Collections** pane. Press **Ctrl+A** to select all the static titles.

 Click to Import

Click the **Import** button to import the static titles into Movie Maker. Movie Maker begins the importing of your static titles. The import can take a minute or more depending on the speed of your computer.

 Review Titles

Scroll through the new static titles that now appear.

 Drag to Storyboard

Drag the **Plus!** static title to your storyboard at the location where you want your audience to see the static title.

 Place Text on Static Title

After you drag a static title to the storyboard, you should place text on the static title. **See 76 Put a Title on a Clip** to learn how to do this.

NOTE

After you import the static titles into your collection, you can drag any title to your storyboard/timeline in your movie to place the static title in your movie.

98 Grab a Fun Pack Music Sample or Music Transition

Before You Begin

✔ **48** Add a Soundtrack to Your Video

✔ **93** About the Movie Maker Creativity Fun Pack

✔ **94** Download the Movie Maker Creativity Fun Pack

See Also

→ **99** Select a Fun Pack Sound Effect for Your Movie

TIP

If you have already imported the Movie Maker Creativity Fun Pack content into Movie Maker, you can skip to step **8** to preview the music samples and music transitions that you can place in your movies.

After you have installed the Movie Maker Creativity Fun Pack, you must import the Movie Maker Creativity Fun Pack contents into your Movie Maker collection before you can use the Movie Maker Creativity Fun Pack content in your movies.

The Movie Maker Creativity Fun Pack music tracks and music transitions provide several music samples and music transitions you can place in your movie. You will place these on the timeline's Audio/Music track so that the music or transition occurs at the appropriate location in your movie. The following steps request that you listen to a couple of the music tracks that you import. As you listen to a music transition track, you might be surprised at how the music seems to lead you from one scene to another.

1 Select File, Import into Collections

You must import the Movie Maker Creativity Fun Pack music samples and music transitions into Movie Maker before you can use the music samples and music transitions. Select **Import into Collections** from the **File** menu.

2 Select My Documents

Select the **My Documents** folder to begin browsing to the Movie Maker Creativity Fun Pack content.

3 Select My Videos

Select to open the **My Videos** folder.

4 Select Creativity Fun Packs

Select to open the **Creativity Fun Packs** folder.

5 Select Music Tracks and Music Transitions

Select to open the folder named **Music Tracks and Music Transitions**.

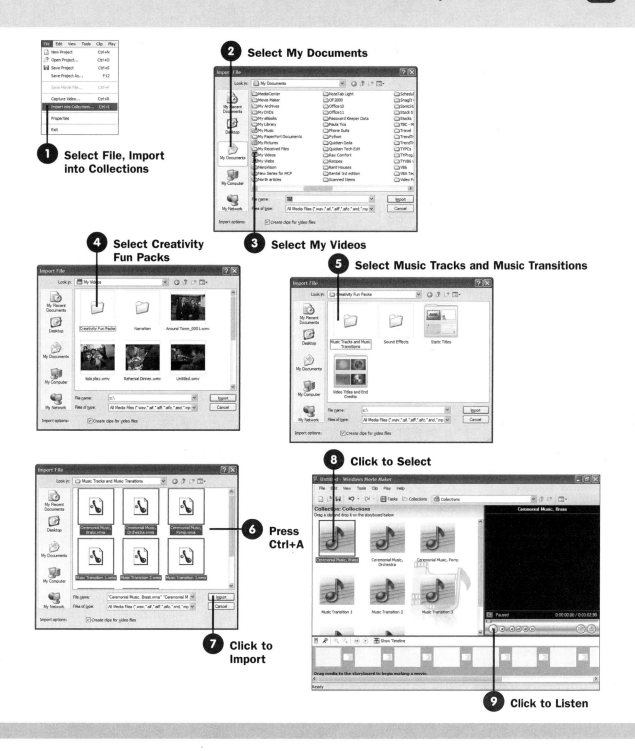

1 Select File, Import into Collections

2 Select My Documents

3 Select My Videos

4 Select Creativity Fun Packs

5 Select Music Tracks and Music Transitions

6 Press Ctrl+A

7 Click to Import

8 Click to Select

9 Click to Listen

6 **Press Ctrl+A**

You'll want to import all the music tracks and music transitions into your **Collections** pane. Press **Ctrl+A** to select all the music tracks and music transitions.

7 **Click to Import**

Click the **Import** button to import the music tracks and music transitions into Movie Maker.

NOTE

After you import the music tracks and music transitions into your collection, you can drag any of them to the timeline's Audio/Music track at the location in your movie where you want the music or music transition to start (see **48** Add a Soundtrack to Your Video and **55** Add Sound Effects to Your Movie).

8 **Click to Select**

Click to select the music track named **Ceremonial Music, Brass.** This music track will remind you of military-related movies you've seen before.

9 **Click to Listen**

Click the **Play** button on the **Monitor** pane to hear the music track. Review the other transitions also to see what new features you might want to add to your movies.

---

99 **Select a Fun Pack Sound Effect for Your Movie**

Before You Begin

✔ **55** Add Sound Effects to Your Movie

✔ **93** About the Movie Maker Creativity Fun Pack

✔ **94** Download the Movie Maker Creativity Fun Pack

TIP

Review all the sound effects—you might be surprised at the range of effects you find. For example, people clapping and cheering at a sporting event might come in handy as low background noise for a Little League game.

After you have installed the Movie Maker Creativity Fun Pack, you must import the Movie Maker Creativity Fun Pack contents into your Movie Maker collection before you can use the Movie Maker Creativity Fun Pack content in your movies.

The Movie Maker Creativity Fun Pack sound effects provide several music effects that you can place in your movie. You will place these on the timeline's Audio/Music track so that the sound effect occurs at the appropriate location in your movie. The Movie Maker Creativity Fun Pack includes sound effects from the following categories:

- Animal sound effects
- Fun random sounds
- Graduation sound effects
- Party sound effects
- Sports

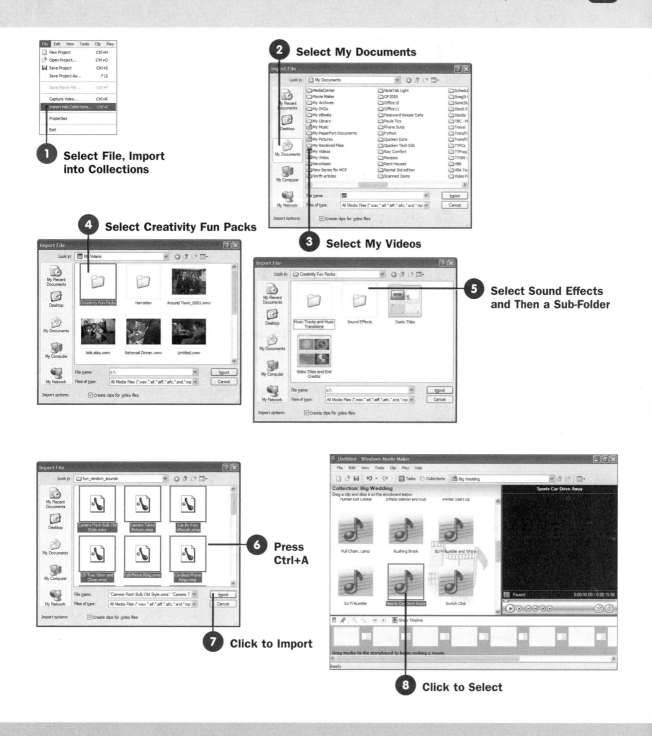

1 Select File, Import into Collections

2 Select My Documents

3 Select My Videos

4 Select Creativity Fun Packs

5 Select Sound Effects and Then a Sub-Folder

6 Press Ctrl+A

7 Click to Import

8 Click to Select

TIP

If you have already imported the Movie Maker Creativity Fun Pack content into Movie Maker, you can skip to step 8 to preview the sound effects that you can place in your movies.

NOTE

After you import the sound effects into your collection, you can drag any of them to the timeline's Audio/Music track at the location in your movie where you want the sound effect to start (see **55** Add Sound Effects to Your Movie).

NOTE

You can repeat steps 1 through 8 to import the sound effects in the other folders within the **Sound Effects** folder.

NOTE

You might have to scroll your collection down to see the **Sports Car Drive Away** sound effect.

1 Select File, Import into Collections

You must import the Movie Maker Creativity Fun Pack sound effects into Movie Maker before you can use the sound effects. Select **Import into Collections** from the **File** menu.

2 Select My Documents

Select the **My Documents** folder to begin browsing to the Movie Maker Creativity Fun Pack content.

3 Select My Videos

Select to open the **My Videos** folder.

4 Select Creativity Fun Packs

Select to open the **Creativity Fun Packs** folder.

5 Select Sound Effects and then a Sub-Folder

Select to open the folder named **Sound Effects**, then open a folder within **Sound Effects** such as **Fun random sounds**. The individual sound effects in that folder will appear.

6 Press Ctrl+A

Press **Ctrl+A** to select all the sound effects in the **Fun random sounds** folder.

7 Click to Import

Click the **Import** button to import the music tracks and music transitions into Movie Maker. You might have to wait a few seconds for the sound effects to load.

8 Click to Select

Click to select the sound effect named **Sports Car Drive Away**. After you select the sound effect, you can click the **Play** button on the **Monitor** pane to review the effect.

13

Enjoying Microsoft Plus! Digital Media Edition

IN THIS CHAPTER:

Anyone who works with digital media should consider obtaining Microsoft's *Microsoft Plus! Digital Media Edition* (*DME*). Movie Maker users are strongly encouraged to use the DME, and many do. This product provides new ways to work with your media, and Movie Maker users aren't the only ones who can benefit from the product.

TIP

Movie Maker (beginning with version 2) is a surprisingly powerful video editing and creation program, as the tasks throughout this book demonstrate. The Microsoft Plus! Digital Media Edition is not a requirement for Movie Maker users, and it does not fill in gaping holes left out of Movie Maker's feature set. However, the DME is a value-added program that increases the power of Movie Maker.

Microsoft Plus! Digital Media Edition offers new ways to work with all of the following:

- Digital photos
- Digital music
- Digital video

Given that Movie Maker supports the integration of all three of these digital media formats, the DME is extremely useful for the Movie Maker user.

The DME retails for less than $20, so it is affordable if you want to accent the movies you make. This chapter explores ways that you can use the DME to improve your videos.

100 Install Microsoft Plus! Digital Media Edition (DME)

Before You Begin

✔ **93** About the Movie Maker Creativity Fun Pack

See Also

→ **101** Add DME Transitions to Your Movies

→ **102** Add DME Special Effects to Your Movies

The Microsoft Plus! Digital Media Edition increases the amount of things you can do with your multimedia work. Consider some of these benefits you get when you obtain the DME:

- **Photos**—Add narration, music, and photo effects before you share your digital photos with others. Movie Maker users can use the photos inside their movies.

- **Music**—Enjoy a music jukebox that plays your digital music. You can also use the DME to record old LPs and cassettes to digital music so you can use them for your movie soundtracks.

- **Movies**—The DME adds 50 new transitions and special video effects to Movie Maker.

- **Portable devices**—Use the DME to download the latest news and music to your PocketPC device. Including the Movie Maker movies you make for your PocketPC, the DME enables you to take your entire entertainment system with you when you're on the go.

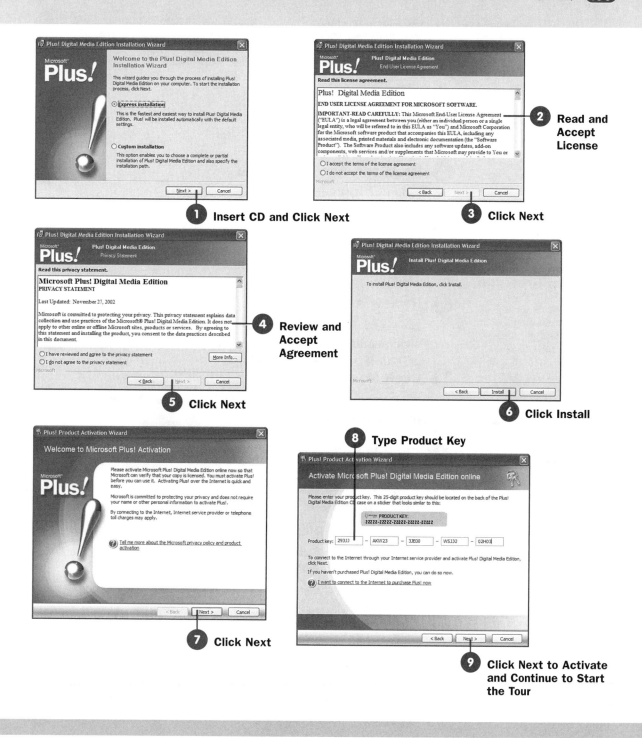

Read and Accept License 2

Insert CD and Click Next 1

Click Next 3

Review and Accept Agreement 4

Click Next 5

Click Install 6

Type Product Key 8

Click Next 7

Click Next to Activate and Continue to Start the Tour 9

CHAPTER 13: Enjoying Microsoft Plus! Digital Media Edition

259

It's obvious how the new movie special effects and transitions will help Movie Maker users, but the other benefits are available as well.

1 Insert CD and Click Next

Insert the DME CD in your CD drive. Click **Next** to start the installation routine.

2 Read and Accept License

Read the legal license (if you're so inclined!) that appears.

3 Click Next

Click **Next** to move from the license dialog box to the privacy agreement.

4 Review and Accept Agreement

Read the DME privacy agreement and click to indicate that you've reviewed the agreement.

5 Click Next

Click **Next** to move from the privacy agreement to continue with the installation routine.

6 Click Install

Click the **Install** button to begin the installation.

7 Click Next

Click **Next** to activate your DME.

NOTE

You'll need an online connection for the activation. Also, grab the DME's box, because you'll need to type the product key that appears on the back of the box.

8 Type Product Key

Type the product key found on the back of the DME CD box.

9 Click Next to Activate and Continue to Start the Tour

Click the **Next** button to activate your copy of the DME. Click **Next** once again to move from the activation dialog box to the end of the installation routine. If you want to view a tour of the Microsoft Plus! Digital Media Edition, click the **Finish** button to start the tour.

101 Add DME Transitions to Your Movies

The Microsoft Plus! Digital Media Edition adds 25 new transitions to Movie Maker. The transitions are rather more creative than the ones supplied with Movie Maker. Some have *fizzle*, *organic*, and *rip* in their names, if that tells you anything about how wild they can get.

Unlike the Movie Maker Creativity Fun Pack's titles and end credits (**see 95** Use the Fun Pack's Titles and **96** Use the Fun Pack's End Credits), when you install the DME, the new transitions go right into Movie Maker and are ready to use the next time you start Movie Maker. You do not have to import them to use them.

 Select Tools, Options

Adjust the default video transition duration if you want by selecting **Options** from the **Tools** menu.

 Click Advanced

Click the **Advanced** tab to display the **Default durations** page.

3 **Adjust Default Duration**

Click the up or down arrows next to the **Transition duration** value to increase or decrease the default time value of the transition effect.

4 **Click OK**

Click **OK** to close the **Options** dialog box.

 Click Show Storyboard

You can more easily see DME transitions from the storyboard even though the timeline has its own Transition track. The timeline's tracks can get squeezed if you have zoomed out too far. To add a transition, you might see its effect better by working from the storyboard. Therefore, click the **Show Storyboard** button to change from the timeline to the storyboard if your movie's timeline is showing.

Before You Begin

✔ **100** Install Microsoft Plus! Digital Media Edition (DME)

See Also

→ **102** Add DME Special Effects to Your Movies

 **TIP**

Unless your movie is a parody or trying to be over-the-top with transitions and effects, don't overdo your transitions between clips. Most of the DME transitions are extravagant, and you should use caution when considering them so you don't make the effect more important than the message. Having said that, the DME transitions certainly have their place, and you will find many uses for these eclectic set of wipes.

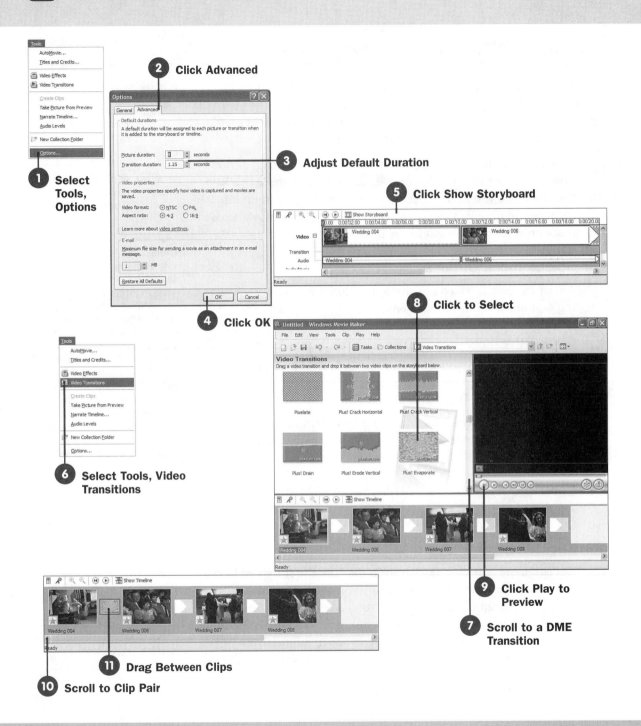

2 Click Advanced

3 Adjust Default Duration

1 Select Tools, Options

5 Click Show Storyboard

4 Click OK

8 Click to Select

6 Select Tools, Video Transitions

9 Click Play to Preview

7 Scroll to a DME Transition

11 Drag Between Clips

10 Scroll to Clip Pair

Select Tools, Video Transitions

Display the video transitions by selecting **Video Transitions** from the **Tools** menu.

 Scroll to a DME Transition

Click the **Contents** pane's scrollbar to review all the available transitions. Scroll down until you see the **Plus!** transitions. From cracks and drains to stars, you'll find a gamut of transitions that greatly accent the transitions you had before installing the DME.

 Click to Select

Click one of the DME transitions to select it. Its thumbnail appears in the **Monitor** pane.

 Click Play to Preview

Click the **Monitor** pane's **Play** button to see a preview of the transition.

TIP

Double-click any transition in your **Contents** pane to see a preview of that transition effect in the **Monitor** pane.

Scroll to Clip Pair

Scroll to the pair of clips between which you want to insert the DME transition.

Drag Between Clips

Drag the transition to the space between two clips on the storyboard.

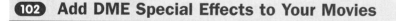

102 Add DME Special Effects to Your Movies

The Microsoft Plus! Digital Media Edition adds 25 new special effects to Movie Maker. The special effects are rather more creative than the ones supplied with Movie Maker. Words such as *wild* and *wildest* appear in their titles, if that tells you anything about how rowdy they can get.

You can turn a plain movie into one laden with special effects with just a few mouse clicks and drags.

Before You Begin

✔ **100** Install Microsoft Plus! Digital Media Edition (DME)

✔ **101** Add DME Transitions to Your Movies

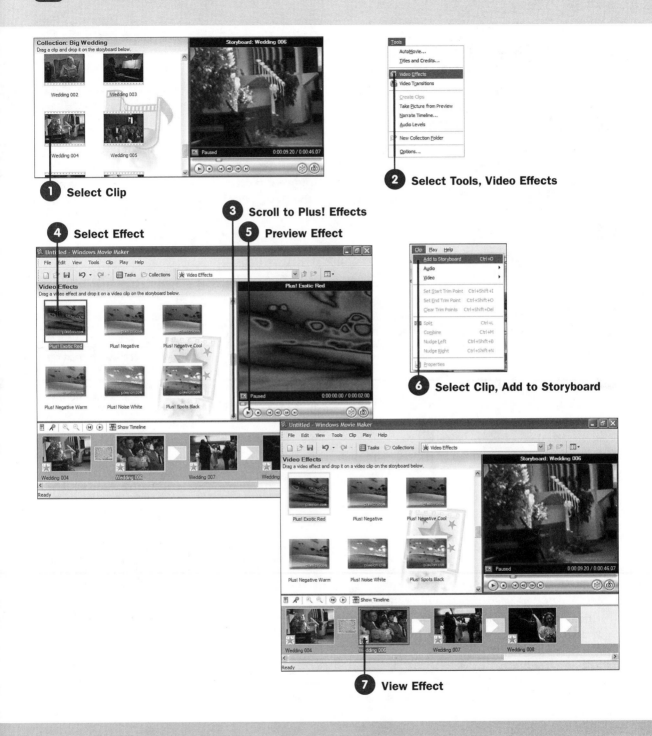

1 Select Clip

2 Select Tools, Video Effects

3 Scroll to Plus! Effects

4 Select Effect

5 Preview Effect

6 Select Clip, Add to Storyboard

7 View Effect

Select **Tools, Video Effects** and scroll toward the bottom of the effects to see the DME effects now available to you. As this task's steps demonstrate, you can select any DME special effect to preview, in your **Monitor** pane, what that effect produces.

Keep in mind that you can apply Movie Maker's special effects, both the regular ones and the DME effects, to all kinds of clips:

- Video clips
- Still picture clips
- Titles and credits

When you apply a special effect to a clip, the special effect appears on both clips if you split that clip into two clips. If you combine two clips, the combined clip takes on the special effects of the first clip. Movie Maker indicates that a special effect applies to a clip by putting a square icon in the clip's thumbnail with a blue star inside the box.

 Select Clip

Click to select the clip on which you want to apply one of the DME's special effects.

 Select Tools, Video Effects

You can display all available special effects in the **Contents** pane by selecting **Video Effects** from the **Tools** menu.

3 **Scroll to Plus! Effects**

Click to select one of the DME's special video effects. All of DME's video effects begin with **Plus!** in their names.

4 **Select Effect**

Click to select one of the DME's special effects. A thumbnail image of the effect will appear in your **Monitor** pane.

5 **Preview Effect**

Click to select one of the DME's special effects. A thumbnail image of the effect will appear in your **Monitor** pane.

NOTE

Special effects are called *video effects* in Movie Maker, although most Movie Maker users still call them special effects.

KEY TERM

Video effects—Movie Maker's term for special effects you add to change the way a clip or movie plays back.

6 **Select Clip, Add to Storyboard**

To apply the effect, select **Add to Timeline** from the **Clip** menu. A boxed icon with a blue star inside appears on the timeline's clip, indicating that a video effect is attached to that clip. If you rest your mouse pointer over the clip's effect icon, the name of the effect you applied to that clip will show.

7 **View Effect**

Double-click the clip that contains the special effect you just added. The **Monitor** pane will show the effect. Enjoy!

About Recording from LP Albums

Before You Begin

✔ **100** Install Microsoft Plus! Digital Media Edition (DME)

See Also

→ **104** Use DME to Capture Music from Old LP Albums

NOTE

The following warning should come as no surprise: Be sure not to use music from record albums in any commercial movie that you make. Using your own LP albums for background songs in your videos won't bother music execs, despite their current excitement about copyright infringements. Just be sure that you own the records, and only use the music for noncommercial videos you make for your family and friends.

Back around the days of Noah, people used to listen to music on vinyl record albums called *long-play albums*, or *LPs*. Compact discs (CDs) had not yet been invented. Millions of those records still line people's attics and flea market shelves. An entire LP fan base has caused somewhat of a rejuvenation of interest in LPs because of their unique sound quality, which today's CDs mask as a result of their high fidelity. It seems the sound of the phonograph needle hitting the record and the background hum that occurs during playback produces a nostalgic sound, and some vinyl albums now command high dollar figures.

How can the presence of LP albums that still abound help you as a movie producer?

Chances are, if you have some of these albums, you probably have not yet replaced all of them with CDs. Yet, you might want to use many of the tunes from these albums as backgrounds in your videos—it makes sense to capture their contents.

LP record albums are not digital like audio CDs. Therefore, you cannot simply transfer their contents, without quality loss, to your computer and play them there. One way to transfer music from your albums to your computer is to record them with a microphone connected to your computer's sound card, but obviously a direct connection would be better.

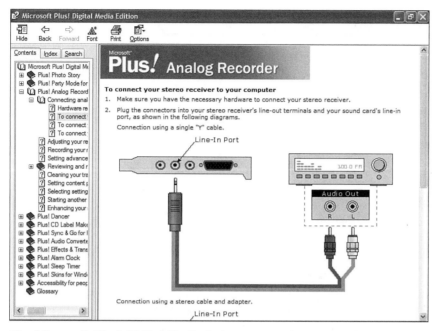

The Microsoft Plus! Digital Media help screens show you how to connect your phonograph to your computer through your stereo system.

If you still own a turntable, connect it to your stereo. If you don't have a turntable, you'll have to borrow one because it's the only way you can play your albums. The sound from a turntable is not strong enough for your computer's sound card's line-in jack to sense. Therefore, you will need to run the turntable through your stereo and then connect your stereo's output jacks to your computer's sound card.

The Microsoft Plus! Digital Media Edition includes the *Analog Recorder* program. With Analog Recorder, after you hook up your turntable to your computer's sound card, you can easily record your records' tracks (see **104** **Use DME to Capture Music from Old LP Albums**). The Analog Recorder includes special filters that reduce the pops and hisses normally associated with LPs and that enable you to divide your recorded LPs into individual tracks, even if you record whole sides of an album at one time.

So, if you have some of those old big band albums from the 40s and 50s that would work well in your movies, the DME comes to the rescue.

 NOTE

Your stereo volume level will probably not match those of your sound card's line-in jack at first. When you first begin recording, the DME provides a way to adjust the volume level.

TIP

Analog Recorder also records from tape recordings that you might want to put onto your computer. As with LPs, Analog Recorder can help improve the sound quality of those tapes as you save their content to your computer system.

104 Use DME to Capture Music from Old LP Albums

Before You Begin

✔ **100** Install Microsoft Plus! Digital Music Edition (DME)

✔ **103** About Recording from LP Albums

NOTE

If Analog Recorder did not break apart your LP recordings into individual tracks, you would have to start and stop your recording at each track on your LP. Recording an album is much faster and requires less effort if you can record a complete side and let Analog Recorder break the side into the LP's separate tracks.

NOTE

A **Welcome Page** dialog box may or may not first appear when you start Plus! Analog Recorder. On this **Welcome Page**, you can get additional information about Plus! Analog Recorder, such as how to connect devices to your sound card and how to improve your recordings. You can click the option labeled **Do not show this welcome page again** if you want subsequent starts to bypass this dialog box.

Blow the dust off your LP albums, connect that old turntable to your stereo, and get ready to transfer that music you haven't heard in years to your computer. With Microsoft Plus! Digital Media Edition's Analog Recorder program, recording your LP albums (and audio cassettes) so you can use their content in movies is simple to do.

One of the benefits that the Analog Recorder offers is that the program will clean your record's contents before saving the music to your computer. The usual hisses and pops virtually disappear when Analog Recorder uses its filters to clean the sound it records. In addition, the Analog Recorder lets you record an entire side of an LP album, and can automatically break apart the tracks into separate recordings.

❶ Start Plus! Analog Recorder

Click your Windows **Start** button and select the **All Programs** option. Select the **Start** menu's **Microsoft Plus! Digital Media Edition** option to display the DME's programs. Start the Analog Recorder by selecting the **Plus! Analog Recorder** option.

❷ Select Sound Card

In most cases, your sound card is displayed in the list labeled **Sound Device**. If not, select your primary sound card from the list.

❸ Select Line In

Select **Line In** from the list labeled **Input channel**.

❹ Click to Start Sound Test

You must ensure that the volume coming from your stereo is compatible with the volume levels of your computer for a proper recording to be made. Therefore, start a rather loud track selected on your turntable and click the **Start** button—the Analog Recorder will detect and set proper sound levels. The test might take a few seconds. When the dialog box displays the message **Detected acceptable levels**, Analog Recorder will have adjusted the sound levels properly and you can continue.

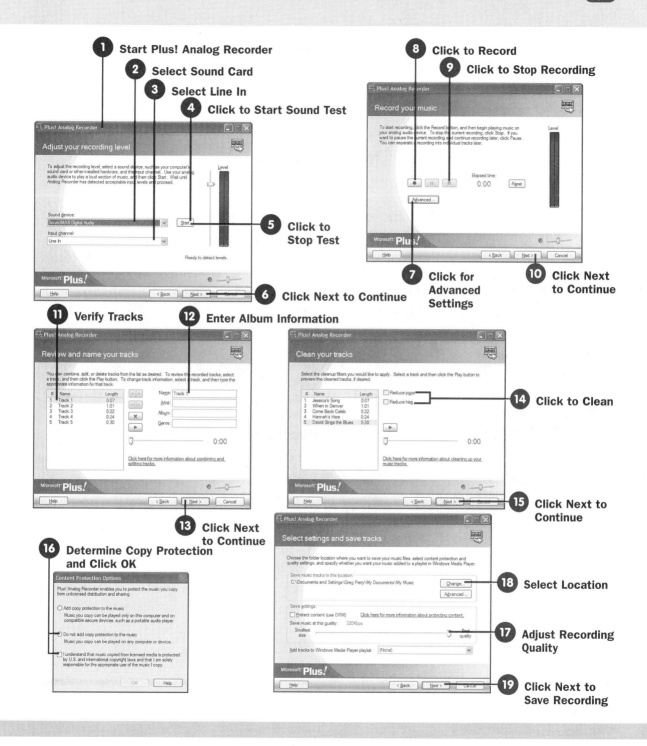

5 **Click to Stop Test**

If you want to stop the volume level test early, click the **Stop** button. Generally, you should *not* stop the test because Analog Recorder can adjust the sound levels if you let the test continue until Analog Recorder stops on its own.

6 **Click Next to Continue**

Click the **Next** button to continue the recording process.

7 **Click for Advanced Settings**

Click the **Advanced** button to indicate whether you want Analog Recorder to break the recording into multiple tracks and other options. If you do adjust the advanced settings, be sure to click **Close** to save your advanced settings and close the advanced options dialog box to return to the Analog Recorder dialog box.

TIP

Normally, you will want Analog Recorder to split your recording into multiple tracks. This puts each song on your record album into a separate recording instead of lumping them all into one long recording on your computer.

8 **Click to Record**

Click the red **Record** button to start the recording. You can now begin playing your record album and Analog Recorder will record it.

9 **Click to Stop Recording**

At the end of the first side, or whenever you want to stop the recording, click the **Stop** button.

NOTE

If you don't want to monitor the recording, you can enter a maximum recording time and Analog Recorder will stop recording at the end of that time period. Use the **Advanced Settings** option to set this option. If you do not enter a maximum time, the recording will continue until you click **Stop**, and if you get sidetracked and let the recording continue unabated, you could fill your entire hard disk with the recording.

10 **Click Next to Continue**

Click the **Next** button to continue.

11 **Verify Tracks**

You now can verify that the tracks were recorded properly by clicking on them individually and pressing **Play** to listen to the track.

12 **Enter Album Information**

You can name the album and artist by filling in the fields at the right of the dialog box. Click on each track and type **Name**, **Artist**, **Album**, and **Genre** information in the fields provided.

Click Next to Continue

After you've entered the track information, click the **Next** button to continue the recording process.

 TIP

You only need to enter the **Artist**, **Album**, and **Genre** field information for one track. Analog Recorder will copy that information to the other tracks. All you need to do for each subsequent track is enter the **Name** information. As you type a **Name**, the name appears in the left column for each track you've recorded.

 Click to Clean

You now can reduce the recording's hisses and pops that may have been recorded by clicking the **Reduce pops** and **Reduce hiss** options.

 Click Next to Continue

Click the **Next** button to select a folder in which to save the recordings.

 Determine Copy Protection and Click OK

Click the **Protect content** option if you want to indicate that your recording is copyright protected. Click the **OK** button to continue.

 Adjust Recording Quality

Drag the slider left or right to adjust the amount of disk space consumed for the recorded tracks. The more disk space you allot, the better the recording.

Select Location

If you want to change the location where Analog Recorder saves your tracks, select a new disk folder by clicking the **Change** button and selecting a new location.

Click Next to Save Recording

Click the **Next** button to begin saving the recorded tracks to your disk drive. The process might take a few minutes. Close the dialog box by clicking the **Finish** button to end the process.

 TIP

If you want to record another album (or the second side of this album), click the option labeled **Start another recording**.

105 Create Labels for Your CDs and DVDs with DME

Before You Begin

✔ **100** Install Microsoft Plus! Digital Media Edition (DME)

 TIP

You need to purchase specialized adhesive paper for your labels. The Plus! CD Label Maker creates inserts for CD and DVD cases and prints lists such as the album's contents on those inserts. You can use plain paper for the inserts, but you need CD and DVD-ready adhesive labels for the CD and DVD labels you create. Record your CD or DVD before attaching the label, because many burners won't correctly write to a disc with a label.

 **KEY TERM**

Playlist—A list of tracks used by Windows Media Player and other programs to keep track of the album name, artist, and track information for recordings on your computer.

When you produce movies and save them on CDs and DVDs, you can write the title on each CD or DVD with a felt-tipped marker, but that looks cheap. Instead, use the Microsoft Plus! Digital Media Edition to create labels for your CDs and DVDs that contain the movie title, your name as producer, and eye-catching graphics.

The Plus! CD Label Maker is a program that comes with the DME enabling you to design and print labels. The CDs or DVDs will play perfectly with these labels, and you can easily print the labels on your printer. This task demonstrates an overview of what you will do to create customized labels for your CDs and DVDs. You can create extremely fancy labels if you dive into all the program's features.

The movies you create have pizzazz, so why shouldn't the labels on your CDs and DVDs?

❶ Start Plus! CD Label Maker

Start Plus! CD Label Maker by opening its program on your Windows **Start** menu's **Programs, Microsoft Plus! Digital Media Edition** option.

❷ Click Next to Continue

Click the **Next** button to begin creating your labels.

❸ Insert CD or Choose Playlist

Insert an audio CD, and Plus! CD Label Maker will load the tracks from the CD that you can select. Alternatively, you can locate a Windows Media Player *playlist* residing on your computer and use that as the basis for your label.

❹ Click Next to Continue

Click the **Next** button after you select a CD or playlist to move to the label selection dialog box.

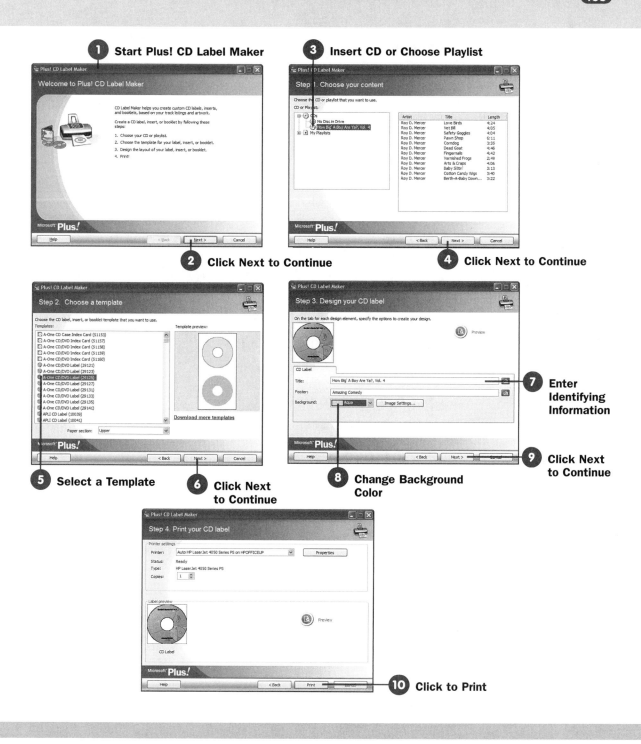

1 Start Plus! CD Label Maker

2 Click Next to Continue

3 Insert CD or Choose Playlist

4 Click Next to Continue

5 Select a Template

6 Click Next to Continue

7 Enter Identifying Information

8 Change Background Color

9 Click Next to Continue

10 Click to Print

Select a Template

Click a template that matches the item you want to print. For example, if you're printing labels that you would apply directly to a CD or DVD, choose a template such as **A-One CD/DVD Label**. If you want to print an insert for the CD's case, select a template such as **A-One CD/DVD Index Card**.

 Click Next to Continue

After you select a template, click the **Next** button to see a preview of your selection.

7 **Enter Identifying Information**

If Plus! CD Label Maker has not already filled in the fields for you, type the **Title** and **Footer** field information. These names will appear on the CD or DVD to which you attach the label.

8 **Change Background Color**

Select a new background color.

 TIP

If you click the **Image Settings** button, a display box appears where you can adjust the graphics on your label or CD/DVD case insert.

 Click Next to Continue

Click the **Next** button to print your label or insert.

10 **Click to Print**

Put your labels or paper in your printer and click the **Print** button to begin the printing. Once printed, if the label meets your satisfaction, apply the label to your CD or DVD. Now your movie really stands out from your other CDs and DVDs.

14

Taking Digital Editing to the Next Step

IN THIS CHAPTER:

TIP

Keep honing your video skills to build on what you have learned throughout these tasks. Lots of great video-editing sites contain forums in which videographers share tips and techniques, such as the Digital Video Editing site at http://www.digital videoediting.com/.

The early chapters of this book show you how to shoot quality videos using your digital (or analog) video camera. By mastering the tasks, you will shoot better video than the majority of all the camera owners in the world. Although this might sound like a far-fetched claim, keep in mind that today's advanced technology combined with low prices puts video cameras in the hands of hundreds of thousands of amateur digital photographers. It's wonderful that this technology is available to so many, but the advanced technology does not replace the need for fundamental camera techniques. Software such as Movie Maker enables videographers to compile and produce the movies they make. In spite of its price (free with Windows XP), Movie Maker provides the beginning filmmaker with enough tools to handle beginning and intermediate tasks.

The Web contains massive amounts of material you can use to hone your digital movie shooting and editing skills.

You can go further with your video productions than Movie Maker allows. To take your video-editing skills further, you'll have to get additional software.

The purpose of this chapter is to show you some of the software available to you if you want to step up your editing skills.

106 About Advanced Movie Production Software

This chapter gives you a taste of the more advanced tools available to you as a digital videographer. These programs pick up where Movie Maker leaves off by giving you professional-level DVD production, and some offer truly advanced video editing features that you'll want to add to your repertoire as you take the next step into movie production mastery.

By performing the tasks that appear in the rest of this book, you'll gain insight into these advanced programs, their primary strengths, and their most useful features:

- Roxio's VideoWave Movie Creator

- Roxio's Easy CD & DVD Creator

- Ahead's Nero Ultra Edition

- Adobe's Premiere Pro

Unlike Movie Maker, none of these programs are free. Given their cost (Adobe Premiere Pro can cost several hundred dollars, although the others are priced under $100), you can expect that they will deliver far more power than Movie Maker. For example, some like to have Roxio's Easy CD & DVD Creator on hand to produce DVDs with complete menu systems and specialized backgrounds and features. Both Easy CD & DVD Creator and Nero Ultra also produce CDs with MP3 audio music on them and provide backup capabilities for your system.

None of these programs is a do-it-all for every videographer. Also, other products compete with these, and some prefer the competition. Video-editing software comes in such a variety of styles for all the variety of videographers out there who want different things.

Read and follow any of the following tasks with the idea in mind that you might want to graduate to one or more of these or similar programs after you take Movie Maker to its limits and decide that you want to step up your video-production skills several notches.

Before You Begin

✔ **1** About Digital Video Production

✔ **84** About Sharing Video with Others

See Also

→ **107** Edit Movies with VideoWave

→ **108** Produce DVDs with CD & DVD Creator

→ **109** Capture, Edit, and Produce with Nero

→ **110** About Editing Professionally with Adobe Premiere Pro

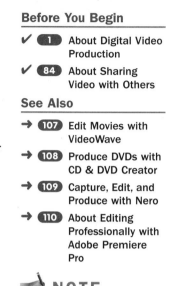

⬛ NOTE

These tasks introduce you to powerful video-editing programs and their features. You won't gain an in-depth mastery of them as you can do here with Movie Maker, but you will gain a much greater understanding of what's ahead as your skills progress.

💡 TIP

Screenshots and trial versions of these programs are often available at their manufacturer's Web sites: **http://www.roxio.com**, **http://www.nero.com**, and **http://www.adobe.com**.

NOTE

These tasks aren't intended to give free commercials for this software. The author finds that each of these advanced programs fills a need when you want to step up your video skills. You'll appreciate the overview of features that await you in such programs.

Free trial version

You can often download a free trial version of advanced video-editing software such as VideoWave Movie Creator on the Roxio Web site.

107 Edit Movies with VideoWave

Before You Begin

✔ **106** About Advanced Movie Production Software

See Also

→ **108** Produce DVDs with CD & DVD Creator

Roxio makes the VideoWave Movie Creator, a software program that enables you to turn raw video footage into an edited movie. You can capture the video directly from your digital video camera or from a capture card. Some video-editing software, especially Adobe Premiere Pro, is especially sensitive to your hardware, and might require a capture card before installing. You can add a soundtrack to the movie as well as trim clips, add transitions, titles, and credits. Of course, Movie Maker does this as well, but VideoWave Movie Creator adds several features that Movie Maker does not support.

VideoWave includes advanced features, such as style *templates*, that many find useful when editing video:

- Embossed and 3D special effects and graphic titles and overlay text enhance your productions.

- A drag-and-drop interface to video CD or DVD makes creating and sharing movies simple.

- DVD and CD menu templates enable you to quickly design a theme around the video you produce.

- StoryBuilder's guided editing feature enables you to select from introductory and ending templates that ensure your titles, credits, and special effects work well together.

- The Storyline editor allows you to fine-tune details such as your movie's brightness, contrast settings, and add and modify advanced special effects such as the rippling of clips (as though reflected from water).

- DVD Authoring enables you to select from a wide assortment of DVD menus that a video DVD player can access.

- Movie templates for all occasions let you create holiday, anniversary, graduation, and other videos with themes.

Think of VideoWave as Movie Maker's older brother. If you want more freedom and special effects than Movie Maker provides, even with the Movie Maker Creativity Fun Pack and Plus! Digital Media Edition, you should consider making the upgrade to VideoWave. Other programs such as Nero (see **109** **Capture, Edit, and Produce with Nero**) and Premiere Pro (see **110** **About Editing Professionally with Adobe Premiere Pro**) also add more elements than Movie Maker can provide, but they require a steeper learning curve than VideoWave for the advanced features.

 1 Capture Video

Capture your video from your graphics card or through a FireWire-cabled connection to your digital video camera. You can also import video and audio from files you've already created, including Movie Maker videos you've saved in the Windows Media Player format.

 NOTE

Each of the products described in this chapter overlaps in some of their feature sets. Some even overlap Movie Maker's features, although the others add more powerful editing and production tools that you don't get with Movie Maker alone.

KEY TERM

Templates—Predesigned StoryBuilder models that contain graphics and special effects you can select that create consistent tones for your various movies.

NOTE

You've seen DVD menus if you've ever played a DVD and selected the extra features found on most of them such as deleted scenes, director's commentary, and actor biographies.

TIP

A huge VideoWave advantage for Movie Maker users is that VideoWave can import movies saved in the Windows Media Player format, whereas the other products in this chapter cannot. Therefore, you can import a Movie Maker movie created earlier into VideoWave and apply VideoWave's more advanced special editing features to your production.

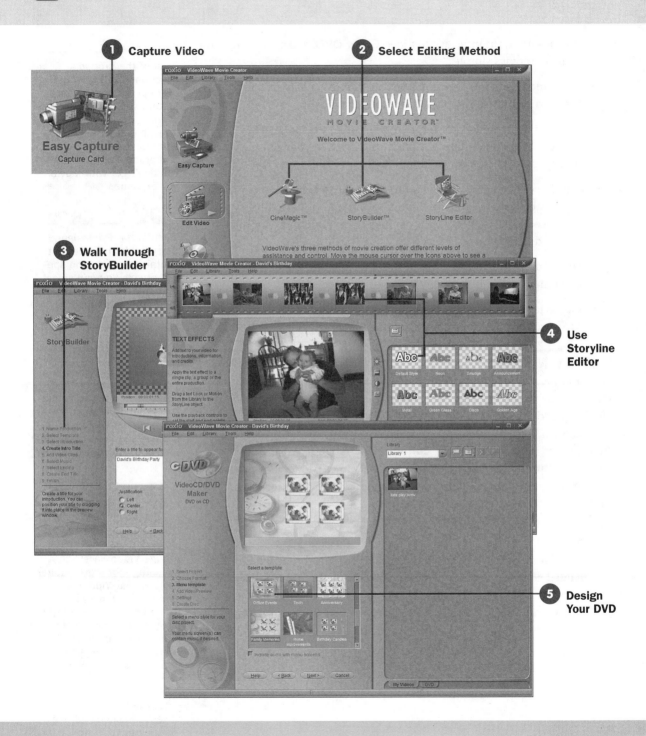

1 Capture Video

Easy Capture
Capture Card

2 Select Editing Method

3 Walk Through StoryBuilder

4 Use Storyline Editor

5 Design Your DVD

2 Select Editing Method

VideoWave provides three tools you can select from to edit your video. Select an editing method you want to use for your video. You can use the **CineMagic** tool, which works very much like Movie Maker's **AutoMovie** tool. Just select the **CineMagic** option and VideoWave creates a movie from your video and soundtrack. The **StoryBuilder** option provides a menu that walks you through your video's creation, and the **StoryLine** editor offers a more detailed timeline approach to video editing.

NOTE

Only use **CineMagic** for video that has a music soundtrack. If your video has narration or conversation, **CineMagic** might edit out part of the speaker's voice.

3 Walk Through StoryBuilder

StoryBuilder (assuming you didn't want to use **CineMagic** to create a final movie) offers a menu on the left side of the screen with options that range from naming your production to creating an end title. The process is much more sequential than Movie Maker's because **StoryBuilder** takes you step by step, in order, as you select options and click the **Next** button. For example, after you select a template style for your movie (such as a birthday style), **StoryBuilder** asks you for the introductory titles. VideoWave's 3D and embossed text styles provide far more options for text than Movie Maker provides (**see 63 Add Titles to Your AutoMovie**).

NOTE

The two biggest advantages that VideoWave offers over Movie Maker are its rich assortment of special text effects (like 3D) and the built-in DVD design that features direct burning from within the program.

4 Use Storyline Editor

If you use VideoWave's **Storyline Editor** (either after you create a movie with **CineMagic** or **StoryBuilder** or without using either of those tools first), you can use **Storyline Editor** to edit your movie in detail using a timeline format. You can edit every aspect of your movie's video or audio, and even select from a wide variety of text styles for your titles and credits.

TIP

After you master VideoWave, you can upgrade to the VideoWave Power Edition and get even more special effects, such as picture-in-a-picture (PIP), where you watch one video in full-screen and a second in a small window, video production for streaming over the Internet, and advanced filtering that provides the same camera effects found in expensive Hollywood cameras.

5 Design Your DVD

After you've created your movie, you can send that movie straight to a DVD or movie on CD within VideoWave. You can design every element of your DVD, including the opening DVD's background picture and the menu used to select different content on the DVD. VideoWave offers a preview of your entire DVD menu and content so you can ensure that your DVD will contain exactly what you want before burning the disc.

108 Produce DVDs with CD & DVD Creator

Before You Begin

✔ **92** About Putting
Movies on DVD

✔ **106** About Advanced
Movie Production
Software

NOTE

Roxio's CD & DVD Creator
cannot use Windows Media
Player files as source files
for DVDs and video CDs.
Therefore, if you want to
transfer Movie Maker
movies to DVD or video CD
using CD & DVD Creator,
you must save your Movie
Maker file in the digital
video AVI format.

If you want the very best tool for a specific job, you should use a tool designed for that job and nothing else. Roxio's CD & DVD Creator is perhaps one of the best applications for creating DVDs and CDs. The blend of simplicity and power can't be beat. Although CD & DVD Creator has no video-editing features, most video editors will want to have CD & DVD Creator on hand because of its wide assortment of DVD-related creation tools.

CD & DVD Creator contains a huge assortment of tools you can use for many areas of multimedia work. Even if you work exclusively in Movie Maker or a video-editing system as advanced as Adobe Premiere Pro (see **110** **About Editing Professionally with Adobe Premiere Pro**), Roxio's CD & DVD Creator can still help you with tools such as these:

- A media player that plays audio CDs and DVDs

- A ripper that rips music from your audio CDs to your computer's hard disk

- Digital photo tools that enable you to design and create printed picture albums, Web albums, and slideshows from your digital photos

- A DVD burner with transitions and animated menus

- Back-up tools back up your hard disks and other media onto CDs or DVDs

- A label maker enables you to design and create eye-catching labels for your CDs and DVDs

1 Start CD & DVD Creator

You can start CD & DVD Creator from your **Start** menu or by clicking the **Roxio Home** icon at the right of your Windows taskbar. When you start the program, you're greeted with a window showing you a list of categories from which you can choose.

TIP

If you also use Roxio's
VideoWave (see **107** Edit
Movies with VideoWave),
the CD & DVD Creator
startup menu lists
VideoWave as an option, so
you can access both pro-
grams from the same interface.

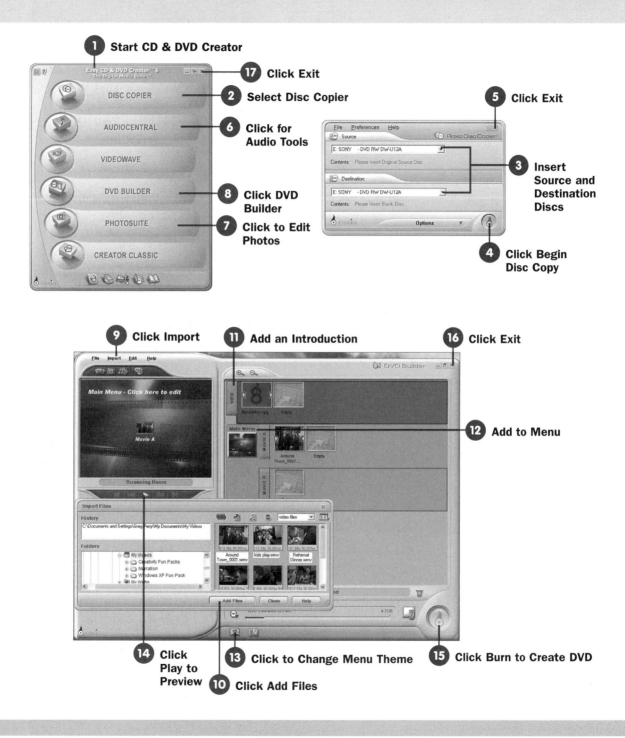

1 Start CD & DVD Creator

17 Click Exit

2 Select Disc Copier

5 Click Exit

6 Click for Audio Tools

3 Insert Source and Destination Discs

8 Click DVD Builder

7 Click to Edit Photos

4 Click Begin Disc Copy

9 Click Import

11 Add an Introduction

16 Click Exit

12 Add to Menu

14 Click Play to Preview

13 Click to Change Menu Theme

15 Click Burn to Create DVD

10 Click Add Files

NOTE

As you see, CD & DVD Creator provides numerous tools for you, the videographer, but provides no video editing tools.

2 **Select Disc Copier**

CD & DVD Creator is considered by many to be the fastest and most accurate copier software available. When you click to select the **Disc Copier** option, CD & DVD Creator displays a copyright notice informing you that you should only copy that for which you own the copyright and then begins the copy procedure.

3 **Insert Source and Destination Discs**

Insert the disc (CD or DVD) that you want to make a copy of in the source drive and put a blank disc in your writable drive. If you have only one drive, CD & DVD Creator will select it for both.

4 **Click Begin Disc Copy**

Click the **Begin Disc Copy** button and the duplication starts. After the copy process, you can copy the source onto another disc or return to the main CD & DVD Creator menu.

5 **Click Exit**

Click the **Exit** button to close the disc copying process and return to the primary CD & DVD Creator menu.

TIP

You can mix and edit audio with the **Audiocentral** tool, and use that audio in any other video production program, including Movie Maker (see **7** About Making Audio a Priority).

6 **Click for Audio Tools**

At CD & DVD Creator's main menu, you can select the **Audiocentral** option to mix and edit audio content that you'll later add to your movies.

7 **Click to Edit Photos**

At CD & DVD Creator's main menu, you can select the **Photosuite** option to edit photos that you might want to use as title and credit backgrounds, or in video scrapbooks you create on CDs and DVDs. Photosuite offers tools such as red-eye removal and sharpness adjustments, so you can correct defects in your pictures before sending them to your production.

8 **Click DVD Builder**

Start Roxio's DVD Builder application by clicking **DVD Builder**.

Click Import

Select from the **Import** menu to capture or (more likely) import a movie file into DVD Builder.

NOTE

Because you can only import video into DVD Builder and it provides no video-editing tools, you'll import the final video you've created in another program, such as Adobe Premiere Pro.

10 Click Add Files

Select the file (or files) you want to put on this DVD and click the **Add Files** button to send them to the DVD project.

11 Add an Introduction

When the user first puts a DVD into her player, the DVD plays any short introductory video you add to the Intro section. (Without an introduction, the DVD will go straight to your menu, or to the first movie if you do not set up a menu.)

12 Add to Menu

Notice the locations for Movie A and Movie B. If you add video to Movie B, a Movie C option will become available. The video content you add will not always be full movies—often you only add one movie. The other video content you add comprises the extra content you might want to put on your DVD, such as outtakes and bloopers.

TIP

Don't add an intro or secondary videos if you want your DVD to begin playing your video as soon as your audience inserts it into a DVD player.

13 Click to Change Menu Theme

Click the **Change Menu Theme** button at the bottom of your screen to change the menu background picture and title format. Various selectable holiday and event menu themes appear. You can change a theme as often as you want before burning the DVD until you find the one that best suits your video.

14 Click Play to Preview

As you add elements to your DVD, you can preview the DVD (including menus you add) by clicking the **Play** button.

15 Click Burn to Create DVD

After you build your DVD content the way you want it, insert a blank disc in your DVD-writable drive and click the **Burn** button in the lower right-hand corner of the screen. DVD Builder then creates your DVD.

16 **Click Exit**

Click the **Exit** button to return to the main menu.

17 **Click Exit**

Click the **Exit** button to exit CD & DVD Creator's menu.

109 Capture, Edit, and Produce with Nero

Before You Begin

✔ **92** About Putting Movies on DVD

✔ **106** About Advanced Movie Production Software

 NOTE

Although Nero is the most feature-packed software described in this book, Nero is not necessarily the best program for each specific job. CD & DVD Creator offers more options for burning media, and Premiere Pro provides far more advanced video-editing tools.

 NOTE

Nero offers an important tool that is surprisingly not found in most other video-editing software: a sound mixer and audio editor that allow you to combine audio from several sources (such as from a music sound-track, as well as a sound effects recording for your movie). You can combine the audio into one and edit it to filter unwanted noises and clean up other parts of the recordings as needed.

A debate rages among advanced digital videographers as to whether Adobe's Premiere Pro or Ahead's Nero is the better tool for the job. In a way, the debate is moot because Nero and Premiere Pro truly are two different products, although both are considered top performers.

Some feel that Nero takes many of the best features of Roxio's CD & DVD Creator (**see** **108** **Produce DVDs with CD & DVD Creator**), such as the label maker and CD/DVD burning tools, and combines them with the feature set of a video capture and editing program that rivals that of Adobe Premiere Pro (**see** **110** **About Editing Professionally with Adobe Premiere Pro**). Nero is certainly the most feature-packaged software on the market, with tools that you can begin using today and others that you'll grow into.

This task provides a glimpse into Nero's various features. Nero provides a free trial with all features available at **http://www.nero.com** if you want to see what all the fuss is about. You can follow this task and delve much more deeply into the product by downloading the trial version.

1 **Select Make Movie from StartSmart**

To have access to Nero's massive collection of tools, you need to begin with StartSmart, Nero's controller software that gives you access to Nero's many tools. Although you can start most of Nero's individual tools, such as the Nero Cover Design program with which you can create CD and DVD covers and case inserts, StartSmart works as a wrapper application that provides one-click links to the other tools. As you rest your mouse pointer over StartSmart's window pop-up, ToolTips appear describing each function that will start if you click on that icon. For example, when you click the **Favorites** category, one of the tasks available to you is called Make Movie. Click the **DVD** icon and then select **Make Movie** from the **Favorites** category to start Nero's movie-making application.

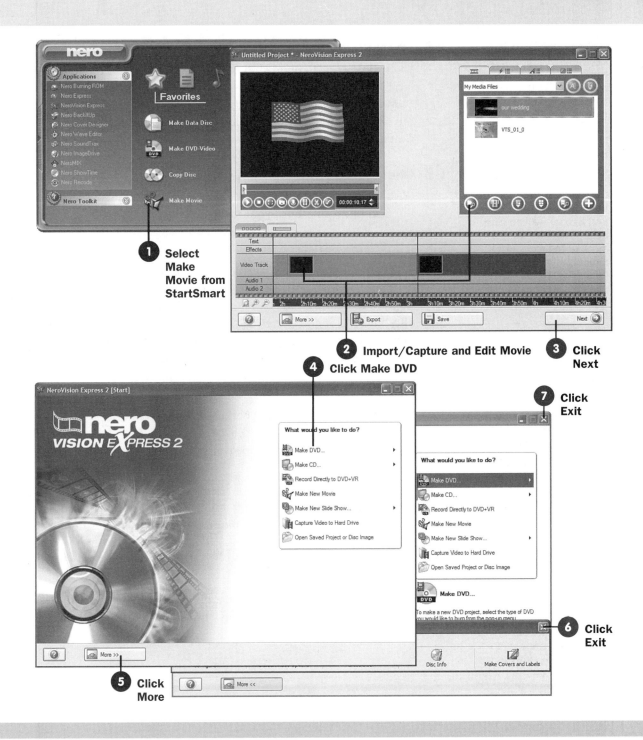

1 **Select Make Movie from StartSmart**

2 **Import/Capture and Edit Movie**

3 **Click Next**

4 **Click Make DVD**

5 **Click More**

6 **Click Exit**

7 **Click Exit**

NOTE

Click the DVD or CD icon in Nero's upper-right hand corner to see all the tools available for that kind of media. Nero's major tools appear by name down the left side of StartSmart, and these categories appear as icons across the right side of StartSmart: **Favorites, Data, Audio, Photo and Video, Copy and Backup**, and **Extras**. As you click each of the six categories, a list of related tasks appears beneath such as those related to DVD production, CD and label printing, and audio editing.

TIP

Note Nero's two audio tracks—they correspond to Movie Maker's Audio track and Audio/Music track.

NOTE

Remember, these tasks just give you a glimpse into the screens of the more advanced programs you might want to consider as your video-editing skills and needs grow.

TIP

Given Nero's everything-but-the-kitchen-sink-approach, if you want to be able to do a lot of things with your digital content, Nero is considered the most well-rounded program you can get. There's only room here to show you some video-production screen samples.

2 **Import/Capture and Edit Movie**

You will now spend quite a bit of time importing video (or capturing it) and editing your movie. Many of the tools are similar to Movie Maker's, except Nero calls transitions *wipes*. You will click the **Capture** button to start a video capture and edit using tools similar to Movie Maker's.

3 **Click Next**

Click the **Next** button after you've completed the movie to move to the next phase and burn your movie to DVD.

4 **Click Make DVD**

You can burn your movie to DVD, CD, or as a movie on a CD by clicking the **Make DVD** option. As you can see, Nero takes you right to the burning stage after you've completed your movie. You also have the option of creating another movie, writing the current movie elsewhere, or making a slideshow disc if you imported digital still images to the timeline when you created the movie.

5 **Click More**

Click the **More** button at the bottom of the screen to see more options. Notice you can make covers and labels for your movie's disc from the window that appears.

6 **Click Exit**

Click the **Exit** button to return to the StartSmart window where you can take advantage of the many other tools Nero has to offer, such as the sound mixer.

7 **Click Exit**

Click the **Exit** button on the StartSmart window to exit Nero if you've been taking this tour along with the task steps.

110 About Editing Professionally with Adobe Premiere Pro

Adobe Premiere Pro (also available as Premiere LE, a slimmed-down version that still contains plenty of power) is considered by most to be the very best video-editing software available for your computer today. Beginners often get lost amid Premiere Pro's tools, but as Uncle Ben once said, with great power comes great responsibility. Just about anything you want to do with digital video is possible with Premiere Pro, and the learning curve often rewards those who tackle the product.

Adobe's opening screen is a little misleading in its simplicity. When you start Premiere Pro, you often see only a **Project** window similar to Movie Maker's **Collections** pane (see **17** **About Collections, Contents, and Projects**), a monitor, and a timeline across the bottom of the screen. After you begin a project and begin selecting from Premiere Pro's menus and buttons, the power behind the opening interface becomes clear.

Before You Begin

✔ **106** About Advanced Movie Production Software

Project window

Monitor

Timeline

Premiere Pro's starting screen looks a lot like Movie Maker's simple and clean interface.

Premiere Pro offers the most power because of its wealth of features. Consider some of Premiere Pro's features:

- Real-time editing—As you import video, you can apply some edits at that time and speed up your editing sessions.

- DVD menu creation and customization—This feature permits direct-to-DVD burning of your movie's project files.

- Multiple and nestable timelines—By adding video and audio content to more than one timeline, you can more easily control transitions from scene to scene and produce special lead-in and overlapping effects not possible with a single storyboard and timeline.

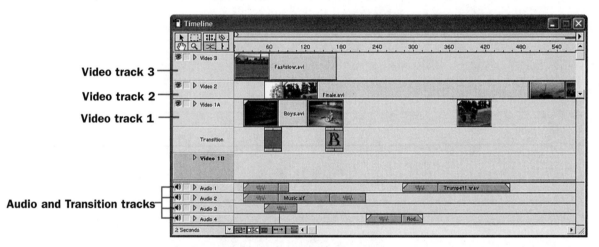

Premiere Pro's multiple timelines allow you to stack many video and audio clips on top of each other and adjust the fade-in and fade-out of each, as well as combine clips more easily.

You can preview each timeline's video in its own monitor pane.

- Massive assortment of filters and effects—Movies shot on video are often crisper and quieter than those shot on film. The difference is often like the difference between the sound of an audio CD and a tape playing. Yet, the makeup of a movie shot on film often gives a more wondrous and cinematic feel to a movie. With one click, you can make a movie shot on digital video appear as though you shot the entire movie on film.

- Built-in audio support with mixer—Wavelength displays show you visually what your audio sounds like, and you can make sound adjustments as well. Mix and edit your sound tracks directly from within Premiere Pro. You can immediately play back portions of your video to ensure you've edited the sound correctly.

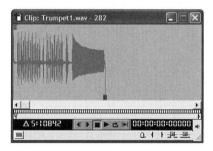

Manipulate your project's audio directly from within Premiere Pro.

- Advanced color correction—Premiere Pro's color-correction tools adjust hue, saturation, and lightness throughout your video or to selected areas of your video. If, for example, glare hits one of your subjects for a few seconds, you can often filter out that glare effect by adjusting the color and lightness of the scene.

TIP

Before moving up to Adobe's Premiere Pro, check Premiere Pro's Web site at **http://www. adobe.com** for Premiere Pro's system requirements to be sure your computer is powerful enough to work with Premiere Pro.

You can specify numerous project settings for your video, including the exact frame size and rate, both of which enable you to create a video in the exact resolution you need or your output device requires.

CHAPTER 14: Taking Digital Editing to the Next Step

Index

B

C

D

How can we make this index more useful? Email us at indexes@samspublishing.com

299

How can we make this index more useful? Email us at indexes@samspublishing.com

301

How can we make this index more useful? Email us at indexes@samspublishing.com

303

G-H-I

J-K-L

M

How can we make this index more useful? Email us at indexes@samspublishing.com

307

How can we make this index more useful? Email us at indexes@samspublishing.com

309

Q-R

S

How can we make this index more useful? Email us at indexes@samspublishing.com

315

T

W-X

Y-Z

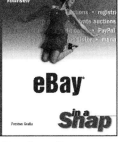

Key Terms

Don't let unfamiliar terms discourage you from learning all you can about digital video. If you don't completely understand what one of these words means, flip to the indicated page, read the full definition there, and find techniques related to that term.

Ambient noise   *Unwanted noise that can creep into your video, such as traffic, air conditioner motors, and echoes off walls, windows, and even your camera.*   135

Analog camera   *A camera that writes to film using continuous signals, requiring the analog signals to be decoded to digital signals before your computer can edit the video.*   6

Aperture setting   *The size of the opening that lets light through the lens.*   49

Audio track   *The audio imported or captured with your video.*   104

Audio/Music track   *Audio you add to your project after you import or capture video and the audio that goes with it.*   104

AutoMovie   *The Movie Maker feature that automatically creates a movie based on clips you select.*   154

Bit rate   *The number of data bits, or signals, used in one second of video.*   102

Bits   *Small data values that, when combined, describe the sound and video of your movie.*   214

Blind carbon copy   *Email terminology, typically designated by the Bcc field, to recipients of an email who are to receive a copy of the email without the primary or carbon copy recipients knowing the copy was sent.*   226

Blue screen filter   *Also known as a chroma key transparency filter, a blue screen filter enables you to create a useful special effect by embedding one video inside another.*   40

Carbon copy   *Email terminology, typically designated by the Cc field, to recipients of an email who are not designated as the primary recipient that appears in the To field. The regular recipient in the To field will see that a copy was also sent to the Cc field's email address.*   226

Channels   *The number of separate audio soundtracks, such as two for stereo. Movie Maker supports one or two channels.*   102

Clip detection   *The process Movie Maker uses to split imported video into multiple clips.*   71

Credits   *Descriptions of who did what at the end of a movie, such as the production staff, as well as a repeat of the stars and head people. Typically, credits scroll from the bottom to the top of the screen.*   186

Cross-fade   *The playing of two clips with a fading-out of the first clip while the next clip fades in at the same time, usually with some pattern such as a swirl effect, and with the second clip completely taking over at the last moment of the transition.*   177

Cutaway shots   *Shots that correlate to a scene but are not imperative to the scene. Cutaway shots help to keep a scene moving without being too distracting.*   34

Depth of field   *The amount of a scene that is completely in sharp focus at any one time.*   51

Digital camera   *A camera that writes to film using discrete signals that your computer can read directly without a decoding device.*   6

Digital image stabilization   *Built-in camera movement sensors that act as shock absorbers. If you move the camera in a jerky motion while shooting, the digital image stabilization corrects for the movement and attempts to keep the picture steady.*   38

Digital rights management   *Encoding of a video or audio file that protects it from unauthorized copying or distribution by programs that recognize the digital rights management system. Also called DRM.*   71

DVD burner programs   *A program you need in addition to Movie Maker that will write your movie to a DVD so the movie is playable on a DVD player.*   215

End trim point   *Determines where the clip stops playback.*   125

Ending playback indicator   *A selected clip's right edge on the timeline.*   125

f-stop   *Numbers that indicate the size of a camera's aperture opening. The formula for an f-stop is a fraction, so the larger the f-stop number, the smaller the aperture opening and the less light that can enter the camera.*   49

FireWire connection   *Also called IEEE 1394, a FireWire connection is a port in your camera that you can connect directly to a PC's FireWire port, allowing you to send video directly to your PC without requiring special decoding hardware, such as a video capture card.*   6

Focal length   *The distance from the camcorder lens to the subject.*   45

Grayscale   *The color description of a film or picture that shows various shades of gray and white without any other color.*   180